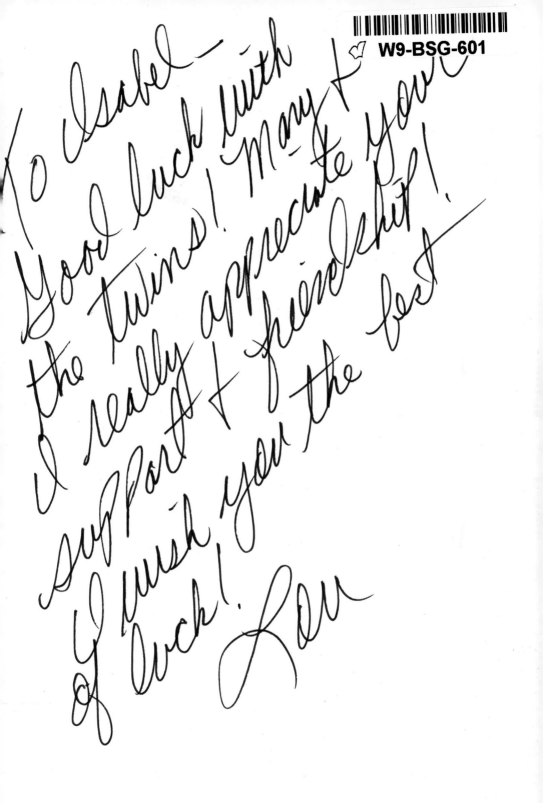

To Isabel –
Good luck with
the twins! Many
I really appreciate your
support & friendship!
I wish you the best
of luck!
Lou

# Winning
# at Illinois

## Lou Henson
### with
### Skip Myslenski

Champaign, Illinois
61824-0673

Cover design and
photo insert layout: Michelle R. Dressen
Book design: Susan M. Williams
Copyeditor: Laurie McCarthy
Proofreaders: Brian J. Moore, Phyllis L. Bannon

10   9   8   7   6   5   4   3   2   1

Library of Congress Catalog Card No.: 89-062927
ISBN: 0-915611-24-4

*We have made every effort to trace the ownership of all copyrighted material and
to appropriately acknowledge such ownership. In the event of any question arising
as to the use of any material, we will be pleased to make the necessary changes in
future printings.*

Sagamore Publishing
a division of Management Learning Laboratories, Ltd.
P.O. Box 673
Champaign, IL 61824-0673

*Printed in the United States of America*

*To my loving and loyal wife, Mary, whose 35 years of unwavering support has always inspired me to go on*

*To my son, Lou, and daughters, Lori, Lisa, and Leigh Anne who have sustained me with their love, devotion, and understanding when I couldn't be there for them*

*To my players, past and present, my other family, who have made it possible for me to successfully carry out my life's ambition—my eternal thanks!*

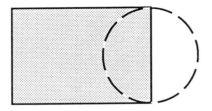

# Contents

# Acknowledgments

I've been involved in many tough games in my coaching career, but writing these acknowledgments is one of the toughest things I've ever done. There are so many wonderful, giving people out there who have assisted me along the way, and that makes it extremely difficult to mention some and not others. So if you read this, and you're one of those who have helped me in some way and your name has been omitted, please accept my humble apologies and thanks. It's only a space limitation that prevents me from recounting everyone's kindnesses.

I got off to a good educational start in the Okay, Oklahoma school system because of excellent teachers and administrators. I am indebted to the late George Hopkins, Joe Eidson, and Harold Nicholson, who first influenced me to become a coach. Thanks to them and my teammates . . . for getting the ball to me!

I will always have fond memories of my collegiate days—of my teachers, teammates, and two special coaches, Bobby Jack Rogers and Presley Askew.

My first coaching break came when Superintendent Tom J. Mayfield and F.E. Atkinson, personnel director, hired me at Las Cruces High. Luitt K. Miller was my principal there, and Rudy Camunez was the athletic director and football coach. Ed Boykin, Keith Colson, Willis Holmberg, and Cal Stutzman ably assisted me. All of these people were great guys to work with, as was the teaching staff and the array of terrific Bulldog players who brought me those state championships. Many of those fine athletes and their parents remain close friends of ours.

One of those, Ray Graham, with whom I taught math, was responsible for my leaving Las Cruces High to join his father, former Hardin-Simmons University Interim President George Graham. The fine people there to whom I am indebted are Dr. Graham; former President James Landis; my assistants, Charlie Horton and Mel Cunningham; Professor Sam Breeland; Wayne Haynes, James Claunch, Dr. Jack Haynes, Hattie Belle Martin, Marlicia Nagy, and Hazel Greggston.

I'm grateful to the NMSU Board of Regents, the late President Roger Corbett, former President Gerald Thomas, Carl Hall, Don Roush, Kay Hafen, Bob Kirkpatrick, all of NMSU, Howard Klein and the entire Aggie Sports Association, the faculty, and my athletic staff, which was composed of Keith Colson, Joe Lopez, Sonny Yates, Joe Muench, Dave Lopez, George Westbrook, Dr. Henry Hosford, Dr. James Tucker, Pat Hill, Jan Rogers, and all of the athletic coaches. To all of my Aggie players, thanks for your excellence! Aggie parents, band, students, and fans, you were great! We also want to praise former *Las Cruces Sun-News* publishers Joe Priestley and Guy Hankins and their crack sports editors, Abe J. Perilman and Joe Muench. We also got great Albuquerque and El Paso coverage from the late Leroy Bearman, Carlos Salazar, Bob Ingram, and Chuck Whitlock. And of course, I would be remiss in leaving out my personal moral support group, the great guys of the Mission Inn coffee club.

I wish to acknowledge my gratitude to the following people at the University of Illinois who have been so cooperative and supportive: the past and present Boards of Trustees; former President John Corbally; President Stanley Ikenberry; former Chancellors Jack Peltason, William Gerberding, and John Cribbet and present Chancellor Morton Weir; all of their respective administrative staffs and our fine faculty; past and present athletic board members; and the late athletic director, Cecil Coleman, who made it possible for me to coach at this great institution. Thanks also to former athletic director Neale Stoner and his associate athletic director Vance Redfern, whose hard work helped propel Illini athletics and facilities to a higher level. I was privileged to work alongside the late great Ray Eliot for a few years, and he was an inspiration to us all.

Present athletic director John Mackovic has demonstrated great loyalty and support for me and the basketball program, which is much appreciated. He and his staff show tremendous organizational skills and leadership. They are associate athletic directors Bob Todd, Dana Brenner, Tom Porter, Dr. Karol Kahrs, Sam Rebecca, Rick Allen, John O'Donnell, Bill Butkovich, Tim Tracey, and Randy Rodgers.

Grants-in-aid, an essential part of any sports program, is headed by the popular Dike Eddleman and his competent past and present staff of Ron Guenther, John Southwood, and Wayne Williams.

The importance of the outstanding academic services team of director Terry Cole, and academic counselors Mike Hatfield (now ticket manager) and Tim Van Alstin, and other counselors and tutors cannot be overstated. Coaches and players alike greatly appreciate those dedicated people.

Former sports information director Tab Bennett, present sports information director Mike Pearson, Dick Barnes, Kent Brown, Frank Reed, former staff member Dale Ratermann, and their support staff give us all a higher profile—thanks, gang!

Our medical and training staff is tops, and we know we'll get quality care with them: terrific head trainer Al Martindale and assistant trainer, our fabulous basketball guy, Rod Cardinal, and their excellent staff; Dr. Steve Soboroff and Dr. Bob Gurtler, our highly capable team physicians. Former head trainer Skip Pickering did a super job for us, and we appreciate his efforts. Thanks also go to McKinley Health Center, where our players receive great care.

No one does it better in the equipment room than Andy Dixon, Kurt Mitchell, and Jesse Ratliff. Terrific job! We also would like to remember retired manager Marion Brownfield and the late Carl Rose for their good work.

Former ticket manager Paul Bunting and Jim Negratti, assistant ticket manager, and that congenial staff have served the public remarkably well.

The best way to a man's heart is through his stomach, and that's why the coaches and student-athletes love Barbara Ward and her superior Varsity Room food staff.

Excellent organization is key to any good summer camp. The people who run my basketball camp have mastered that skill. Thanks go to associate athletic director Tom Porter, Linda Horve, and Bromley Hall's duo of Jim Phillips and Jim Graham and their efficient workers. We are so proud of our outstanding high school coaching staff and guest lecturers who make our summer camp the biggest and best in the state.

Through the concerted efforts of past and present strength coaches Bill Kroll, Pete Hoener, Leo Ward, and Dwight Daub, our Illini continue to be the strongest and best conditioned team in the country. This fact is in no small measure due to the great weight facilities donated by "Illini Lou" Proano—special thanks!

We deeply appreciate our loyal film crews under the direction of Jimmy Phillips, who provide us with opponents' game tapes. These are Lee Feldman, Carroll Dukes, Bruce Carroll, Bob Evans, Bill and Sean Gaston, Bruce Trapkus, Dave Natelson, Russ Cardinal, William Hendrickson, Todd Salen, and Bill Thompson.

And of course, the other women in my life are very special: Dorothy Damewood, Janann Vance, Phyllis Gordon, Mary Haring, Frances Yeats, Kathy Topolski, Laura Curtis, Janice Revell, Linda Michael, Mary Gallagher, Marsha Goldenstein, and Cindy Butkovich...those luncheon dates are great!

Sincere appreciation goes to Dr. Bill Nugent, executive director of the U. of I. Foundation, and his staff for their keen interest and assistance in our athletic program.

What can we say about executive director of our wonderful Alumni Association, Lou Liay, and Don Dodds, director of the C-U Alumni Association? They're always organizing trips in support of our teams, getting loyal Illini together, sometimes with Dan Perrino's talented Medicare 7, 8, or 9. We're grateful to them and all those fantastic, loyal alumni!

Our fabulous Rebounders Club, the support group of the century, which was so faithful and loyal, even through the lean years, deserves so much praise from our staff and teams. Orville Holman is the current president. Past presidents who have served are Wayne Norrick, Bob Eisner Jr., Dale Cozad, Dave Piper, Bob Evans, and Doug Mills. Other past and present board members include Bill Thompson, Bill Gaston, Louise Ellis Cochran, Gene Suggs, Jim Wright, Dave Diana, Lloyd Engert, Jim Fink, Clarence Shelley, Leonard Flynn, Dick Lord, Deane Stewart, Joe Hallbeck, Harold Moe, Wayne Young, the late Bob Johnson, Tom Rochford, Harold Hopkins, and Jack Everette.

The Illini Spirit groups are second to none and support us in every way. They are Gary Smith's Illini pep band and Chief Illiniwek, the cheerleaders, the Illinettes, the Orange Crush, and many other groups too numerous to mention. Kudos to all of you!

Every coaching staff needs wheels, and the providers of those bright, shiny autos are Bill Hopper, Win Smith, Kent Shirley, and Miles Schnaer. A million thanks!

There are literally hundreds of behind-the-scenes people who assist in so many ways. Among them are former Assembly Hall director Tom Parkinson; present director, Wayne Hecht, his office staff and maintenance people; and the Assembly Hall game personnel, which include statisticians, timers, scorers, PA announcers, ushers, and game officials; the Huff Hall staff and management; and the IMPE staff of Tony Clements, Craig Stinson, and others.

If I ever get any leisure time, I call upon my group of bridge buddies to help me relax with a few hands. These consist of Bill Thompson, Ken Perry, Wayne Young, Bob Corley, Larry Stewart, Jerry Johnson, Pete and Paul Coleman, Bob Suter, Lowell Garner, Bob Brunson, Lee Eilbracht, Bob Schmisseur, Dick Barker, Manford Morrow, Tom Harrington, Bob Manley, Bob Steigmann, Vic Feldman, Don Laz, Steve and Mike Hartman, Bob Markus, Bill Nugent, and Glenn Walker. Three no-trump!

Our Big Ten conference has been so fortunate to have had superb leadership in the persons of the now retired Wayne Duke and his trusted assistant John Dewey. This same high level of leadership will continue through our new commissioner, Jim Delaney, and his capable assistants, Clarence Underwood, Rich Falk, and the entire staff.

I'd like to express my sincere appreciation to the media for the fair and accurate coverage that my team and I have received throughout the years. I've especially enjoyed getting to know many of you on a personal level.

A coach is only as strong as his staff, and I feel I've had the best. I will remain indebted to the following assistants, for they have given me their all. They are Tony Yates, Les Wothke, Dick Nagy, Jimmy Collins, Mark Coomes, Scott Nagy, John Gianinni, Bob Hull, Dan Smith, Bob Hildebrand, Bill Molinari, Larry Lubin, Mark Bial, Steve Carroll, Levi Cobb, Mark Pittman, Don Maurer, Brian Dutcher, Roger Lowe, and Dave Kreps.

Our secretary Dorothy Damewood is second to none—efficient, dedicated, and loyal, like the rest of our people. We all love you Dorothy!

Some of the most unheralded people who put in a great deal of work for practically no rewards have been our terrific managers. We salute you!

To sign off with these acknowledgments, I'd like to recognize the dozens of people who have contributed to this book in some way. Of course, I must start with my main man, Skip Myslenski, who does have a decent jumpshot, but "too much thinking has slowed his feet." He still might make the team if he'd get a different hairstylist. Skip, a million thanks for your superb efforts. Thanks also to my editor, Laurie McCarthy, for her sensitivity to my words and thoughts—and deadlines.

And to my wife, Mary—what would I have done without you? If this book sells, you'll get your cruise.

To the wonderful people at Sagamore Publishing: Joe Bannon, president; Peter Bannon, executive vice president; Susan Williams, production coordinator; Michelle Dressen, marketing coordinator; and Brian Moore, administrative assistant—we thank you for extreme dedication and expertise in publishing this book. (And girls, I'm sure your raises will soon be forthcoming!)

Those many others who helped gather information, and assist me in many other ways, you have my heartfelt thanks. These are: Lou Jr., Lori, Lisa, Leigh Anne, and Laurie Henson; Linda Coomes; Professor Juliet Walker; Bill Wiegand; Loren and Lex Tate; Dick Barnes and his SID staff; Dorothy Damewood; Bill and Cheryl Thompson; Lou and Mary Liay; John O'Donnell; Jim Wright, Orville Holman; Charlie Bellatti; Eddie Groth and his NMSU staff; Keith and Evelyn Colson; Joe Lopez; Don Seamster; Wayne Haynes and the H-SU administrative staff; Judge Fred Green; Jim Benson; Mark Jones, and the Champaign Public Library.

*Although I have dedicated this book to my players, past and present, I would like to take this additional opportunity to extend my endless appreciation to all of you and to your parents. May God bless!*

# The "Lou Do"

Fans argue about it. Commentators analyze it. Newspapers and magazines write about it. A song has been written about it. Even one of my players, Kendall Gill, kids about it, telling me that I need to get myself some Grecian Formula.

I'm sometimes asked about my team's prospects for the season, but that is usually the third subject people want to talk about when it comes to the University of Illinois basketball program. I'm often asked about the high school recruits I've lined up for the next year. That is the second item discussed when it comes to the basketball program I head. But neither of those topics, nor any other, can touch the one that tops the charts. It is the undisputed king, the reigning champ, the unchallenged, unassailable, number-one focus of attention whenever a conversation gets around to me.

It is my hair. It is—and I almost feel as if I should have a drum roll here—the Lou Do.

OK. First of all, it is all my own hair, and I do not wear a toupee. My family is always asked about that, and my wife Mary has a stock answer now whenever she hears that question. "If he were going to wear a toupee," she says, "he'd certainly get something that looks better than that!"

But people continue to debate the issue all the time. We once had a call at home from a bunch of guys in a bar up near Kankakee, and the one on the line said he desperately needed to talk with Mary. "We got a bet going here and I need to get the true story," he said when she got on the phone. "Does Lou wear a toupee?"

"How'd you bet?" she asked him.

"I bet he did," he said.

"You lose," she informed him.

Another time, at a game, two students sitting right behind her were having the same argument. Finally she just turned around and said, "He is not wearing a toupee."

"Oh, OK, Mrs. Henson," they said, quickly realizing who she was.

Now this is not to say that some people don't think I need one, which is a fact my whole family came to realize one Saturday evening when we were watching the news on television. We all viewed the clips from our game that afternoon and laughed at how prominent my bald spot looked on the screen. Not three minutes later our phone rang. The caller owned his own toupee shop in Danville, and after introducing himself he said, "Lou, would you consider a hairpiece? I think I can help you."

"Look," I said, "I really appreciate your interest, but I don't think so." Of course, what he wanted to do was give me a hairpiece and then advertise the fact.

Now to go back. Around twenty years ago, in 1968 or 1969, I was coaching at New Mexico State, and I wore my hair in a very short crewcut. I had a lot of hair back then, but it was naturally light and I was in the sun so much that it  faded out and left me looking bald. It was so bad, in fact, that my family calls the pictures of me from that time my "Yul Brynner shots." So eventually I decided to start letting it grow out, and it was during that time that Mary and I took a trip to Las Vegas.

While we were out there I went to a barber, and after he looked me over, he said, "You know, you can do a lot with your hair."

"Like what?" I asked him. See, even though I was letting it grow out, I wasn't doing anything with it.

"Here's what you need to do," he said, and then he combed it into the style I still wear. So that's where the Lou Do started, with a barber in Vegas.

Now I admit that I've gradually lost some of my hair since then, but the colors, the other thing people wonder about, are all natural too. Gray and brown, with a little red thrown in. Three colors. That's just the way it is.

I often refer to the Lou Do in speeches now and tell people, "Hey, look. I just take and do the best I can with what I've got. I've always taken a little and tried to do a lot with it. Heck, that's just the way it goes."

On other occasions I kid about Michigan State coach Jud Heathcote, who combs his hair straight forward. "I think Jud should change his style, wear his hair like me," I say at those times. "But he won't change. He probably enjoys looking like Caesar."

But my favorite story, the one I particularly like to tell, concerns Dick Vitale. He's the bald-headed announcer for ABC and ESPN who came in to cover a game of ours for the first time, and then spent half the telecast talking about my hairstyle. In fact, he's the one who nicknamed my hairstyle, the Lou Do; he calls his the Dickie Do. I couldn't understand it. "Here we have a great ballclub, a club that's ranked in the Top Ten, and he's spending all this time talking about the Lou Do." You know, I finally figured it out. Dick is just a very jealous guy!

But I still don't know how to respond to the mother who walked up to me one day and said, "Lou, can you believe my son? He wants a Lou Do."

# 1

## They Shoulda Been in Pictures

**D**ick Nagy, one of my assistants, is standing near halfcourt, and he hears the sound. "It was like the crack of a rifle. My heart just went into my throat," he says later. Jimmy Collins, another of my assistants, is standing under the basket, and he sees it happen. "My life flashed before my eyes. I thought, 'Fate. It's frowning on us,'" he will say. But I am at the other end of the court, and so I neither see nor hear Kenny Battle slip on some water that has leaked in through a tear in the roof of the Minneapolis Metrodome.

Then a hush settles over that huge building, and turning I notice him lying prone on the floor with Collins and team trainer Rod Cardinal hovering over him. What's going on? I immediately wonder.

Steve Cameron, Sports Editor of the *Decatur Herald and Review* is standing near the sidelines and he, too, sees Kenny go down. He is the only media person near the scene, and as I pass Steve on my way to Kenny, he tells me he thinks it's bad.

"Can you believe it?" I ask Nagy. "Our biggest game of the year, and he slips on water. We need to check the floor from now on. We need to check everything."

But a lot of players slip during the year, and I still don't think that Kenny is seriously injured. I really don't. I feel Kenny will be OK, and that's what I tell people. "People fall and bruise themselves all the time," I tell them. "Don't worry. He'll play."

I am near the end of my thirty-third season of coaching, my fourteenth at the University of Illinois, and the following evening we'll be facing Louisville in a semifinal game of the 1989 Midwest Regional. But now, before heading back to our hotel after this practice session, we have to meet the media, who immediately bring up Kenny's mishap. "The floor's slippery. I don't think it's a very good floor right now," our forward Nick Anderson tells an assembled mass of writers.

"I sure hope they get the leak fixed," says Kendall Gill, another of our players.

"First of all, the floor. It's a beautiful floor, a good floor," I say when it's my turn.

I say that, first of all, because I do think it's an excellent tournament, and that was just one of those things that I don't think is anyone's fault. I don't think you can condemn people just because they have a leak in the roof. But there are also a lot of little things you must be aware of as a coach, and one of those is not to dwell on the negatives. One or two little things come up. After a while you learn to push them aside, or they'll affect the way you do your job.

You've got to be able to handle adversity. "It's not the stimulus or the stimuli. It's how you react to it." That's one of the first things I heard from my late father-in-law Ben Brantner, and I think of that any time I'm faced with a tough situation. You have to be like a golfer who can't let a bad hole affect his play on the next and the next hole. The poem, *One Day At A Time*, given to us by the late

Cecil Coleman, the former Illini athletic director, has been a source of comfort to me for years. I keep it next to my bed on the nightstand, and it goes like this:

*There are two days in every week about which we should not worry, two days that should be kept free from fear and apprehension.*

*One of these days is* **yesterday** *with its mistakes and cares, its faults and blunders, its aches and pains. Yesterday has passed forever beyond our control. All the money in the world cannot bring back yesterday. We cannot undo a single act we performed: we cannot erase a single word said—Yesterday is Gone!*

*The other day we should not worry about is* **tomorrow** *with its possible burdens, its large promise and poor perform-ance. Tomorrow is also beyond our immediate control. Tomorrow's sun will rise, either in splendor or behind a mask of clouds—But it will rise. Until it does we have no stake in tomorrow, for it is yet unborn.*

*This leaves only one day—*Tomorrow! *Any man can fight the battle of just one day. It is only when you and I have the burdens in those two awful eternities—*yesterday and tomorrow*—that we break down.*

It's difficult to overcome adversity and concentrate on the present. It takes a lot of self-discipline and training, but it is something you need if you hope to survive as a coach. It's just strange how some things develop. Many years ago in New Mexico,

I was having lunch with a very successful businessman and I said to him, "John, you're really successful. How did you do it?"

"Lou," he said, "I *plan* success."

He made a big point of that, how he planned for success, and here I thought the guy was a genius. But people change, times change, what goes around comes around. Eleven or twelve years later, he filed for bankruptcy. So things can be going great for you, you can think you're doing a great job planning and all, but sometimes things just happen. Things like Kenny Battle slipping on water that leaked in through a roof.

"Can you believe this is happening to us?" I ask Mary when I finally get back to my hotel room. She is there with some other members of the family, and—as is our habit—we spend a long time discussing what occurred that day. I next visit with my brother Ken and his wife Ellen, our son Lou, daughters Lisa, Leigh Anne, and Lori and her husband Mark Wojciehowski, and their two and one-half- year-old daughter, Catie. Little Catie should be a real basketball fan—during the first thirty days of her life, she attended three major college basketball games in three major cities, Tulsa, St. Louis, and Chicago. But I pass most of this Thursday evening looking at more tape of Louisville.

I've already spent four days going over these same films with Mark Coomes, one of my assistants, but now I just want to go back and look again. I want to make sure we know everything we're going to do. I don't want to be shocked. I never want an opponent to do something that we haven't seen, since all it takes is one or two plays to cost us a close game. I just don't like surprises. That's why, next March when we play Michigan, we will have seen every game they've played until that point. Indiana, same thing. The other top three or four teams in the Big Ten, same thing.

It's probably something I don't have to do, and young coaches in their first jobs might not do it. But I look at it like this. I think you can be a good student and work pretty hard and get yourself a good grade, maybe a B. But if you want to move up to another level, if you want to get an A, then you have to put in twice the time. I think it's very difficult to make that final jump. So, while I don't necessarily have to watch all this film, it gives me a certain amount of satisfaction and occasionally something new does pop out at me. I want to be sure I see that. It reinforces my thinking, my confidence. I don't want to be wondering about things. I like peace of mind. I like to control everything I can possibly control. I don't believe things just happen. I think there's usually a reason.

I know that's not always the case, but I remember a big argument I had one day with Dick Nagy. "Hey, coach," he shouted at me in exasperation. "Don't you believe some things can just happen?"

"Dick," I told him, "I don't operate like that. I think you can control a lot of things." In coaching, as in a lot of other professions, you can't control everything, and I realize that now. But it took me a long time to accept that, to understand that there are certain things you can't control. And the less time spent on them, the better. But that's still hard for me to do. By nature, I still want to change things that I can't. We all want to.

I'm ready for bed around midnight, but first I check with our excellent trainer, Rod Cardinal, on Kenny's condition. "It's coming along. He might be able to play," he tells me.

I believe him. With Kenny's personality, after all the toughness he has shown in his years at Illinois, I just think he's going to play. I can't believe he's going to miss a game, and I don't think about him again until the next day. That night I sleep well. We had prepared all week. We had reassured ourselves by going over the tapes. We'd done everything we could do.

The game is not scheduled until 7:00 on Friday night, but that morning I awake at 5:30 and immediately slip another Louisville tape into the VCR. As I watch, I make notes of some of those things I want to talk about at the team's afternoon skull session. Then around 8:00, I meet Mark Coomes in the hotel restaurant for a cup of coffee.

Three hours later, we're back at the Metrodome for our shootaround, and here it finally dawns on us that we have a problem. Kenny can't shoot, can't get loose, can't do the stretching exercises being handled by his teammates. "Does it hurt you?" I ask him.

"No," he says. But he's dragging his right leg, the leg with the damaged knee, and although we still hope he can play, we are now concerned enough to start making alternate plans.

"Can you believe this is happening again?" I ask my assistants when we get together. I'm thinking back then to 1984, the last time an Illinois basketball team was this close to the Final Four. That year Efrem Winters played the regional championship game with a sprained ankle and was a virtual nonfactor in our 3-point loss to Kentucky. Now there's a problem with Kenny, and for short moments it plays with my mind.

"Why does this have to happen to us?" I think.

"Why shouldn't it happen to us?" I then answer myself.

I know I have to go on, and so now I discuss our two options with my assistants. We can push Steve Bardo, our fine point guard, up into Battle's forward position, and start Larry Smith at the point. Or we can simply insert Marcus Liberty into Battle's slot and hope he plays big for us.

We decide pretty quickly on Marcus, but we really don't know what to expect of him. He's young, playing with us for the first time after sitting out a season, and he's coming off a couple frustrating first-round games in Indianapolis. So we know we have to be careful here, and we don't tell him that he could be starting that night. We don't go up to him and pat him on the back and tell him, "Marcus, Ken's gone. You're going to have to do it." We play it down. We don't have any long sessions with him. We go along as if nothing has happened. We don't want to put any added pressure on him.

But deep down, we as coaches know, we could be in trouble. Without Kenny it's going to take a great game to beat Louisville. When you've looked at as much film as I have, you have a good idea of what could happen, and now I fear that the little leak in the roof could cost us the championship. For I know Denny Crum's Louisville team is hot and good enough to win the national title.

As a coach you are also a psychologist, and one of the things you are always trying to do is instill confidence in your players. You can do that in a variety of ways, but one example I always remember involves a guy named Gordon Wood, who won something like a dozen state championships while coaching at high schools large and small in central Texas.

This one time he had his team down in Austin for a title game at the University of Texas and was in the locker room getting ready for a practice. As the team dressed, a manager came up to Wood and said, "Coach, I forgot to pack the jocks." Wood, instead of getting angry, just reached into his pocket, pulled out some money and said, "Here, John. Take this money, go down to the athletic supply store, and get those jocks. And, John, next year when we're back here playing for the championship again, don't forget those jocks."

Just like that, he let all the kids standing around know just how much confidence he had in them, and no one can give players confidence like a coach. You've got to know how to do it. But by treating Kenny's injury as an everyday occurrence, by going along as if nothing terrible had happened, we were hoping Marcus would have more confidence when he finally learned that he would be starting against Louisville.

That afternoon when I get back to the hotel, I jot down on a sheet of paper some points I want to remember during the game. It will be in my breast pocket that evening in case I need to refer to it. Then at 2:45 I join the team for our pregame meal. Years ago, thinking it would help them remember, I would have told them to be seated at 2:44 or 2:47 or something like that. But I don't do that anymore.

At the meal, I sit at the far end of the table, away from the players. But when we are finished eating I get up, mingle with them, and stress some points I want them to remember. "I don't want you in the lobby visiting with people. Go to your own rooms," I tell them. "I don't want you talking to anybody between now and game time."

I'm fairly predictable in situations like this, and I'm treating this game like any other, despite its obvious importance. I want to be careful not to do anything out of the ordinary, for it's unbelievable how some players think. If I'm wearing a certain sport coat and we win some games, I'll wear it again. I know it doesn't have anything to do with winning, but some players might. We have some players who think they're going to have a bad game if they miss their first two or three shots. You check into a hotel, a lot of them will remember, "Hey, we got beat the last time we stayed here." That's why you'll see teams changing hotels even if the first was a good one. Coaches know it has nothing to do with the result. But it could have an effect on your next game if the players believe it did.

It was quite a distance from our Metrodome locker room to the floor, and so that morning during our shootaround, I'd had a trainer time just how long a walk it was. When I did that, I saw one of my assistants roll his eyes in a way that said, "Why's he doing that?" I did it because I wanted to know, I did it so we could make the best use of our allotted time.

Our hosts, Neal and Sally Johnson, who have been assigned to us to help make our stay more pleasant, do just that; they were unbelievably considerate and efficient and tended to our every need.

That night, according to plan, and thirty minutes before our game with Louisville, I send the players out for their warmups. Mark Coomes and I remain behind and there, for the final time, we discuss strategy. As we talk, three maintenance men walk in and start cleaning up the room. This is an unexpected intrusion and Mark asks them, "What are you doing here?"

"This is the way we do it with pro teams," he says, and since we are in the Minnesota Twins' locker room, we go along with their routine.

We just ignore them and then as I do before every game, I go to the chalkboard, divide it into columns, and write out those things I'll discuss with the players just before the game starts. On offense, I note, we want to penetrate, go right at them, try and get their big guys in foul trouble. Number two, we definitely feel we can fast break them, get it down, and get some easy shots. Number three, we want to pound the offensive boards. Number four, we want to show some patience in our set offense. And number five, we want to screen on the perimeter with the man being guarded by their big man, All-American center Pervis Ellison.

Our defensive strategies go into a second column, and in the third I write some general reminders. "Play hard," is one of them. Then in the final column, I note the matchups we'll open with, and there I write the initials "ML" opposite "KP." They stand for Marcus Liberty and Louisville's Kenny Payne. When Marcus returns to the locker room, he'll know for the first time that he's starting. We didn't want Marcus out there warming up and worrying about starting. And later, during my pregame talk, I'll attempt to minimize his situation even further. "Seven or eight of you guys will play tonight," I will tell my team then.

I don't put much stock in who's starting and intentionally play down that role. I de-emphasize it in hopes of keeping the pressure off Marcus.

Ten minutes before the start of the game, the players return to the locker room. I tell them to go to the restroom, to do whatever they need to do personally to get ready. I don't believe in long talks at moments like this—I may go ten minutes on a normal game, but on a big game like this I go only six or seven. There's no need to be emotional. We've taken care of that during the week. So we just recap what we want to accomplish, go over what I've written on the board, and then it's time to play. They're warmed up, and we don't want them to get tight. They're loose, and we don't want them to do a lot of serious thinking. "Hey," I finally tell them, "we've come too far to lose this one. Let's go out and get them."

That's about all I say. That's all I have to say.

In situations like this, I'm conditioned and I'm able to control my feelings. I know some people say they can't eat, they can't sleep, they can't do this or that. But that doesn't really bother me anymore. You never adjust completely to going out for a big game. At least I don't think you do. If you're competitive and trying to beat people, you don't, but you learn to control it.

It's like being a veteran actor or actress: they always say they never quite get over stage fright and rarely go on stage without feeling a little bit of that. That's exactly the way it is in coaching. You always have a certain amount of stage fright and nervousness and concern over a game, and you never get over that. But it's like a guy who has to give a speech on a Friday. If he's inexperienced, he'll relax on Tuesday, Wednesday, and Thursday, then be afraid on Friday. But if he's experienced, his greatest fears will come on Tuesday, Wednesday, and Thursday, and he'll be pretty relaxed on Friday. He knows then he has to put everything else aside. He knows then that he can't afford to be afraid because now it's showtime.

Just 89 seconds into the game, Marcus announces himself with a basket over Ellison, and begins a performance that erases all the questions we had about him. There are other early encouraging signs as well, but then—after only 2:34 of play—Lowell Hamilton goes up for a rebound, comes down off balance, lands awkwardly, and hops off the court, his injured right ankle dangling in the air.

"Can you believe what's happening to us?"   I ask my assistants.

"You know what you gotta do, man. Go and do it," Hamilton tells his replacement, Ervin Small, as they pass near the bench.

"We believe in you. Just play hard and do the things you do in practice, and we'll be all right," his teammates on the court tell him.

"How's Lowell?"  I ask Cardinal.

"I think he's going to be OK," he tells me at first.

"I don't think he'll be able to go back in," he tells me minutes later.

So we lost Kenny, and now we've lost Lowell, and as a staff we are down, really down. We know it's going to be a tough game, and even though we're playing well, we know that when the chips are on the table, you don't lose two starters and win against a team like Louisville. You might do that at home during the regular season. You don't do that on a strange court in the NCAA regionals.

"How in the world are we going to win this game now?" I think. "What are we going to do now? No way we win now," I think.

We all feel the same way, my assistants and I. No one thinks we're going to win at this point, and if they do they don't know anything about the game of basketball. But how I feel and how I act are two different things. No matter what I feel, I try to act the same. At moments like this, you don't share your negative feelings.

There is a timeout shortly after Lowell goes down, and as I look into the faces of my players, I wish I had a camera. They are obsessed with this game. They are determined to win this game. They are screaming at each other, encouraging each other, firing each other up. They have pulled for each other all through the season, but here the feeling is special. Their looks of determination, I've never seen anything like it before. I've never seen a group so fired up. It doesn't make any difference to them. They're going to win this game. They're on a mission.

Their response, the determination they show here, turns out to be the key to the game. They know what's happened, but they don't care. Usually we're the ones pounding on the clipboards, telling them this, telling them that, encouraging them not to give up. But here we don't have to do that. Time and time again during the season, we've gotten them involved in games, gotten them back into games, told them they can win games if they only do this or that. But here the roles are reversed. I was down when those two guys went out but now, seeing how they feel about it, I'm ready to go. They get me going.

Remember how you felt watching the movie *Hoosiers*? Remember how you felt watching this small school that didn't have a chance take on the big guys, and how you responded to the courage its players showed? That is the feeling I have right now, and I wish I could get a picture of the moment.

When they go out, the courage they show, the way they hustle their guts out, that's basically what a lot of coaches stand for. For those coaches, it means more to have their teams outwork their opponents than it does to win, and I am one of them.

I am basically a private man who does not publicly display his emotions. But when this game ends, I have some trouble controlling my feelings. Kenny has scored only 4 points, while limping through fifteen minutes. Lowell has scored the same while limping through thirteen minutes. We have also had an NCAA tourney record—thirteen shots blocked by Louisville—but somehow we've won, 83-69, and I can't help but lower the mask a bit.

When I meet the media, I show more emotion than I ever have after a game, and my voice is shaking slightly as I say, "Let me tell you, like I've told you all year long, this club does things they're not supposed to do. They showed they've got guts. They will not die. You have to beat them. Let me tell you. In thirty-three years of coaching, this is one of the most outstanding victories I've been associated with."

I don't say it, but I also feel it was the most remarkable game with which I've ever been associated. When you think of Ken Battle, you think of someone who leads in every facet of the game. On the floor, on the bench, in games, in practices, wherever he is, he's going to be leading. Leading by example, that's Ken Battle.

Ken's leadership was not missing in that game. As a matter of fact, I think it was present before the game and throughout it as well. First because all the other guys thought he could play. He's durable and plays all the time, so even after he went down, they just knew he was going to play. When they saw him out there limping and dragging his leg, his leadership was even more apparent; and they looked up to him, respected him for his supreme effort. I know it moved me to see this guy, this competitor, just wanting to play, and trying, trying and limping and dragging his leg. It moved me to see that, and it had to move the team as well.

I think seeing Kenny and Lowell attempting to play after they were injured motivated the team to the point that they were determined not to lose. Their personal tenacity was instrumental in inspiring the team to the emotional level they needed to win.

Later that night, after watching Syracuse defeat Missouri, I return to my hotel suite and immediately begin watching tapes of the Orangemen, whom we will play for the regional championship on Sunday. Mary soon goes to the bedroom, closes the door behind her, and is off to sleep. But I stay up until 3:00 in the morning studying the one team that now stands between us and the Final Four.

We have a dozen of their games on tape, but after viewing just a few of them, I'm struck with the exceptional abilities of the Orangemen. "They're a lot better than I thought they were," I say to myself. I'm also growing more impressed with their point guard Sherman Douglas. I've heard Dick Vitale say he's one of the top two point guards in the country, but I never believed that. Until now, I thought he was wild, out of control, just a gunner. But after watching him on film, I realize he's a great point guard. He scores when he needs to. He sets up his guys. He does a great job for them.

"Mark, I didn't realize how good Syracuse was. They're an unbelievable team. Jim Boeheim has done a great job with them," I tell Mark Coomes when I join him for breakfast after three hours of sleep.

He just nods in agreement. He's watched all the tapes I've just seen, and so he already knows that.

"And Douglas," I continued, "he's one of the best in the country."

"You're right," he agrees. "He's got great control of the game."

Douglas is the primary topic of our conversation at that breakfast. Later, when we meet with Dick Nagy and Jimmy Collins, I tell them too just how good I think Syracuse is. We know we have more depth than they do. We know that defensively we're probably a better team. But we all agree that if you give them an inch, they can kill you.

We coaches have made our discovery, but we don't share our new knowledge with the team. We don't want them to start thinking that Syracuse is better than they are. We don't want them to start doubting.

Normally I will tell them how good our next opponent is or come close enough to telling them so that they think I'm right every time. It's another instance when the coach has to play the role of psychologist, and this is how I will do it for a Thursday game for instance: on Monday and Tuesday, I'll build up our opponent and tell our players just how good they are. "They're a great rebounding team," I might tell them.

"Their forward, hey, he's the best shooter we're going to see all year, " I might say.

"You're going to get your noses bloodied playing these guys," I might warn them.

Now you can't go too overboard and exaggerate, or they'll see through you and lose confidence in you. But the worst thing I can do is put our team on the floor and have our opponent play better than I said they would. So I want them to get a little scared—that helps make them pay attention to what I'm saying.

But on Wednesday and Thursday, I'll start getting positive. I might tell them if they do this, do that, they're not going to have any trouble winning. Now I want to get it into their heads that this is a team that we can beat. I won't turn completely around and say, "Hey, these guys aren't very good." But I will say, "Now their forward, we can control him. Play him tight and make him give the ball away, and he's not going to hurt us at all."

But here, for the Syracuse game, I can't do any of that. I don't have the time to take them down, and then bring them back up again. If we had four days before the game, I would do that. But we have only thirty-eight hours, so I never mention to the players just how good I think our next opponent is.

There is a media conference at 11:00 on Saturday morning and then at 1:00, it's off to the Metrodome for practice and a report on our wounded. Battle appears much better, and I'm encouraged when I hear Kendall Gill say, "He's back to being the old Kenny Battle, running his mouth off and stuff like that." We are now fairly certain he will start on Sunday. But Lowell, his ankle swollen, is back at the hotel receiving treatment, and it's highly doubtful he'll be able to play against Syracuse.

So our attention again returns to Marcus Liberty. During the afternoon I spend much time with my assistants discussing whether we want him to start in Lowell's place. His youth is one concern. It's very difficult for a veteran player to put together two good games, to have great games back-to-back, and for a young guy, it's just expecting too much. Another concern is Derrick Coleman, Syracuse's strong and rough center. Marcus is more of a finesse player, and we're not sure we want Marcus guarding him. So we think of starting the more rugged Ervin Small. We know you can't let a great player like Coleman get started. If he gets off early, there's nothing you can do with him the rest of the game.

I have one final concern that I don't even share with my assistants. It involves not only Marcus, but our whole team, and I think of it often in the thirty-eight hours that separate the end of our Friday game and the start of Sunday's. I wonder throughout that time about our team's emotional state.

People say I never get emotional, and many feel you have to be emotional to coach. I have emotions like everyone else, but I feel I'm a better coach if I restrain them. I want to be a stabilizing influence on the team. If a player makes a great shot, I don't want to jump up and cheer. And if he makes a bad play, I don't want him to think it's the worst thing that could have happened to us. Somewhere in between is where I want to be. I believe you can play on emotion for only so long, and then it's going to catch up with you. It's difficult to play two great games in a row and even more difficult to play three. But if you can play game one and game two and keep your emotions in check, then you'll be OK for game three. That is the way the great UCLA teams did it under the incomparable John Wooden, who has been more successful than any other coach in the history of sport. Over a twelve-year period at UCLA, Coach Wooden's teams won ten NCAA basketball championships. I am confident that no other coach will ever duplicate that feat. Those teams played with remarkably controlled emotion, and that is exactly the way I like for our team to play.

I believe there are certain steps you have to take to get ready to play, and I don't like our guys going out and depending totally on emotion. I'm against that. I know you can't win without emotions, and I have to get the team ready to go. But it's a matter of degrees, and I don't want them too high. Your emotions can take you only so far and then they run out, so that doesn't do it. That's also why I don't give pep talks before games.

So back to the Louisville game; for the public it was a great victory, but for me it was a miracle game. It was a game in which we expended a lot of emotion, and any time there's a lot of emotion in a game, I immediately wonder about the next one. Sometimes in tournament play, you can reach an emotional peak and play a couple of games in that state. But after thirty-three years in coaching, I don't need a psychology book to tell me of the possible dangers. I've seen it too many times. I know that when you play on emotion, it costs you. And then you better be good enough to win without it.

I didn't discuss any of this with the coaches. I didn't let the team see my concerns. But I wondered just how much emotion we would have left when we went out to play Syracuse.

Two rows of fans, packed ten deep, are lined up in our hotel lobby as we leave for the Syracuse game. As I pass through them, I simply nod and continue on my way. I don't like to be bothered at a time like this. That's just the way I am. I climb onto our bus after barely acknowledging them. "Wait a minute," I think as soon as I sit down. "These people spent all this money to come up here to support us, I should at least talk to them a little bit."

I get up then, exit the bus, and go back inside. "Hey," I yell to them. "You know I really crave attention, and since you applauded me when I came out the first time, I figured I'd come back for more." Then I get serious and tell them how much we appreciate their support, how I'm not sure whether we as a team are number one, but they as fans certainly are. Then I get back on the bus.

I firmly believe that you have to be alert for games, that you have to concentrate for games; and that's why I initially walked through those fans without acknowledging them. It's the same reason I don't sit around relaxing and talking with my family the morning of a game. If you're doing that, if you're having a good time, it's taking a toll on you. And I like to be fresh.

That's also the reason we have certain rules with our players. At home, you can't do much about it, but when we're on the road, we don't want parents dropping by and visiting with them. They drop in, talk to them about the game, tell them to be sure to do this, be sure to do that. They think they're doing the kids a big favor, but they're actually hurting them. The players don't need that. We'll tell them everything they need to know. We don't need the parents doing that.

But the worst thing that can happen is to have your players standing around the lobby and talking to people, to every alumnus who wants to talk to them. We tell them they have a specific fifteen or twenty minutes to mill around and visit. But other than that, if we see them in the lobby, we want them to be passing through. "Do not stop and talk," we tell them, "be thinking about the game."

To me, it's just playing the percentages, and although the percentages don't always work out for you, I'll always play them. I'm going to do it that way, and I'm not going to change. I believe any time you start veering from your normal course of action, it's going to come back to haunt you. I believe you've got to decide what's right and then make sure you always attempt to do it that way.

As the team warms up to face Syracuse, Mark Coomes and I are in the locker room talking over our options. The possibilities have been discussed in detail over the last thirty-eight hours, but we can't be sure which way we'll go until we get reports from the court.

Every five minutes a staff member, either Gary Bruner, Ryan Baker, Jimmy Phillips, John Gianinni, or Scott Nagy, rushes back to tell us how Kenny and Lowell look. "Real well," they say about Kenny, and so we decide we're going to start him. But the reports on Lowell are not so encouraging, and again we debate whether to start Marcus or Ervin in his place. Ervin's stronger, we know that, and he's a veteran who's very good at blocking off the boards. But we finally settle on Marcus for the obvious reason: we have to keep up his confidence.

We know Ervin's performance won't be affected by whether or not he starts. But Marcus could be affected, and to win against Syracuse we know we need him to play.

"Explain to me what happened out there!" I scream at my assistants.

"What's he doing out there?" I yell a minute later.

"Where's our rebounding?" I wonder a minute after that.

It's not yet midway through the first half of the Syracuse game, our most frustrating half of the season, and I'm not looking for any answers to my questions. My assistants know they're not supposed to answer. They've learned not to answer at times like this. I'm solemn. I'm mad. I'm upset. Man for man, I know we're a lot better than Syracuse defensively, but we're giving up a lot of easy baskets. We're not supposed to be doing this, we're not hustling. We're not going to the boards either, and that's just killing us too.

It's a combination of things. We're flat. We're breaking down. We're doing things fundamentally that we normally don't do—and Syracuse is playing really well. We're trying anything to get our team going. We put Lowell in and then pull him out once more after we see him struggling, put him back in, then pull him out after he again struggles. "Coach," he tells me, "I've either got to sit or play. It's hard for me to go in and out. I have to get loose."

"Lowell, you've got to play," I say back. "We just can't leave you out there. You have to be effective."

"You have to hustle," I tell the entire team during timeouts.

"You've got to get back."

"Hit the boards. They're just killing us on the boards."

"You've got to dog Douglas. Don't let him penetrate. He's killing us there. If he's going to beat us, make him beat us from the outside."

None of it helps, and our breakdowns continue. One or two breakdowns, I expect that in a game. But when there are this many, I know something's wrong. It's our emotion. We had just been too emotional in the Louisville game, and now we're paying for it. We're playing with no emotion at all.


I'm in the hallway outside our locker room with Jimmy, Dick, and Mark, and together we're analyzing the first-half statistics. We're down to Syracuse by 7, and we're lucky it's not much worse. We're not shooting the ball as well as Syracuse; we're turning the ball over more than Syracuse is; and we're being outhustled by a Syracuse team that is burning us with too many easy baskets. Nine of their eighteen first-half field goals, the shot chart tells us, have been layups.

The four of us spend three minutes looking at these figures and discussing what they mean, and then we open the door and rejoin the players. They are quiet. They know when they play well or poorly, and when they play poorly they just sit there and don't talk.

But I'm mad, and right away I start in on them. I start with the stats to show them just how bad they're playing, and then I go down each player individually. I talk to them about not doing those things Illinois basketball is based on. Hard work. Doing their jobs. There's no hidden agenda. They know exactly what they're supposed to do, and there's nothing better than a group of guys that puts out 110 percent and does those things. But there's nothing worse than a guy who doesn't do what he's supposed to do, and that's exactly what I tell them.

I'm not yelling, but my words are pointed. "Hey, look," I say, "we only ask you to play forty minutes. That's all. Forty minutes. Now is that asking too much for you to play hard for forty minutes? You know, we've come a long way. We've put too much into this season to give it to them. Now, if they can beat us, they beat us. And if they beat us, let them take it. But you guys deserve a chance to go to the Final Four, and I never thought I'd see the day when you gave that chance away."

"You guys have overcome a lot of adversity to get here, so let's not give up now. Don't give it to them. Hey, you guys, you're handing it to them without a fight."

I think if you can have your club mad when they go into a game, and if the talent is close and the other club isn't mad, then you're probably going to win. That's why I don't like to play a team that's mad. That's why you don't do anything to get a team mad at you.

So if you can get a player mad at halftime, many times he'll go out and play great ball. It's the same with a team. If you can get them mad at halftime, they often respond. You get after them and a lot of times it helps. It just depends on the situation.

All of our coaching staff agree that that's the way we are. We reward success, we reward effort. We may pat them on the back or be nice to them. But if it's not there, we swing the other way. We expect them to do certain things, and when they don't, we're not just going to sit back and take it. We'll try changing it first with talking. If that doesn't work, we'll try changing it by hollering. And if that won't do it, a player will be asked to find himself a place on the bench. If a guy knows he can make mistakes and stay out there, you'll never correct his problems. So we're just not going to tolerate that.

In this situation, most of the guys had played poorly, so we got after all of them. It was probably the toughest I'd been on them in a while, but I wanted to jar them. I wanted to try and shake them up and get them going. We felt that would help us turn it around, and we left the locker room thinking we would play better. But we weren't certain that would be enough to win. We certainly didn't know that because we knew Syracuse was a super team.

Nick Anderson opens the second half with a short jumper, then Kendall Gill follows with a 3-pointer from deep in the left corner, and—after Coleman makes a foul shot—Kenny Battle bangs in a running jumper from the right of the lane. We are now back in the game, down only 47-46, and that trio is on its way to scoring 45 of our 50 second-half points.

I believe that things are fairly basic in ball games and that games are won with momentum. So if anything positive happens, you want to build on it and keep it going. You want to keep it going as long as you can. So in the second half, we got out quick and started playing pretty well, and when we got a timeout I acknowledledged that. You're not going to win many ball games unless you think you can do it, so as soon as we started doing some things right, I started talking to them. "We're on our way now," I told them. "We're going to win this thing now."

Gill spins in a reverse layup off a pass from Battle, and Coleman goaltends on Nick's jumper from the left baseline. Now, with 15:38 remaining in this game, we've finally pulled even with Syracuse at 50. But the Orangemen, proving to be as good as we feared, immediately go back up by 4; then Nick closes that to 2 with a thunderous dunk off a lob from Larry Smith.

It's depressing for your opponent if you can get a jam or two, and it can really be uplifting for your own club. So I could sense right then that our players felt they were on their way.

Then you start building. Sometimes, even when your team is still playing poorly after starting poorly, you'll tell them they're playing better. You'll tell them their defense is picking up even if it isn't, that they're more alert even if they're not, that they're getting to the ball quicker even if they're still a step slow. That helps them. That makes them think they're playing better than they really are, and confidence means so much in sports. So much.

I've used that trick in the past, but the encouragement I was giving them here reflected the way I truly felt. I felt we were playing a great second half.

We tie the game at 62 on another 3-pointer by Kendall, but Syracuse comes right back and goes up by 4. We tie them again at 68 on Kenny's driving jumper, and then he gives us our first lead in nearly twenty-eight minutes with a layup off a pass from Nick. Now it's Syracuse's turn to tie us, which they do with 6:43 remaining. But we immediately go up by 4 on Nick's rebound of a Battle miss and a jumper by Kendall from the top of the lane. We stretch it to 6 with 4:30 left on a Bardo jumper from the left of the lane. Still Syracuse is not cowered, and they're back to within 3 with just over a minute to go.

I know one coach who used to tell his players, "Gentlemen, if you have the game tied with five minutes to go, I'll win it for you." He's no longer a head coach and you can see why. But even then I couldn't believe he'd say that. We don't believe in operating like that.

Our philosophy is to "win over forty." The idea is to win the game over its full forty minutes, to play tough and hard over the full forty, and to try to wear the other guy down. It pays off for you, and we always want our guys to believe they're in better condition than anyone they'll ever face. All year we prepare them for a game that may be tied at the end, and we're continually telling them, "Hey, you're the best conditioned team in the country. If it's close with five minutes to go, you're going to win it. If it's tied with a minute to go, you're going to be fresher than the other guys."

It's a bit of brainwashing, but we also really are in great condition. I don't know of a team in the country that's in better condition than we are.

Douglas has the ball now as the clock ticks down toward a minute, and he whirls past Larry Smith and penetrates to the right baseline. In the first half he did this with impunity and created countless easy baskets for his team. But here Lowell Hamilton, playing on an ankle he won't be able to walk on a day later, cuts him off. It's a textbook play, the kind of play we weren't making in the first half. And now Douglas, suddenly trapped, throws a pass toward Coleman. But Larry Smith, in another play from the textbook, intercepts it, while Douglas fouls Hamilton. Sixty-two agonizing seconds later, we're on our way to Seattle and the Final Four.

"We saw on film," Larry will say after our 89-86 win, "that when Sherman gets stuck, he usually goes to Coleman. So I just stepped in front of him."

"We're the kind of team that doesn't burn out at the end," Hamilton will say. "We're the kind of team that juices it up at the end."

Kendall Gill falls to the floor and is soon joined there by Nick Anderson and Larry Smith. The rest of the players are smiling, hugging, waving their fingers in that traditional signal that declares them number one, and then they gather to take turns cutting down the nets. Nick grabs me, tells me to take my turn atop the ladder. "I felt good that he thought enough of me to ask me to do that," I will later tell the media. "But when I came back down the ladder, Nick said, 'Coach, what I wanted to do was embarrass you in front of all the fans. I didn't think you could get up there.'"

I then look for Mary, who is still trapped in the stands, and the players gather at halfcourt and break out in a rap song led by Kenny Battle.

*They call me Kenny B*
*Shoo-wop, shoo-wop*
*My number is 33*
*Shoo-wop, shoo-wop*
*I get the score from Kenny G*
*Shoo-wop, shoo-wop*
*And don't forget the lob from Larry*
*Shoo-wop, shoo-wop*
*Lowell-ski will grab the rebound*
*Shoo-wop, shoo-wop*
*Old Nick will jam it down*
*Shoo-wop, shoo-wop*
*On the court it's what we do*

*Shoo-wop, shoo-wop*
*Small and Liberty will do it too*
*Shoo-wop, shoo-wop*
*Oh, but I forgot old coach Lou*
*Shoo-wop, shoo-wop*
*He's the head of this Illini crew*
*Shoo-wop, shoo-wop*
*To Seattle we will go*
*Shoo-wop, shoo-wop.*

As they rap, I'm doing radio interviews, television interviews, and newspaper interviews on the court. And then I'm taken into a room to talk to a mass of assembled media. My reactions have been muted in comparison to the players', and since that fits my public image, many of the questions are about my emotions. "I could have run around kissing people, but I didn't," I answer. "I feel great. I feel great. But we still have some business to take care of."

I'm aware of everything that's going on, but I control my emotions, I display only those I want people to see. So I restrain them until I finally meet alone with the players in the locker room, where I echo much of what I said two nights earlier. I tell them it was one of the most remarkable games I've ever been involved in. I tell them how much courage they showed after playing such a poor first half. I tell them how they continue to surprise me.

But deep down I feel even more. Deep down, I realize suddenly that I've never felt better, because I know what they've put into that game. Deep down, I know this is a remarkable team, that I enjoy coaching because they put it on the line every time out.

The crowd in our locker room is thinned out now, and only a few writers are still milling about. Some are standing with Mary, who is visiting one of my locker rooms for the first time in thirty-three years, and I decide to have some fun. "Let's go, Mary," I say to her. "If we hurry, we can get home to watch *Murder, She Wrote.*"

Since it's Sunday evening, I just happen to think of one of our favorite shows, and I have to use it. It perfectly fits the perception people have of me as unemotional. But by the time we get home that night, the mystery show is long over, and Mary and I and some of the family settle back to watch a tape of the Syracuse game.

# Every Gallstone Tells a Story

This season, now rushing toward its climax, actually began twelve months earlier and right after our disappointing 3-point loss to Villanova in the second round of the 1988 NCAA tourney. The coaches got together then to analyze our strengths and weaknesses, and before they departed for the summer we visited with each player to discuss what he needed to work on before the next year began.

First is Steve Bardo, our point guard and tremendous defender who played his high school ball at Carbondale High under the highly capable Doug Woolard. We tell him that we want him to become a better scorer and to rebound like Nick Anderson. He has shown that he can be a tremendous rebounder, but he hasn't done it with the consistency we feel he should have. We want Kendall Gill, whose high school mentor was the well-regarded Ron Brauer, to improve enough to be able to play the point if he needs to, and we want him to concentrate on becoming a better shooter. We know we're going to need some 3-point scoring. We have been terrible at that, and we feel Kendall is our best chance there. But he's a straight-up shooter who doesn't have very good form or very good wrist action, and we feel he needs to work on weights and get stronger so he can correct that.

We feel Larry Smith needs to have more drive; he needs to work at his game harder and just improve so he can play on this level. Nick has had a great sophomore year, so we just talk to him about his total game; he needs to become a better ball handler and defensive player, and he needs to work on taking the ball to the basket. We basically encourage him to hone his skills.

Kenny Battle, who's listed at 6-foot-6 in the program but really is only 6-foot-5, needs to become a better outside shooter so opponents can't jam him with a big guy inside. We want him to be able to play the perimeter, both to make us better and to give him an opportunity to play pro ball. Kenny played high school ball for the winning Gordie Kirkman and for John McDougal for two years at Northern Illinois University. Coach McDougal has been both a mentor and close friend to Kenny, and they share a very special coach-player relationship. Lowell Hamilton—we just want him to improve fundamentally on the little things. When he was in high school, it was not uncommon to see him travel six or seven times in one game. His ball handling needs work. Things like that.

Marcus Liberty's situation is a little different since he just sat out a season because of academic ineligibility. So I tell him, "Marcus, you're one of the finest talents we've ever recruited, and you were an outstanding high school player. Many think you were the top player in the country in your class. But that was on a secondary level, and this is the Big Ten. It's a vicious league, and to be successful on our level you must pick up some strength. You must pick up some muscle. You need to learn to put the ball on the court and take it to the basket and *create* a little more."

We take pride in the physical conditioning of our players, and that's why I have stated to the media on more than one occasion that I feel ours is one of the best conditioned teams you'll find. We believe in weight training and our players work extremely hard. We are blessed with an exceptional weight training program and some good people who oversee it. Strength coaches Bill Kroll and Peter Hoener worked diligently for years to upgrade our program and facilities. Strength mentors Leo Ward and Dwight Daub are carrying on with those concerted efforts. Today we have one of the premier weight training facilities in the nation thanks to a phenomenal gift from former University of Illinois baseball player and alumnus Lou Proano. Not only did Proano finance the weight training facilities, his contribution also made possible the construction of one of the country's finest college baseball facilities, Proano Stadium, which is on our campus.

So basically, the message to all of my players is the same: If the team is going to improve, they need to perfect their skills and build their bodies; each player needs to work and take care of himself.

Drug abuse has permeated all levels of society with a stranglehold so tight that civilization may never be able to free itself. Forty years ago the major problems that confronted athletic coaches were broken training rules involving a few beers or cigarettes. Now the major problems facing coaches of athletes are not only broken training rules, but broken laws, broken bodies and minds, and ultimately, broken lives. The whole world watched and was horrified as some of the greatest amateur athletes in recent years were stripped of their Olympic medals. A staggering percentage of others were prohibited from Olympic competition because of failed drug tests. Professional athletes have had highly successful and lucrative careers cut short or never reach fruition because of drug abuse. At the college level and below, athletes have been dismissed from teams and have ruined their educational opportunities when they let drugs become a part of their young lives. We have seen drugs ruin reputations, destroy family relationships, and in some cases, cost athletes their lives.

Athletes are a small segment of society, but because they are involved in high-visibility activities, some people will say, "It's another jock involved in drugs again." But the evidence shows that the college athletes are no more involved in drug use than the general student enrollment; in fact, slightly less.

Many colleges and universities have implemented drug testing programs for their athletes that have proven to be  major deterrents to drug use. The University of Illinois has been one of those, and I fully agree with this step. If our concern is for the general well-being of our athletes, then we have to stand behind the drug testing and drug education programs. They disperse information on drugs and substance abuse, and if any of our athletes have a problem, they can get help.

The drug education and testing program here at Illinois consists of random sampling for drugs, including anabolic steroids. This is done several times a year with both men's and women's sports. We have an excellent system that appears to be working very well.

It is my personal opinion that all colleges and universities should have drug testing and drug education programs. In fact, I think that anyone whose occupation makes him or her directly responsible for the lives of others should be required to submit to random drug testing  and be exposed to drug education at their place of work.

If you worked, you were praised. Then you were special. If you didn't work, you were ridiculed. Then you were put down.

That was the way it was in my family while I was growing up. The value of a good work ethic was impressed on me early.

My home was a cramped farmhouse two-and-a-half miles north of Okay, Oklahoma (population 300), where I was born in January 1932. I was the fifth child in a family of six boys and two girls: Alma, who died in infancy; J.D., who was killed during the Korean Conflict; Bill, who owns an electrical business in Wagoner, Oklahoma; Jim, a retired construction boss, also of Wagoner; Rose Mary, a homemaker who is married to J.W. Yates, formerly of Wagoner and now living in Dallas; Don, restaurant owner in Pryor, Oklahoma; and Ken, restaurant owner and former high school and college basketball coach. For most of his life, my father Joe supported us by toiling as a sharecropper. Our home had no electricity, no running water, and a backyard outhouse. Our quarters were so cramped that I shared one bed with two of my brothers. We changed spots on that bed once a week, which meant that once every third week I had the uncomfortable honor of sleeping in the middle.

At an early age I was up and out by 5:00 in the morning to help milk our thirty cows, feed the calves, skim the milk, and prepare the cream for sale to the creamery in Wagoner, some eight miles away. My biggest concern in those days was making sure the cow didn't step in a bucket of milk—and if it did, how to remove its foot without spilling the milk. My later duties included chopping cotton, picking corn, and raking hay, which was one thing I could do at a young age even though I wasn't a very healthy child and always had problems with the heat.

I'd faint all the time, and the memories of those spells are still acute. One day while raking, I started feeling bad, so I headed toward a shade tree—and that's the last I remember. When I came to, I was under the tree. Another time I was in a Christmas program in grade school and suddenly pitched forward, and hit the floor chin first. I still have the scar to prove it. Next thing I know, I'm outside the building being revived. You couldn't afford to go to doctors back then, so I never had my problem diagnosed. I didn't even visit a dentist until I had graduated from college.

Those fainting spells seemed to clear themselves up later on. But even when I was suffering from them, they didn't stop me from getting interested in sports. I played some tennis, some baseball, ran a little track, and about the time I entered junior high, I nailed a flimsy wire rim onto a tree and began playing basketball. A pair of rolled-up socks served as my ball back then. When I finally got the real thing a few months later, it was a $3 model that was too light to shoot when the wind was blowing.

But sports were really considered frivolous in my home, and my dad thought they were just a waste of time. He would often get mad at me for playing them, and my interest in them was never discussed. He would never see me play. He would never see me coach. Ever. The big thing back then was the work ethic.

There is a theory that claims that if you teach a youngster until he's six, he will seldom stray far from those early lessons during his lifetime. If he does, the normal tendency would be for him to revert eventually to his childhood learnings. I believe that and I think I'm living proof. I was drilled early on in the work ethic, and in my coaching today it still dominates me.

I don't think you can accomplish anything without a few brains, but more importantly, I believe you have to be a self-starter; you have to be willing to work. Time and time again I've seen people with ability and players with ability not utilize their talents and just waste them. That's why, philosophically, I feel it's so important to bring a player along slowly.

Assume I recruit a player like Marcus Liberty. He has some pretty good offensive skills, and I let him come in and score 18 points a game while not rebounding, not playing good defense. If I let that happen, he'll never be a complete player. So you put him on the bench because you expect him to attain a certain level of success in all areas, in all phases of the game. During Nick's first year, he was our leading scorer, but we didn't start him all the time. Instead we put him on the bench because he wasn't doing some of the things we insist on. That's basically what we did with Lowell all along; and he got better and better. The thing is, if you want a sound player, don't give him his candy first. Because if you give him his candy first, you're never going to get him to eat his vegetables.

It's a bit like sanding down a piece of wood before finishing it. Here we have to break the player down before building him back up. We get high school stars, and we have to break them down and get the defense, get the discipline, get them to play hard. Ken Battle has been the only exception to this rule; he may be the only player I've ever had that I felt played hard all the time. During practice I'd even go over to him and put my arm around him and say, "Ken, would you slow down? I think you're going too hard." But the rest of them have to learn that; they have to go through this breaking-down process and learn the fundamentals, how to play hard. We know they're not going to like it while they're going through it, but we also know it's good for them and makes them better players later on.

That's why, when we recruit a player, we say to him, "Look, do you want to come to Illinois and play for a top ten or top twenty program and get a great education? Now, do you want it up front

or later on? If you want it up front, don't come here. If you want
to go to a school, start immediately, not play good defense, and not
become a complete player, don't come here. But if you want to
come here, start from the bottom in some areas of the game, work
and become a complete player, well, we want you."

So we establish that early. But even then they have no idea,
no concept of what it's going to take to be a complete college
player. In high school they're at Level B, where they've succeeded
pretty easily. But to get up here to Level A, the time and energy
and effort needed is just so much greater. There's a huge difference
in the way you compete on the high school level and on the college
level, and players realize that only after they've been here a year or
two. They'll drop by then and say, "Gee, coach, I didn't realize you
had to play this hard." But what you have are players who are used
to scoring 25 points a game and dominating. Suddenly they run
into opponents who are as good or better than they are. In high
school, they could make mistakes and still get their points. In
college, they make mistakes and they're costly. That's why, on this
level, one of the most important things is getting a player to work
hard, to instill the work ethic.

Indoctrination. The key in coaching or in any other profession
is indoctrination. I don't drop everything on the player at one time.
But over a period of time, I slowly indoctrinate them into what I
want.

So now, whenever a couple of players drop by the office
during the off-season or even in-season, I talk to them about
different areas of the game. It may be defense. Then I grab Ervin
Small and say, "Look, Ervin, here's the way we put our feet." After
that we'll talk about defense for five minutes. Or maybe it's

rebounding. Then I say to Lowell, "Hey, Lowell, it's too bad we have a one-man rebounding team."

"What do you mean, coach?" he asks.

"I mean we're a one-man rebounding team. Nick leads our team in rebounding, and the other guys around him don't rebound like he does. They don't hit a lick on the boards."

"Hey, that's going to change next year. I'm going to beat him next year," he says.

"Look," I say. "Talk is cheap. Let's see what you can do on the court."

I issue the challenge right there, and sometimes I see them looking at each other, kind of laughing, giving each other the eye. But I'm doing this for a reason. I want them to know how important I think rebounding is, along with team basketball and all those other things you need to do to win. It's almost like the subliminal suggestions in commercials. So in the hallway, sometimes I just grab a player and start talking about blocking out, demonstrating how he should do it. Sometimes I do it in an airport. The players are wondering what I'm doing. People walking by are looking and thinking, "Is this guy crazy?"

But I'm doing it for a reason. It's all indoctrination, brainwashing the player about those things he should be doing. It's the whole idea of getting across important points at a particular time. And since it's so unexpected, the time to do that might be in the airport, or the hallway, or in my office. There's a time and a place for everything, and sometimes you can get a point across more effectively away from the court than on it.

I'm not just doing these things for no reason. Most of what I do has been thought through carefully because basketball is my life. Basketball, my family, and not much else.

Back in Okay, long before I knew I would be spending my life in basketball, one of my best friends was a boy named Lancey Nichols. He lived on the neighboring farm, about a mile away, and his dad Frank sold *Bluebook Spellers* to supplement the income he made from his fields.

Frank Nichols was what you would call a sharpy, and when he approached potential customers about buying a speller, he'd always open his pitch with a sweet-sounding proposition. If they could find a word in the book that he couldn't spell, he'd give it to them free. What those customers didn't know was that Frank had the ability to spell every word in that book both backward and forward, and so it was no surprise that he never had to give one away.

That was just the way Frank was. He delighted in challenging others, and one day he pulled Lancey and me aside and taught us to play checkers. Our board was rough-hewn wood, and our pieces were nothing more than old bottle caps, but I quickly fell in love with the game. I was soon able to beat Frank, which ended my matches with him. But I continued to play checkers and still find it a great source of relaxation.

I learned one other thing from Frank Nichols back then, both while listening to his spelling challenges and across a checker board. I learned to compete, and I quickly fell in love with that too.

Some years back I had a gall bladder operation performed by an excellent local surgeon, Dr. Michael Russo, who is now deceased. Before I went under the knife, Dr. Russo asked if I wanted my gallstone saved so I could get a look at it. I told him that I did. I got along so well after my surgery that just four days later I called up Bill Thompson, Larry Stewart, and Jerry Johnson, my bridge-playing buddies, and we played around the tray table for several hours in my hospital room. When I lost, I accused the others of taking advantage of a drugged hospital patient. But that didn't seem to rouse much sympathy.

Shortly after I got out of the hospital, Bob Evans went in to get his gall bladder removed as well. He's a dear friend of mine, a great guy who served five years as president of our Rebounders Club. One day we got to talking about our mutual experience.

"My stone was huge," I told him.

"Mine too," he said.

"Did you save yours?" I asked.

"Oh sure," Bob replied.

We went on like that for a while, and finally I looked at him and said, "I'll bet you a steak dinner mine was bigger than yours."

"It's a bet," he said.

Now there was no way I could win that bet since mine wasn't all that big. But the next week Mary and I were going over to the Evans's for coffee and I had to do something. So I went out to our back yard, found myself a nice-sized rock, and put it in my pocket. "OK, Bob, show me your gallstone," I challenged as soon as I was in the door of his home.

"Here it is," he said, showing me. I then pulled my garden's contribution from my pocket, compared it, and immediately proclaimed myself the winner. But the story doesn't end there. Later over coffee, Bob admitted that he had gotten his stone from his garden. I confessed that I'd done the same, and we all had a good laugh. But it was still a competition, and I was glad I had won, even though it had only involved comparisons of bogus gallstones.

I am riding during the off-season to a grants-in-aid function with Dick Martin, our fine TV announcer, and John Mackovic, our football coach and athletic director. Our conversation meanders through various subjects related to sports and finally settles down on the reputations and practices of various coaches.

"Lou," Dick then says, "you're not that demanding a coach, are you?"

"Dick," I reply, a little surprised, "why, sure. Sure I am."

Then it's his turn to be surprised—a response, I'm sure, that would be shared by many people if they saw me at work. Dick's misconception, one that seems to be held by many people, was from judging me by my public image. That portrays me as a nice guy, as a father figure, as good natured. And off the court, I do try to be that way. If I look outside and see that it's raining, and someone else tells me that it's not raining, I probably won't contradict that person. I would just let it go. I'm a fairly easy-going guy in my personal life, but that's not the way I am on the court.

I grew up playing checkers, dominoes, cards, and competing. In my home, in my family structure, if you didn't compete, even for sleeping space, you didn't survive, and I've carried this attitude since childhood: that everything in life is basically competition. I don't hunt. I don't fish. I don't play golf. I used to play some tennis, but I don't anymore. But bridge, checkers, and dominoes, I still compete in those games when time allows.

Speaking of checkers, during the Final Four one of the television networks shot some footage of me playing checkers with our assistant sports information director, Kent Brown. And just recently I experienced a first. Stevie Jay, the very popular afternoon talk show host on local radio station WDWS, challenged me to a game of checkers on the air. Each of us just described our moves as we went along, but luckily the game didn't last that long—did it Stevie?

One Saturday morning Mary and I drove to Springfield to play some bridge with Bill Ridley and John Homeier, two former Illinois players, and Bill's wife Jo. We got there around 1:30 in the afternoon, sat down, and instead of playing with two decks as people normally do, we always play with six. That way there's no wasted time between hands; the dummy could make the cards while the hand was being played, and we could just keep going. So we sat down to play at 1:30, stopped to eat a great dinner at 6:00, then played again until midnight. This was competition, not a social event. Neither Bill Ridley, John Homeier, nor I like to be social in situations like that. When Mary and Jo tried to discuss a hand, we stopped them.

"Look," we told them, "we don't want post-mortems. Just play."

On another occasion, we played bridge with Steve, Mike, and Jeff Hartman and their wives at their lakehouse for thirteen consecutive hours. After breakfast the next morning, Bill and Ann Cofel and John and Ann Healey, a few of their friends, joined us for several more hours of bridge. Competition, it's what I'm about.

It's the same thing on the court but very few except those directly involved have any idea of my personality when I'm out there. It's all business, and we want it done right. I have to do it right. My assistants have to do it right. The players have to do it right. I'm a perfectionist there, that's just the way I am. I mean, it's a hard-nosed business, and I tell our guys, "We have two hours and we're not going to waste a minute of it. We're going to go out there, and I don't want you wasting your time or mine. We're going to get it done, and we're going to do it to the best of our abilities."

I once read an article about the actor Dustin Hoffman, who's often accused of being a perfectionist when he's shooting a film. When people talk about him in that way, it carries a negative connotation; but in this article he pointed out that you wouldn't want a heart surgeon  operating on you if he or she wasn't a perfectionist, and you wouldn't want an attorney representing you in court who wasn't a perfectionist. Luckily, I haven't needed a heart surgeon, and I've had the good fortune of acquiring the services of two great attorneys who have  also been close friends, the late Wm. Byron Darden of Las Cruces, New Mexico, and my present legal counsel, Tom Harrington of Champaign.

Some players might think of me the way a lot of people commonly think of Hoffman, but here's a story that will help explain my attitude.  One day I was visiting with a Peoria friend, Dick Corley, who got three  degrees from the University of Illinois and then went on to become a very successful plastic surgeon. "You know, Lou," he said to me, "the worst years I ever spent were the first years I practiced. I was such a perfectionist then and expected everyone around me to be perfect. I lost nurses and secretaries right and left. I put tremendous pressure on them. They couldn't work for me. Even the good ones would come in and be nervous and not confident of what they were doing. Finally I relaxed a little bit, realized they were going to make some mistakes. And then my life around the office became much better. We were more produc-tive, and people would stay with me. I no longer had unrealistic expectations of them."

Back in high school, when I first started coaching, I was much like my friend  Dick was when he started his practice. I expected too much, and if a player made a mistake during a game, I immediately pulled him. Sometimes I made him go down to the end of the court and do pushups even while the game was  going on. But now, even though I still think I'm a perfectionist, I might realize that a guy is going to throw the ball away. Or a guy is going to miss a shot. But there's a big difference between missing a shot and picking up your pivot foot and traveling. You do that, and I'm on top of you. I'm going to scream. That's just concentration, and I've seen NCAA playoff games lost because some guy travels. There's no excuse for walking.

That's why, in the middle of an important practice session, I may take the ball and spend five minutes faking and putting it on the floor. I may do this twenty-five times. Then I'll look at the players and say, "If I'm fifty-seven and can fake and put the ball on the floor without traveling, is it too much to ask you guys to do it? You guys are traveling all the time. Why not do it right?"

You can't expect a player to do something he can't do. If you make that mistake, you're going to damage his confidence and ruin the individual. So we make sure he stays in his comfort zone and just does those things he does well. But traveling? Hey, that's one mistake we can eliminate, and so we concentrate on it.

In that way you can be a perfectionist. And in basketball, being a perfectionist is not condemnation. It's what any competitor should want to be.

When I was in the eighth grade, my family moved from Okay to Wagoner, and I began competing in basketball in an organized way. In my first game for Wagoner Junior High, where I was coached by Mr. Ashley, I scored 13 of my team's 15 points. I would end the season as my team's leading scorer.

But the most lasting influence from that year was an English course I took that was taught by Mrs. Nicholson. Her husband Harold just happened to be the superintendent of schools back in

Okay, and also the coach of my team in the following summer's Wagoner County baseball league. I was immediately impressed by Nick, as we all called him, and decided then to return to Okay for high school, where another fine educator, George Hopkins, was our principal.

My father was still complaining bitterly that I spent too much time shooting baskets and not enough on my chores. But after a sales pitch as good as any I've since used on a recruit, I did convince him to give me $3.95 from our meager family budget to buy my first good pair of tennis shoes. They were, coincidentally, white high-top All Stars by Converse, the company I now represent. But by transferring, I was ineligible as a freshman at Okay High. So I didn't get to play for the school until my sophomore season, although I practiced every day with the team.

My coach that year was a decorated World War II hero by the name of Joe Eidson, whose dad owned a second-hand clothing store in town. We were all impressed by his toughness, which he had shown by surviving a German concentration camp while his weight dropped from 180 to 70 pounds. But this year he also touched me with his kindness. He knew my family, like many others, wasn't that well off, and so he let me trade in my worn pairs of shoes for the best available at his father's store.

Joe resigned as coach before the start of my junior year, and Harold Nicholson, "Nick," appointed himself successor. Every morning, through all my four years at Okay, Nick drove me the eight miles from Wagoner to the school and then, since he arrived so early to fulfill his obligations as superintendent, he let me into the gym for an hour of early-morning practice. Not surprisingly, he turned into something of a role model for me. It was during my time with him that I first started thinking of coaching as a profession. I admired him because he had distinguished himself in the field of coaching, and today I still carry with me much of his philosophy.

The idea of becoming a coach was nurtured through the two seasons I played under him. But there was one game, the final game of my junior year, that was something of a benchmark. We were then in the state Class C playoffs and going up against our bitter rival Onapa, whom we had defeated two weeks earlier by 35 points. But before our rematch, Onapa decided to use a defense that was little-known at the time, a defense now called the match-up zone. By employing it this time, they won by a point, 47-46.

The defeat was heartbreaking, but a seed had been planted. I was suddenly very much interested in this thing called coaching and the strategy involved in it.

There was no such thing as a Final Four back then. Colleges were playing national title games, but they weren't any big deal.

I do remember listening on the radio when Adolph Rupp's Kentucky team beat Hank Iba's Oklahoma State team for the 1949 title. And once I saw former DePaul coach Ray Meyer bring a team into Oklahoma State. But the status of the game and the profession of coaching is so much different now. It's not even close, which is why I once told a reporter that if a young man came to me and asked whether he should choose college coaching as a profession, I would tell him no. Put it this way: If I started again, I probably would still be a coach. But I wouldn't advise other people to do it. I have the right temperament, I've weathered the storms, and I've been fortunate. But to understand what I mean, just look at the pressures now and all that's involved.

For the eleven years between 1939 and 1949, the first eleven years of NCAA title games, the total gross receipts were $911,633. In 1989, each team in the Final Four received $1.25 million. So start there, and then consider this. You've got 293 schools trying to be one of the 64 that get into the NCAA playoffs, which means that each year 229 are not going to make it. Now you know what the people around those 229 schools are thinking. The players, the president, the student body, the student newspaper, the boosters, and the fans are all going to be wondering why their team didn't make it.

But go further now and consider the odds of those 229 teams ever making it. Think about it. Of those 64 who do make it, you can probably write in 25 or 30 that will be there eight out of ten years. Then in certain conferences, you've got teams that will make it every third year or so, which means you're looking at roughly 200 schools that may never get to the playoffs—and if they do, it's going to be a rarity. But the people at those schools see all that money out there and start wondering why they're not getting a piece of the pie. That's true, that's reality, that's what's happening. Coaches know. They're surrounded by all these people who watch as $250,000 is awarded for just making the tournament, $1.25 million for the Final Four. And these people are thinking, "Why not us?"

It goes even further than that, and Illinois is a good example in which just getting to a post-season tournament is not enough any more. We've been to seven straight NCAA tournaments, so what would happen if we won only eighteen games and went to the NIT instead? How would people react? The season would be deemed a failure. Would they even come out to watch us play? They wouldn't do so enthusiastically. So the teams that have been going have to continue going, or the coach risks losing his job. It's a fact of life in basketball today, this pressure to win the big bucks.

Then there are the other pressures. You're under pressure to follow the NCAA rules, and they're more severe than ever before. Any one of us can make a mistake, and suddenly you and your whole staff can be fired. But the rules are so complex, all kinds of things can come up. That's why your faculty representative to the NCAA is so important, and we're lucky to have a guy like Professor John Nowak. He's been outstanding and has made great contributions to our institution at considerable personal sacrifice. Others who have aided us in the interpretation and compliance areas of Big Ten and NCAA regulations are Chicago-based attorney Mike Slive and his staff.

Once two of our Chicago players appeared in a summer All-Star game for which no admission was charged, but soft drinks were sold. Since they didn't sell tickets, we thought they were all right. But the concessions generated income, and that fact made these two guys ineligible according to NCAA rules. So we had to petition the NCAA and get things straightened out. But that's why I say people like John Nowak and Mike Slive are so important to our program. They answer all kinds of questions, questions you didn't previously have to worrry about.

You're also under pressure to graduate your players, and everyone's watching that. Years ago, if a player went out on the town and got into trouble you never heard about it, even in the local papers. But if a player from New Mexico gets into a fight in a bar now, you read about it in Chicago. And that's pressure too. Finally, a college coach today has so many factions he has to try to please: the administration, the faculty, the students, the boosters, and the media—you take a certain amount of flak from each of them. You have to be able to handle that, and I think my personality has allowed me to. But you have to have a thick skin to manage that, and a lot of people don't have that.

Sometimes I sit back and long for those early days. But being a realist, I know that all of these complexities are part of the game now. The hassles can sometimes get tiring, but it's not all bad. For the most part I enjoy my work.

The people you're around every day affect how you get through all those hassles. When Neale Stoner, former athletic director, and his assistant Vance Redfern, and their staff were here at Illinois, I enjoyed working with them, and they assisted me in many ways in building our program. Mike White, former U. of I. football coach, and his staff were supportive of us, and we had a good relationship. Now I have more good people to work for in the persons of John Mackovic, my present athletic director, and his associates, Bob Todd and Dana Brenner. And, of course, I have been so fortunate to have great staffs with which to work. My present assistants are some of the best in the country. Dick Nagy, Jimmy Collins, Mark Coomes, and Scott Nagy are not only super guys to be around, they're personable, hard-working, and as loyal a group as I've ever seen.

Of course, one thing hasn't changed about the game. Thirty years ago, a coach was a teacher, and today he is still a teacher; it's just a different teaching situation now. It's more complex, it's more intense. Your margin of error is smaller, and unless you're lucky and at one of those schools that always gets great players, you better be good. But still, it's teaching. You still have to teach. My goal in high school was to attend Oklahoma State and play for Hank Iba, the legendary coach and renowned teacher who won back-to-back national titles in 1945 and '46. But neither he nor his staff saw me play, and so at Nick's urging, I turned down some offers from small four-year colleges and enrolled at Connors A & M, a junior college in Warner, Oklahoma.

My coach there was Bobby Jack Rogers, who had played on Iba's championship teams and demanded that we play defense for a full forty minutes. He was one of the toughest and most demanding coaches I've ever been around—a strict disciplinarian. In my first year there, he guided our team to the National Junior College Tournament. Rogers left for East Texas State College after that year, where he won the National Association of Intercollegiate Athletics (NAIA) basketball championship.

After my freshman year I set off for Freeport, Illinois, looking for some lucrative summer employment. In high school, I had worked at Austin Watkins's poultry house in Wagoner, and there I tested the cream we purchased from the local farmers; killed, scalded, plucked, and cut up fryers; and almost got fired for the only time in my life while selling eggs to a neighborhood lady. "Are these eggs fresh?" she asked me.

"Yes," I assured her.

"Are you sure they're fresh?" she asked again.

This time I didn't answer her immediately. Instead I grabbed an egg, cracked it on the rim of a barrel, broke it into my mouth, and swallowed. "Oh yes, ma'am, they're very fresh," I said, at which point she gasped, dashed from the store, and later jeopardized my job with old Mr. Watkins by complaining about the "fresh" young clerk.

Now, after listening to a glowing sales pitch from a canning company recruiter, I left Connors for Illinois to take a job that was supposed to pay high wages and include free lodging. But when I and some of my teammates finally arrived in Freeport, we found that the house we were expected to live in was a rat-infested,

World War II barracks, and that our salary was much less than advertised. We immediately dashed to the nearest employment office, which sent us off to Lanark (population 1,400) and the Green Giant Canning Company.

We intended to stay only until we earned gas money home. But when we were each given work at 80¢ an hour, we decided to sign up for the summer. I was assigned to work in the brineroom, where I stood over a vat and mixed the water, salt, and sugar solution that was eventually pumped into the canning room and sealed into cans of peas and corn.

That summer and the next two as well, I basically worked twenty-four- hour shifts, and got by with quick naps atop the sugar and salt sacks piled in a corner of the brineroom. If I needed to rest during the pea pack, my partner at the time had to work doubly hard to cover for me, and later I'd return the favor. If the need arose during the corn pack, which used less brine than the peas and was a one-man job, I could get my work done early and then get my rest.

My teammates and I, whom the townsfolk called Okies, found ourselves rooms to rent, but I primarily used mine only for a quick shower and to change my clothes. I slept in its bed only when it rained and the canning company was forced to shut down.

I met Mary Catherine Brantner the last month of the last summer I worked for the Jolly Green Giant. On our first date, the evening of August 1, 1954, we saw a Doris Day movie, *Calamity Jane*, at the White Pines drive-in theatre in Polo, Illinois. I guess you might say it was "love at first sight," because starting that day, we dated for thirty-five consecutive days or nights, depending on when I could arrange my work schedule to get free from my twenty-four-hour shift, so we could go on picnics, walks, or see movies.

I returned to NMSU in September to begin my senior year and play my final season of college basketball for the Aggies. I made the long drive back to Lanark during Christmas break, and took Mary to a dance in the high school gym. There, beneath the basketball goal trimmed with mistletoe, as the band played their final selection, I asked her to marry me. "Grow old along with me, the best is yet to be" is the line of poetry I borrowed from Robert Browning to whisper in her ear. A few days later we headed for Oklahoma so she could meet my family. Then we went to Las Cruces, New Mexico, where we were married by a justice of the peace at 2:00 p.m. on December 29, 1954.

I was warming up on the floor of Williams gymnasium, resuming basketball practice after Christmas break at exactly 2:30 the same day. Thirty-five years later, perhaps the best has been, we don't know. But Mary knows one thing for certain: we have grown old together. If you stay in this coaching business long enough, believe me it will make you *old.*

When I returned to Connors after that first summer in Lanark, my new coach was former Arkansas coach Presley Askew. Like Iba and Rogers before him, he impressed the importance of defense upon me. And that season I finally started playing it with the tenacity necessary to be successful. I also led the team in scoring. So when Coach Askew left after that season for New Mexico State, he offered me a scholarship, which I immediately accepted.

Coach Askew's methods were gentler, but he was as much a disciplinarian as Rogers had been. In my three years with him, I learned the value of that virtue, as well as many other intangibles that go into successful coaching. Coach Askew is one of the most intelligent, personable men ever to coach the game. We players loved to listen to his homespun humor and the phrases he used to weave into his coaching lectures. The players all loved and respected him because he treated everyone with dignity. He will soon be eighty, and he remains very active. He still sends letters of advice to me, and as a sign-off in beautiful bold script he'll pen this philosophical phrase, one that has held us both in good stead throughout the years: "Keep Sawin Wood."

I continued being indoctrinated into man-to-man defense, and it would take me a long time to realize that a team could play a good zone defense too. The zone defense was considered a "sissy" defense when I was in college. If you played it you were not considered good enough to play a man's game. There was a lot of macho involved in that attitude, and for a long time, in my own mind I downgraded coaches who resorted to zones.

But the man-to-man defense is still one of the foundation blocks of our philosophy at Illinois. I also think it's easier to teach and play a zone than man-to-man. In a zone, you basically just stand around in an area and make your opponent shoot from the outside. Man-for-man, first of all, you've got to be able to cover a driver. Then you've got to cover a cutter, you've got to cover in a screening situation, you've got to cover when you're on the ball, when you're away from the ball, and at the same time you've got to help your teammates out. There's no comparison in the degree of difficulty between the two.

I may be exaggerating a bit here, but I can pretty much teach someone to play zone in one afternoon on the chalkboard. For someone to learn to play good man-to-man, it takes at least a year. That's why it's easier for a young player to break into a team that plays zone most of the time, and why some of our young players spend time on the bench no matter how good they are offensively.

If we let our defense slip, it undermines our whole philosophy. If we let a new guy on the block come in and play, even though he isn't playing good defense, his teammates (who've worked hard at it for three years) are going to see that and think, "Why do I have to do it?" That's why it takes a bit longer for players to rise in our program, but they'll be better in the long run.

This philosophy was drilled into me while watching Hank Iba and while playing for Eidson, Nicholson, Rogers, and Askew; and I've followed it as long as I've coached. Back in the late Sixties, when I was coaching at New Mexico State, the same Jimmy Collins who is now my assistant was then my fine-shooting sophomore guard. We were scheduled to play a great Purdue team that was coached by George King, the present Purdue athletic director. That team featured the high-scoring Rick Mount. Since it was billed as one of the important games of the season, I was flown into Chicago for a press conference. "Mount's a great player," I told the writers there. "But we have a guy, he's probably not as good as Mount, but he's close. He's a very good player. Jimmy Collins."

Most of them knew nothing about our team with the exception of *Chicago Tribune* sportswriter, David Condon, who coincidentally grew up in Las Vegas, New Mexico, with our team physician Dr. Henry Hosford and his brother Professor Phil Hosford, who at the time was serving on the NMSU Athletic Board. In fact, Hank and Phil had been members of a neighborhood group dubbed "Condon's Gang." So Dave was well aware of our NMSU team and its potential. The other writers present appeared to be skeptical of my comparison of Collins with Mount, and soon one of them checked a roster sheet and said, "Coach, this guy you're talking about, you left him out of the starting lineup."

"That's right," I told him. "Jimmy probably won't start, but that doesn't mean he doesn't have good offensive skills. We just think every player should attain a certain level of success or excellence defensively before we move him in there, and he's getting better at that all the time."

Well, all the writers smirked at that, but then we went into Purdue and beat them 87-80. That team would go to the Final Four the following season. Mount shot eleven-of-twenty-three and scored 27 points in thirty-six minutes of play. Jimmy shot six-of-ten and scored 13 points while playing only a dozen minutes. But that's a good example of what I believe. Here we had Jimmy, a tremendous player. We didn't start him and played him for less than a third of the game. We let him work his way up, and he was a better player for that. He was one of the most prolific scorers who ever played for me, as well as being an excellent defensive player.

You teach what you are. You hear that all the time in educational circles, and there's so much truth to it. You may fool people for a while, but sooner or later, you'll be found out. You must practice what you preach. That's another old cliche, but as sound a maxim as you'll find. If I just talked defense, my players would see through that. So I've got to put a player on the bench and tell him, "Look, this is the way we're going to do it, and when you do, you'll play." If it takes Jimmy Collins not starting and sitting on the bench, then that's the way it's going to be. If it takes Nick Anderson not starting and sitting on the bench, that's the way it's going to be as well. We're going to play good defense.

At Illinois, we define that in two ways. We go by points allowed and by our opponent's field goal percentage. To me, the latter is the better barometer. Points are an important part of it, of course. But holding down the opponent's shooting percentage, that's the best way to do it.

When considering only athletic skill, we judge a potential recruit strictly in terms of offense. If he doesn't have offensive skills by the time we get him, there's little we can do to help him. But defensively, he probably hasn't been taught a lot, and I can teach anybody to play defense.

We want guys who can score, and the most precious ones are guys who can really *create*. If they're the right kind of people and can score and create, those are the ones we recruit. We tell them, hey, don't even worry about your defense. If you're willing to work at it, that's all we ask of you. We're not going to take anything away from your offense. We're going to let you score, we're going to score in the 80s, 90s, sometimes over 100. We tell them that on the offensive end, we're going to help you. We're going to hone your skills and run patterns that will assist you and help the team. We tell them, hey look, you're an 80 percent offensive player, and we're going to move you up to 85 or 90 percent. But defensively, you're very weak you're a 30 percent player there, and we're going to get you up into the 90s. All you need is to be willing to work.

Joe Dumars, the guard for the world-champion Detroit Pistons who's renowned for his defense, once said that to play it well, you always had to know where the ball was, you always had to know where your man was, and you always had to have the "want-to." He was right, and the last is the most important. It's most important because you can make mistakes defensively, and if you "want to" badly enough, you can still cover your man. It's the most important thing because there's nothing glamorous about playing good defense. Playing good defense is a dirty job; playing good defense is not much more than hard work. And no one can play good defense unless he wants to.

I've coached some exceptional defensive players over the years. At New Mexico State, three of the exceptional ones were forwards Ernie Turner and John Burgess and guard Rob Evans. Slammin' Sam Lacey is the best shot-blocker I've ever coached. Here at Illinois, Bruce Douglas and Derek Harper led the Big Ten in steals several times. Doug Altenberger was one of the best position defensive players; his value was in his ability to defend various sized opponents. Big George Montgomery and Efrem Winters were our best defensive combination against inside people. Neil Bresnahan was a 6-foot-6 defensive dynamo for us. Of course, Steve Bardo was selected Big Ten Defensive Player of the Year just last season.

So the first thing I, as a coach, have to do is make a player want to do it. Then after a while, they play good defense just because they want to. Then you've got him. Once a player does it because *he* wants to, then you have something. But when we get them, they don't play good defense because they *want* to, they play good defense because they know they *have* to in order to play. "If you're going to play here," we tell them all, "you're going to have to play the other end of the floor."

We'll explain it to them. "Look," I'll say, "how much time are we going to have the ball? Let's say we shoot it on the average of every fifteen to twenty seconds. That means you're going to spend about half your time on offense."

"OK. That's right," the players will agree.

"So," I'll ask right back, "how much time does that mean we're spending on the other end of the court?"

They'll all laugh about that, but I've made the point that they spend at least half of a game on the defensive end. "Now," I will ask them, "how are we going to win games if we're mediocre defensively? How can we do that?"

After a while, someone will say, "Well, coach, we can't."

"That's the point. That's why we've all got to play good defense." And then I move on to a bit of brainwashing. "Now, P.J.," and here I'll look at Bowman. "Bardo over there is playing great defense already. Now since he's doing that, don't you think you should help him? Isn't it important for you to play good defense too?"

"Sure, coach. All of us have to do it," he'll say.

"Well, Steve," I'll turn to Bardo. "If you're the only one who plays defense, and we let guys play in games who don't do that, don't you think that after a while you might not play it quite as hard?"

I don't expect an answer, but that's just common sense. If someone's out there doing the dirty work, he wants everyone around him doing it too. No one's going to go out there and sacrifice his body drawing a charge if his teammates aren't willing to make that sacrifice too. That's why you need everybody to do it; that's why you need everyone wanting to do it. It's just that simple.

Coaching principles and techniques that I learned from my own coaches and others are just as valid now as they were back then. When I discuss basketball with Lee Cabutti, the excellent retired coach from Champaign Central High, we both agree that the techniques we used early in our careers are still sound. The players have changed; they're so much better now. But in many ways I'm doing the same things my coaches once did. Fundamentally speaking, the game of basketball has remained the same.

Coaches' monetary rewards, however, have changed drastically. Many great coaches of past eras never made any big money. Bob Knight and I have talked about this a lot, about how coaches' salaries have escalated so much. When he started at Indiana back in 1972, he was making something like $16,000, and he didn't make much more for a long, long time. I took the New Mexico State job in 1966 for $10,000, and when I was hired at Illinois in April 1975, my salary was $30,000, which was very good for the time. Attractive fringe benefits were nonexistent.

All of that changed when television increased its involvement with college basketball. To understand the situation fully now, all you have to do is look at the contract Rick Pitino signed with Kentucky in the spring of 1989. It was for seven years and worth a reported $6 million. Some coaches now have shoe contracts worth $150,000 per year and show up at games in $600 suits. The contracts we sign for radio and TV shows are also much more lucrative now, as are summer camps and speaking engagements.

Sports is big business now, and although I liked it better when it wasn't, I know none of us can do anything about it. But the material things ... well, I believe it's important that you make a living and do well for your family. But I still don't believe that money can buy happiness. I know that old saying, "But it can keep you comfortable while you're trying to get happy." And I know that some people probably criticize me for spending maybe only $200 for a suit when other guys are spending $600. But I tell people who ask me about that, "Listen, the most enjoyment I get in life is to win a ball game or to see a player really improve or to know that he's getting his degree." Things like that just happen to make me feel good.

New cars? Early on at Illinois, in exchange for a short

television commercial, we were given the use of a new Corvette. After a few days I said, "Send it back. That's not me. Get me a station wagon." It's not image or anything, it's just me. I had an old car when I got to Illinois, and the only reason I drive a new car now is because it's furnished. Mary and I still live in the same modest house we bought when we first settled in Champaign, and for the last fourteen years, I've spent three or four mornings a year just hanging around Delbert's, John Watkins's clothing store down in Arthur, Illinois. It's a small town, but I'll go down there, spend two or three hours, just hang around the store and drink coffee and talk to people.

Everybody knows who the head basketball coach is down there, and a lot of kidding goes on. "John," I'll kid Watkins, "if you gave me my clothes instead of just giving me a discount, then you could say you provide the wardrobe of the Illinois basketball coach. That would be pretty impressive."

"Lou comes down here on Saturday morning, my busy time," he'll tell his customers. "He drinks my coffee, makes me buy him lunch, and hangs around my store. When he leaves, he picks up a pair of socks and charges them."

The Delbert Taylor family owns The Villa, a clothing store for women across the street from John's place, and Mary checks out the latest fashions there as John and I make our rounds. We may wander into the Tintype, a photography studio that is owned by one of our basketball photographers, Mark Jones; we may stop at one of the restaurants for coffee, or drop by Dick's pharmacy where we can get ice cream sodas, "green rivers," and cherry colas made the old-fashioned way.

A large segment of the people who live in and around Arthur

are Amish, and as we walk along Main Street, we watch as the horses and buggies with their quaintly dressed drivers move along the thoroughfare. When we finally leave this quiet village, our last stop may be at Erland Kondrup's cheese factory.

Another getaway for us is at Mary's hometown of Lanark, located in northwestern Illinois. Here we visit relatives and friends several times a year for special occasions such as weddings, family reunions, or anniversary celebrations. More than sixty years ago, Ben and Hassie Brantner, Mary's late parents, purchased a 180-acre farm three miles east of Lanark and raised five daughters and five sons there. Herbert Hoover Brantner, politics unknown, otherwise known as "Hub," bears the dubious title of "Illini Basketball Expert In Residence." He has retired from farming but not from "coaching"; nor have brothers-in-law Sam and Max Brantner, Dean Miller, Virgil Coomes, or Don Earp. Had I met with this crack advisory team before the Final Four Michigan game, the outcome might have been very different!

And if sister-in-law Marcella Earnest of Austin, Texas, and brother-in-law Bob Brantner of Nova Scotia, Canada, lived closer, I feel certain that they too would have gladly contributed more expertise. Thank goodness most of the sisters-in-law, Liz and Thelma Brantner, Shirley Miller, Becky Coomes, and Carole Earp, are only good fans who cheer on the Fighting Illini instead of assisting the head coach.

I know this sounds corny, and I do enjoy big cities like Chicago and all they have to offer. But visits to Arthur and Lanark are important to me. They take me back to my roots. I've never felt that people prove their worth by getting rich or by purchasing another car. I've never felt I had to move to the high-rent district just because someone else is moving there. I've always felt confident enough to be who I am and I refuse to let people pressure me into being what they think I should be.

A congratulatory card I once got from my daughter Lisa's best friend, Lindie Carden Stenzel, explains my feelings best. On the front of it was Ralph Waldo Emerson's definition of success:

> *To laugh often and much; to win the respect of intelligent people and the affection of children; to earn the appreciation of honest critics and endure the betrayal of false friends; to appreciate beauty, to find the best in others; to leave the world a bit better, whether by a healthy child, a garden patch or a redeemed social condition; to know even one life has breathed easier because you have lived. This is to have succeeded.*

## In the Beginning

The experts' preseason rankings start appearing in early fall, and as they dribble out, there we are among everyone's favorites. In Dick Vitale's *Basketball* we're tapped as the second-best team in the country, and he writes, "Forget past disappointments and high hopes. The depth and athleticism of the Illini spell a big, big year." *The Sporting News* puts us at number three and declares, "Illinois's lofty ranking stems from its unmatched collection of superb mid-sized athletes who can generate a wealth of firepower." We're number five in the pages of *Street & Smith's*, and in *Sports Illustrated* we're number seven.

"I think," I tell my assistants, "that we can end up anywhere between first and seventh in the Big Ten." I'm not kidding. Early, at this point, I really do think this team might end up in the middle of the pack. Michigan is just loaded. Iowa's loaded. Ohio State, we don't know what to expect since they've just had a great recruiting year. Indiana, they're always a threat. I think we could very easily wind up in the second division.

Here's the thing. The previous season we as a team were last in the Big Ten in free-throw shooting and last in the Big Ten in 3-point shooting. We are very concerned about that since the unwritten rule of thumb states that if a player doesn't shoot well as a sophomore, he won't shoot well from then on. Then Phil Kunz, whom we were counting on to back up our front line, tells us he's going to transfer; and Jens Kujawa, our starting center and best post defender, decides to return to his native Germany and play for a club team and a $90,000 salary. We are scrambling now, just trying to keep our heads above water while attempting to replace those two. We sign Rodney Jones out of New Mexico Junior College, who played for Ron Black, only to find out that he can't make the grades and will have to sit out the season. So here we are without a true post man and with a team that was ranked last in some very important shooting departments. And that gives us some reservations about our future. We have no idea how good we will be. We don't know what to expect.

I stayed on at New Mexico State to get my master's degree in education, and then I began my coaching career with a single expectation. Someday, somehow, I wanted to win a state high school championship.

This career choice, I felt, was a natural for me. I had been taking administrative courses and thinking of going into that field, but then I sat back one day and tried to be logical. "Look," I told myself, "you've spent your whole life playing this game, and you've had the luck to do it under tremendous coaches. They've taught you the game. You enjoy it. You know what you're doing. Why not? It's not something you have to do. If you end up not liking it, you can break away and do something else."

That was how the decision was made, and I tried to get into coaching as soon as I graduated from State. But my application to a small school in the tiny town of Maxwell, New Mexico, was turned down. So I returned to the university and finished my graduate work in twelve months. I was now married to Mary and we were living in a men's dormitory, where I was pulling down $150 per month as head resident. She too was working while going to school, and on the side I was making another $75 per week running a laundry service. I also refereed games and helped coach the NMSU freshman team. Between us we were making enough to buy a new, gas-guzzling car.

The next year I signed on to teach math and coach the B team at Las Cruces High School, and we had to sell that car and buy down. It hurt, but I'd suffered a cut in pay and was now taking home only $271 per month. Then, just two years later, varsity coach Vernon Yates retired to run a Spudnut shop. The door opened for me and I was elevated.

I found many of the players I had coached on the B team now trying out for the varsity, such guys as Joe Lopez, E.W. Wright, Don Mullins, Lee Jensen, Harley Pettes, Jimmy Apodaca, Tommy Sullivan, Buster Deerman, Ed Boney, Ed Melendres, and Greg Robles. Our familiarity with each other would turn out to be a key to our eventual success. But no one expected any kind of success when our season opened. And after we went down to El Paso, Texas, and got beat by 16 points by Ysleta High, even I was a little concerned. We were still an average team in December, but suddenly, in early 1959, we caught fire, went to the playoffs, and earned a spot in the state tournament.

We were scheduled to open against a good Albuquerque team, but we were given no chance to win. We won, 54-51. That earned us a spot against Ralph Boyer's sterling Carlsbad team, which was comparable to many of the better ones you find in Illinois. Again we were given no chance to win. They were bigger than we and blessed with three players who would go to college on scholarships. But we won, 48-47. That put us into the finals against Clayton, and even here we were given no chance to win. We won by 7. So in my first year in my first head coaching job, my expectations were fulfilled.

As a young coach, I just couldn't wait for the first practice of a new season. I would spend the days in my office working and thinking, planning, and calling coaching friends and former college teammates to run ideas by them or pick their brains. Some of these were my brother, Ken; young Pres Askew, son of my coach at NMSU; former assistant Cal Stutzman, who'd moved back to Nappanee, Indiana; and college teammates Wesley Jarman, Raymond Gann, Don Butler, and Bill Cleary, all of whom have remained good friends. I'd ask them for information and we'd exchange ideas. If I gleaned only one useful bit of information from all this talk, I'd feel it was time well spent. I'd be pumped up and wouldn't sleep well a night or two before opening practice.

That feeling is still there to some degree, but as October 15, 1988, and my first meeting with my latest Illinois team approach, I'm much more relaxed. I've spent most of the summer in my office plotting; we know what we want to do. I'm looking forward to the new year and the challenge of seeing how much we can improve between this day and the opening of the season.

We gather the team around us and almost immediately set out to indoctrinate them further into concentrating on those areas we feel are important. "Larry," I say to Larry Smith, "do you think we can win the Big Ten this year?"

"Yes. Of course we can, coach."

"Guys, do you realize that we've led the Big Ten in defense for four consecutive seasons?" I ask. "Do you realize that in eight categories, we led the Big Ten in seven of them? Do you realize that? P.J. Bowman. What does that mean to you?"

"Well, coach, it's pretty darn good."

"It's more than pretty darn good," I tell them. "You know what that means? That speaks for the character of this team. That speaks for the type of people you are. You know, you're willing to get on the floor, and you're willing to play defense. That may not mean a lot to you, but it means a lot to me. Now, Andy Kaufmann. Do you think we can do that this season?"

"Sure, coach."

"Now look, guys," I go on, "I don't know how many games we're going to win this year, there are just too many variables involved. I don't know how many of you will get sick, how many of you will be injured, and I don't know how many times another team will get hot on us. We don't know that. But there's one thing we can do, and that's every time we step on the floor, we can play our game. We can put the most we have into every game, and we can't do anything about those other things. But if there's even a single play—if, say, we have seventy defensive plays and seventy offensive plays—if you let down on a single play and we lose a 1-point ball game, it should be hard for you to go home and live with yourself. Every play is important. Not only the last play, but the first play, every play of every game. Guys, do you realize that during the season we're going to have maybe fifteen games that will be decided by 5 points or less? Now you do the things you're supposed to do, and you can hold your heads up high after those games, whether you win or lose them. Play hard, do the things you're supposed to do and can do, and we'll be OK."

On this day I don't want them to think that everything hinges on winning and losing. It's more important that they think of the fundamental things they need to do, and that's what I spend five minutes talking to them about. Then we roll up our sleeves and go to work.

We won two more state titles in my second and third seasons as head coach at Las Cruces High School, and the fourth year my team was favored to win the state title again, but we were upset in the quarter-finals. Just after that my thoughts turned to college coaching. I had two excellent players on my ball club that year, 6-foot-8 Charles Cleek and 6-foot-5 Dave Olsen, both of whom were being heavily recruited by major universities. I was in constant contact with both head and assistant coaches, among them Ned Wulk of Arizona State, Bruce Larson, of the University of Arizona, and Texas Tech's Gerald Myers, excellent coaches all. I was just a high school coach, but they were kind enough to talk basketball with me and about coaching on the college level. About that time, Hardin-Simmons University in Abilene, Texas, invited me to interview for their head coaching job. And as luck would have it, Bob King, the head coach at the University of New Mexico at Albuquerque, called on the very same day to see if I'd be interested in assisting him.

Bob King was relatively new to the state and looking for someone with connections to its high school coaches. I was the logical choice because of my success at that level, not to mention that I had two fine prospects that he could use. Bob called me often for a couple of days and offered me the princely salary of $6,500.

The Hardin-Simmons head coaching position was immediately a bit more appealing to me because I'd be my own man. I thought I had a good chance to get it since the university's acting president, Dr. George Graham, just happened to be the father of a fellow Las Cruces High mathematics teacher and friend, Ray Graham. Ray had been singing my praises to his dad for years, so Dr. Graham was kind enough to give me an interview. "I may take the job if you'll let me integrate the team," I told him over the phone before going to Abilene. Dr. Graham didn't give me a definite reply then, but he assured me that the issue would be settled by the time I arrived.

This was 1962 in conservative West Texas, and the school had never had a black player on the basketball team, nor any black student at all. But my ball clubs at Las Cruces had been integrated, and I insisted that be the case here as well.

I agreed to the interview, but as Mary and I drove toward West Texas, we stopped four different times so I could call King and talk to him again about the New Mexico assistant's job. I was very interested and I liked Bob, so I considered turning back. Still I kept going and finally arrived in Abilene early on a spring evening. Some sights look better at night, and Hardin-Simmons proved to be no exception. Its campus looked beautiful to us as we drove through it on that evening of our arrival. It turned out to be almost as pretty as it seemed that first night, and I decided to take the job after meeting with Dr. Graham and the athletic board. They informed me that they would let me integrate the basketball team and that my salary was to be $5,500.

In terms of my career, it was probably a mistake to take the job, a mistake that turned out all right. But there was some attraction in taking the gamble, in being my own boss, and in building my own program. H-SU had won only eight games the previous year, and their gymnasium was a converted airplane hangar. Normally I don't take that kind of chance, and when I'm coaching a game, I certainly don't. We're not going to go out and triple-team the ball and use tricks like that. We're going to stick to the basics. But when it comes to the coaching profession, a lot of us do poorly at picking our jobs because of our aspirations. We all have expectations of moving up, and when we have that opportunity, most of us will take chances we normally wouldn't take.

We've all made mistakes because of that, me included. But I've been fortunate. Mine have worked out.

During my interview I was given the green light to recruit blacks. With that assurance and the job secured, I took my $1,000 recruiting budget, climbed into my old Volkswagen and headed east toward Mississippi. Most Southern colleges were not then recruiting blacks, and I hoped to attract some of that state's excellent junior college players, since our H-SU team needed immediate help. My plan would not be put into practice without many anxious moments, however.

For it was at this time that Dr. Martin Luther King and the Freedom Marches were very much in the news, and the civil rights movement was in full motion. Racial tensions had rarely been higher; some people were being jailed, and others were being killed. An out-of-state license plate made you a suspected person in that combustible state. You were then, to its whites, an Outside Agitator, a "foreigner" intent on stirring up trouble. Whenever I stopped for gas, the station attendant warily eyed my Texas plates and gave me a look that was part suspicion, part hatred. They didn't want anybody from out of state coming in. And they'd always ask me, "Whaddya want? Where ya going?"

"I'm the basketball coach at Hardin-Simmons, and I'm just here to recruit some players," I answered any time this happened.

I wanted them to know.

I would drive into the black community, where I would end up staying in some coach's home. I had to be careful about being seen coming in and out of the black area of town. These gracious black coaches and their families were aware of my plight and were kind enough to house and feed me until I finished my business with them. They had been visited by very few white coaches, if any, and no white coaches from a Southern university. They went out of their ways to be hospitable and to guide me to players they felt could play at our level.

On one of these trips I stopped at Okalona Junior College, which is now closed. I wanted to look at a player I'd heard about named Art Haynes. His coach, Dolan Faulkner, readily introduced me to Art, and then he pulled me aside and said, "I've got a couple other guys you should look at. They're playing this afternoon, and you should stay and see them."

I did, and as his team played, Faulkner pointed and said, "Now this guy's Ambrose Kirk, 6-foot-1, a good player."

"Yeah," I said, and then I pointed to a 6-foot-2 guard I had spotted. "But what about that one? He's a heck of a player."

"That's Nate Madkins," Faulkner said.

"Where's he going?" I asked.

"Well, I guess he hasn't decided," Faulkner said.

"He's the one I want," I declared.

I wound up recruiting all three of them: Haynes, Kirk, and Madkins. None of them had ever seen the campus, but they were the first blacks ever to attend Hardin-Simmons. All of them played on the team and really contributed. But Nate Madkins was special. He became one of the best college players ever to bounce a ball. Dick Nagy, now my assistant, would be his teammate, and I've heard him say that Nate was the best he ever played with. I've had very few players who could score at will like he could. He'd get between 30 and 40 points in tough games, and in a game against West Texas State, he scored 52 points. He was one of those dominating players like Michael Jordan. I'm not saying he was as good as Michael Jordan. But back then he could beat his man just like Jordan does today.

My recruitment of blacks from Mississippi continued throughout this bitter period of racial strife, even during the long hot summer of 1964, when three young civil rights activists, Michael Schwerner, James Chaney, and Andrew Goodman, were killed by whites when released from the Neshoba County Jail on June 21, 1964. They were buried on a remote farm, where their bodies were not recovered until some six weeks later. Those were grim times for blacks and any white sympathizers, so I took great care in my travels within those boundaries. To this day, I keep in touch with some of the warm-hearted people with whom I came in contact during those troubled days.

New Mexico was a fairly liberal state in the early Sixties, but when you were near the border that separates it from Texas, you found people whose attitudes weren't so open. I took a high school team to a tournament in that area one season, and while we were there, we stopped as a team to eat in a restaurant. We were served without incident, but later, when a couple of my black players went back alone for a soft drink, they couldn't get served.

So I had some idea of how my now-integrated Hardin-Simmons team would be received as we traveled through the South. And I took care to make certain we wouldn't end up in a troublesome situation. When we had to stay overnight in a city, we always called hotels in advance to make sure we didn't try to stay at one that wasn't integrated. We would never go into a restaurant without taking the same precaution. And often on road trips, our players ate sack lunches or at drive-ins. Blacks could get served at drive-ins if they stayed outside, but not if they went inside the doors.

Throughout the South, drinking fountains and restrooms still had signs above them, those degrading signs that designated some for the use of "Whites," others for the use of "Coloreds." And on the road we ran into fans who taunted our players with racial epithets. No school dropped off our schedule because we were suddenly integrated, but there were some that refused to schedule us because of that. We were playing a lot of Texas schools and, well, it was just a real problem.

The whole season was a new experience both for our players and for many at Hardin-Simmons. Nate Madkins, for as great as he would become, failed to make a shot when we played at Oklahoma State that first year, which was also the first game he ever played before white people. I remember it clearly for that reason and because it was my first college game as a coach. There I was trying to coach against a legend in his own time, Henry Iba, a man who had coached more years than I had lived. Back on campus, Nate and the others who had come with him from Okalona were never abused physically, but they were ignored by some, and remarks were made by others.

Ed Murphy, now the head coach at the University of Mississippi, where our son, Lou, Jr., will be a graduate assistant this year, was one of my white players that season. He roomed with and spent much time with Ambrose Kirk during the year. He remembers other students leaving a cafeteria table as they approached to sit down, and he remembers players walking away from a pool table if they came in and called winners. The minimal abuse that Art and the others got was really nothing compared to the treatment they received back in Mississippi. But here, unlike there, they had no black culture to disappear into, they had no place to hide. They had to be around whites.

Whites, in turn, also had to learn to live with blacks. I can vividly remember looking up from practice one day and spotting my secretary, Hattie Belle Martin, staring at the team. She didn't stay there for long, but when I got into my office the next day, she quickly walked in and said, "Lou, I can't stand it."

"What's wrong?" I asked her.

"Lou," she said, "I can't stand to see our white boys out there with the blacks."

Hattie Belle was around fifty at the time and a fine person, but she had never seen people of different races play together before. That's just the way it was back then.


I had won three state titles in my four seasons at Las Cruces High and when I took the Hardin-Simmons' job, I was a confident young coach. My team was going to be dependent upon some dozen junior college players I had recruited out of my Volkswagen. My new position was one of the most challenging I could have taken. But still, as I approached my first season in Abilene, I was thinking, "Hey, coaching? There's nothing to it. It's pretty easy. Don't worry. You're going to win."

We lost nine of our first ten, and I felt I was doing such a poor job of putting the team together that I sat down during the Christmas holidays and decided to put in a new offense. I should have known better. I'd heard coaches say you can't do this, you just can't change your offense in the middle of the season. But we were doing such a bad job and losing our games anyway, I thought, "What do I have to lose?"

I spent five days putting in a new offense. But after using it for just a few games, I junked it, went back to my old ways, and we played 60 percent ball the rest of the way. So I learned a lesson early. I learned to listen to the advice of experience, and it's something I try to pass on now to young coaches when I lecture at clinics. Some young coach will inevitably come up to me, start talking strategy, and then say, "This is the way I do it."

"It's probably a pretty good way," I'll often tell him. "But there's a better way. You know why I know that? Because I made that same mistake too."

I was only thirty years old when I got to Hardin-Simmons, and I admit that I thought I was doing a great job because I'd been winning at Las Cruces. But I know now that I wasn't the coach at thirty that I was at thirty-four; and that I certainly wasn't the coach at thirty-four that I am now. But it's amazing—as you get older and gain experience, people sometimes say the game has passed you by. And in some cases it might have. If you lose your enthusiasm for it, sure, the game is going to pass you by. And if you ever do lose your enthusiasm, you should get out. That means you've probably stopped growing. That you've probably stopped trying to improve your knowledge. That you don't go to clinics, that you don't talk to other coaches, that you're running the same offense you've run for years.

But if your enthusiasm is still there you're going to be a better coach. You don't want to knock young people, you want to build them up. And you certainly don't have to be fifty-seven to be a good coach. You can be a good coach at thirty. But I remember a quote of Sir Ralph Richardson, the great British actor, who on his eightieth birthday said, "I'd like to learn a little bit more about acting before it's too late." Now isn't that something?  But that's it in a nutshell.

That attitude defines experience for me.  To me, someone is experienced if he has devoted time and intellect to achieving a goal—in my case, to putting out good teams and winning.  So you're always striving to learn a little more, to pick up something you didn't know before.  That's something I always do.  Always.  I talk basketball with people at clinics.  I talk basketball with people at camps.  I watch basketball games all the time.  Some coaches say they don't like to watch other games, but I do.  I might have something else to do, but watching games is enjoyable for me, it's my relaxation.  It's not work to me, it's like my hobby.  I'm always trying to find something new.

I'm not the only one.  Most coaches do that, and we all know what everybody else does.  That makes it interesting.  That defines your challenge for you: Year after year, season after season, you have to take the combination of players you have, put them into slots, and then use your knowledge to build your team.

You don't make major changes.  You don't want to become too complex and overcoach.  We've all been guilty of that, and it's the worst mistake you can make.  But every year, every season, it's different.

I laugh about our preseason ranking.  I really do.  Here we are going into the season without a true post man, without any real size, and with a team of terrible shooters.  And people have us ranked number two, number three in the nation?  I laugh about it.

I don't mind it since it's great publicity for our program, and

I also know that Illinois now never gets the chance to rebuild. After so many successful seasons, we're just expected to be good. I understand that, and I understand that I can't control those expectations. I try not to allow the extra pressure to affect me, but when it puts extra pressure on your players, its detrimental—especially if they end up losing some early games that they're expected to win.

Since the public's expectations are so high, the fans will start questioning the players. "What happened to you guys?"

"That team was ranked below you, how'd you lose to them?"

"What's wrong with you guys?"

If that happens, the players can start doubting themselves and putting more pressure on themselves. And my aim, the aim of any coach, is to keep the pressure off the players. Also, if the public gets down on your team, it can affect the outcome of a lot of games. If we're in a tough game and have a negative crowd, we're probably not going to win. But if we have a positive crowd and they're happy with us, that fact could help us win.

I know a lot of people feel I'm too pessimistic, but you know what a pessimist is? An optimist with experience. And my experience has proven to me that I can't afford to show optimism to the public or to the media. In private now, most coaches are very optimistic and feel that if they have equal talent, they're going to win the game. But not too many coaches want the public or the media to know what they really feel about their team, and that's why you hear us give the pat answers we do.

"Well, coach, what about your team? How's it going to do this year?"

"Well, I don't know. We're a little bit young. We're small. We don't play good defense. We'll have to play well to win."

The public laughs when they hear answers like that and they think, "Oh, the coach. He wants to make everybody think that they don't have anything this year. Then when they have a good year, it makes him look good as a coach." Now with some people, I'm sure that could be part of it. But basically, anything we say is aimed at giving our team a better shot at winning. And one of the ways we do that is to keep the pressure off. That's what that answer is trying to do.

"Well, coach, how many games do you think you'll win this year?"

That's another common question, but what happens if I say twenty-five, and we end up winning only twenty-two? I'm going to pay for it because I told them twenty-five, and now I've disappointed them. That'll hurt a lot of people because your fans, your boosters, your alumni are always going to think your team is a little better than it really is. They want to think that, and there's nothing wrong with it. But as a coach I just can't afford to be up-front with them.

Again, it's not wanting to put the pressure of expectations on your players or risking that their confidence will be shaken if they don't match those expectations. That concern is also one reason we schedule the way we do.

If we play Metro State, coached by one of the brightest young coaches in the business, Bob Hull, the public thinks, "The reason Lou's scheduled Metro State is to build up his record." And sure, that has a little bit to do with it since we have to win so many games to get into the NCAA tournament. But the big reason we schedule that way is to make our team stronger, to give it a chance to mature and gain confidence. That's why we do it.

It's the same thing in football. "I'd like to play one of the smaller schools in the area," John Mackovic said to me recently. Sure he needs another victory to help him get a bowl bid. But he's seen, we've all seen too many seasons ruined if you take on three or four Top Ten teams before you get into your conference schedule. That can just kill you. Your players may lose, or they may get injured and lose all their confidence before their real season even starts.

Most of the things coaches say and do are planned. That's why I'm not optimistic in my public statements about the coming season, and that's why our schedule looks the way it does. We have eighteen Big Ten games, and we know every one of them is going to be a war. Then we have Missouri, which is always a good one. Then we have our tournament, two more pretty good games. Other than those, we want two or three games that are going to be easy; and maybe five that we should win, but that'll be good tests for our team. I'm not trying to pad our record by the way I schedule, as a lot of people think. It's all just part of building the team up and taking care of its confidence.

I'm sports-minded and I love sports, but I have found over the years that fans can be a funny breed. That's why I'm careful in what I say to them. For many of them, I've come to understand, have their egos involved in my team.

I once received a call from an old friend from Oklahoma, Gary Allen. I used to work on his dad's farm. We asked him and his family to have dinner one night, and while we were eating, he made a request. "Lou," he asked, "could I get a picture with your autograph on it?"

"Why, sure. I'll send you one," I told him, but I was a little surprised. Here was a guy I'd known all my life wanting an autographed picture, so I asked him, "Why would you want one?"

"It's like this, Lou," he told me. "There's this guy in my office who has an autographed picture of Bobby Knight, and when you guys play Indiana, we fight like cats and dogs. So I want a picture of you for my office wall."

Now that's a good indication of what I'm talking about. It's not just the game or winning and losing. It's what has transpired before the game. Fans' pride, their ego, they're wrapped up in our team. Back at Hardin-Simmons, there was a mentally handicapped fellow who came to all of our games. He was our barometer on how the fans were feeling about me. The way he acted toward me after a game was a reflection of the attitude of the townspeople he'd been around. If people were feeling good about my coaching tactics, he'd come by and be friendly. If he had heard criticism of me, he would stay away for two or three days.

We have fans at the Assembly Hall, people I know, who cannot sit and watch in a close game; they have to get up and go outside. Bridge-playing friends of ours, Elinor and Bob Corley, watch our games on TV from their Florida home when they can't attend, and Elinor is a basket case while she watches. She paces in front of the TV, and when it's close she has to leave the room. I can understand that because as a fan myself, I'm convinced that it's harder on me to watch a game when I'm pulling for one particular team than it is to coach a game. When I just have to sit there and pull for the team, I get nervous. It's unbelievable. If the team I'm pulling for loses, I can get over it pretty quickly, but some fans will be depressed for a week, maybe two.

People like them will remember that loss too, and I see it all the time. When a school brings in a new coach, he's the new kid on the block, and most fans are gung-ho. But the rule of thumb is

that initially at least 20 percent of them are against you.  At least
20 percent and maybe more.  Then as his time at the school goes
along, and the team loses some tough games, the guys who bet on
those games may have lost money and become disenchanted.  So
if you've been in a place fifteen, twenty years, you're going to run
up against fans who'll remember a game you lost ten years before,
and they're still going to feel you should have done something to
win it.  So it's just inevitable that you pick up a few critics along
the way.

A few of those critics actually form clubs.  Once in a while, I
subject myself to mental abuse when I mingle with local sports
groupies just to get a feel for the pulse of this segment of fandom.
For example, there exists in Urbana-Champaign a small exclusive
band of individuals who have aptly tagged themselves "The King
and His Court."  This once "blacks-only" group was formed for the
soul (sic) purpose of meting out cruel and unusual punishment upon
the head of any unsuspecting basketball coach within the boundaries of Champaign County.  The soul (sic) monarch, who happens
to double as chairman of the "Membership Committee of One" is
Lonnie Clark, King Lonnie, or His Majesty, as he prefers to be
called.  Assistant King Bruce Nesbitt reportedly is organizing a
coalition among the ranks in a treacherous attempt to dethrone the
king.  The court, approximately twelve in number, is composed of
persons who are solemnly pledged to make life as miserable as
possible for poor vulnerable coaches such as I.  On rare occasions
I am invited to join them for the explicit purpose of giving them
the vicarious pleasure of castigating a live target.  Needless to say,
I turn down most of these invitations unless I find myself in a very
masochistic mood.

My confidence, which had been so high when I arrived at

Hardin-Simmons, was shaken by our poor early-season perform-
ances, and I soon began to think that I was doing a poor job. I
started feeling the pressure, and worse than that, I started feeling
sorry for myself. "Why are these things happening to me? Why
aren't they happening to other people?" I kept wondering.

I felt I was the only one in the world who was under pressure,
and when I went out to lunch with good friend Wayne Haynes, I
promptly spent an hour crying on his shoulder. I complained about
how bad I had it, about the poor attitudes of my players, about the
difficulties I was having as a high school coach getting spoiled
junior college kids to accept the challenge of a major college
schedule. I complained about personal problems. "You know those
two dorms Mary and I take care of?" I asked, referring to the two
dormitories we oversaw as head residents. "I got a janitor for each
of them. And now one's complaining that the other one is
sweeping his stairs and letting the dirt come over into his area. Can
you imagine? Here I've lost nine of ten, and I've got to take care of
problems like that." Wayne was a Hardin-Simmons grad; a used car
dealer, whose business slogan is "Everybody drives a used car"; and
a staunch Southern Baptist. He just let me moan away. But after
he patiently did all this listening, he looked across at me and said,
"Lou, you need to check your attitude. All I've heard for the last
hour is your complaining about how tough you have it. You think
you're the only one who has problems?"

Then he told me something of himself, how as a young boy
back in the Forties, he fell from a tree while picking pecans and
severely damaged his arm. They amputated at the elbow, then at
the shoulder, but the infection continued to spread. They thought
he was going to die, and they said to his parents, "Look, we have
this drug that the military has been experimenting with. If you'd

like, we'll try it on your son."

"Go ahead," they told the doctors.

Wayne was the first civilian in Texas to whom this "miracle drug" was administered. The drug was penicillin, and it saved his life. Shortly after that, his grandmother's gas kitchen stove blew up, burning her to death. Then in his twenties, his older sister was killed in an auto accident only two blocks from home.

After listening to Wayne, my problems paled in comparison. I needed that lecture at that particular time—it really helped me put things in the proper perspective. We all have a tendency to think our problems are worse than other peoples.'

Those good folks at H-SU, like Wayne, were kind and supportive of their new young coach and his family. Mary and I and our three youngsters, then ages two, three, and four, lived mostly in campus dormitories to help out our down-to-the-penny budget. Convenience was a factor, too, as Rose Fieldhouse, our gymnasium, housed my office. Since Mary was taking a full load of classes, she found it very easy to walk to all of them. In addition, I was always right on the scene to check up on my players' activities. Busy days all, but made more enjoyable by warm, enthusiastic friends and fans.

We went 10-16 in my first season at Hardin-Simmons, which wasn't too bad for a school that hadn't been winning that much. And then we ran off records of 20-6, 17-8, and 20-6. That restored my confidence and made me believe in myself again, but I still had a burning desire to become a better coach.

As a young coach, I was fairly inflexible in pursuit of that goal. After practice one New Year's Eve, I called the team around me and told the players they had to be in their dorm rooms at a certain time. "Be there," I warned, "because we'll probably check on you."

We did check, and we found that a player we had from back East wasn't in his room. Now in that era, and as a relative newcomer to coaching, I was extremely strict with the training rules. When the player finally did show up at 2:00 in the morning, I was in the lobby waiting for him. "That's it," I told him. "You never play for me again."

He was one of the few players I've ever permanently kicked off a team, and I realize now that I was too harsh. There's nothing wrong with being a little flexible on certain issues. Some things you can't fudge on, but in this case I should have found another way to penalize him. I should have remembered a lesson Presley Askew had taught me back when I was coaching at Las Cruces High.

On that occasion we were getting ready for a trip, and I told my players to be in their homes by 10:00 the night before our departure. When that hour came, I started calling and asking to speak to them and learned that two of my key players had missed the curfew. Shortly after that, I spoke to Coach Askew, who was then at New Mexico State. "You've got a heck of a ball club. Things seem to be going along great," he said, and he was right. We were one of the top-ranked teams in the state.

"Well coach, I think I've got a problem," I said to him. "I can't take a couple of the guys on our next trip."

"What? Are they sick or something?" he wondered.

"Well, no," I said. "They weren't in at 10:00."

"Lou," he said. "Let's talk about this for a while. Now why do you want to penalize your team and everybody else just because a couple of guys didn't get in at 10:00?"

"But coach," I said, "we have rules, we have to go by the rules."

"That's right, Lou," he said. "But isn't there some way you can do that and get their attention, let them know they were wrong without punishing the rest of the team?"

He was right, and although I don't remember exactly what we did, we took the players on the trip and handled the problem in a a different way. He made his point. There's always more than one way to handle a situation.

I think our players at Illinois have flexibility and not too many rules. They can talk to the media any time they want, although I tell them not to be negative about another school, its players, or a teammate. They can express their views, but I ask them to be positive. Now that may seem like too much of a restriction to some people, but I think you have to have that or they'll end up hurting morale, hurting teammates, and hurting a lot of others as well.

We have an 11:00 curfew the night before games. If we're playing at home, we check them into the Chancellor Hotel, and the only time they can leave is to go out for food at McDonald's, Merry-Ann's Diner, or Pizza Hut, all just across the street.

When I first started coaching, I always demanded that the players wear coats and ties when we traveled, but that kind of rule goes back to ego: wanting people to think how nice your guys looked in airports and how that was such a good reflection on the coaching staff. It meant a lot then and still means a lot. But after watching players get on the bus and take off their coats and loosen their ties so they can relax, I thought, "Let's be realistic." Sure, it's important for people to think highly of our team. And it's important for us to be good representatives of our school, but we want to be realistic about it. So we changed the rule.

I don't require that they wear coats and ties now. At New

Mexico State we had some players who didn't have enough money to buy themselves coats. Before one trip, in fact, I told them, "Guys, you can wear trousers, sweaters, jackets, anything that makes you look nice. We just don't want you wearing tennis shoes."

After practice that day, one of the players went up to one of our assistants, Rob Evans, and said, "Coach, I don't have a pair of shoes." And it was true. He was from such a poor family, he didn't own a pair of shoes.

We forget that some of these kids don't have very much, and that's why I really feel that we have to start giving players a stipend of $50 or $100 a month based on need. Now I'm not saying "pay to play." But a lot of the problems that we have in college basketball now arise because players don't have any source of spending money. I think if you gave them that stipend, you would eliminate a lot of those problems. I think the NCAA, the people in its Kansas office, feel the same way.

Think of it. Back when I played we were getting $15 a month laundry allowance, and that went a long way. We didn't have to worry about spending money. We could go to the movies, we could get clothes out of the cleaners, we could buy toothpaste and all of that. Now, what would that $15 be worth today? Maybe $100. Maybe $150. But we're back at zero, so what happens is this: A team might be getting ready to go on a trip, and a player has his coat in the cleaners. He can't afford to get the coat out, so he goes to one of the coaching staff and says, "Coach, I have to get my coat." Most coaches at one time or another have helped a kid get his coat out of the cleaners. What I'm saying is that a stipend could eliminate a lot of stuff like that.

We need a stipend, it would be helpful to many. But the reason it hasn't happened is very simple. Take the University of Illinois: We have roughly nineteen sports and 400 to 500 athletes. That means $40,000 a month coming out of the budget, and there aren't many institutions in America that can absorb that kind of expense.

Well, break it down then. Let's just give it to the basketball and football players. After all, the athletic budget at the school is between $13 and $14 million, and those two teams generate all the income other than maybe $50,000 to $60,000. Now you're talking about $11,000 a month, $110,000 for a ten-month program. For a school like Illinois, that wouldn't be too much. But now you're discriminating against nonrevenue-producing sports, and opening up a whole new can of worms.

So while most football and basketball coaches believe that revenue-producing participants should receive a monthly allowance, nothing gets done, and we continue to have our problems. The cheating is there, you can't deny it. But I don't think it's as widespread as some would think, although it's probably worse than others think. You read about it more, and it appears that more schools are being put on probation than ever before, so you have the impression that more cheating is going on than ever before. Maybe that's true. We all know how much money is involved in college basketball now, and that probably does influence the way some people operate.

I guess I have to agree with Dick Nagy, who along with Jimmy Collins does the majority of the recruiting for me here at Illinois. "Since the dawn of time," he is fond of saying, "whenever money has been involved, whenever there's been a big business, there has been cheating. It's the same thing in athletics. You take the money out of it, take the TV and media out of it, and you won't have it."

There was very little money involved in college basketball during my years at Hardin-Simmons. Even after I rebuilt that program, my lifestyle wasn't what you would call luxurious. Mary and I still lived with our three young children in a college dorm, and we were still shopping at Abilene Salvage, a store that sold damaged furniture at a discount. Incidentally, some of that furniture is still in use today!

But money didn't mean that much to me, and I was long used to living on a tight budget. I'd grown up that way, and when I coached at Las Cruces High, our finances had been so tight I couldn't afford a soft drink. It wasn't that it cost very much. I just had no money for it. That's when I started drinking coffee, which was free in the faculty lounge.

My situation wasn't unique. A lot of today's older coaches went through times like that. But here in Texas, the people had money. But I never asked for anything. I never looked for a lot of fringe benefits, and I never pushed for a higher salary. So maybe they were taking me for granted when I finally did ask to have something done. When we were living in the men's dormitory located across the street from the gymnasium, I asked to have my back screen door fixed—not a *new* screen door—just to have the old one fixed.

I called university maintenance several times to make that request. The more I called, the longer I was ignored, and the larger an issue it became to Mary and me. There was a problem with the flies and mosquitoes, and it was annoying. But more than that, it was a matter of principle. I'm a big believer in the little things. Block out, take the good shot, pick up the loose ball, then you don't have to worry about the big things. So while this may sound stupid now, that broken screen door became a symbol for Mary and me.

Jim McGregor, Presley Askew's successor at New Mexico
State, walked out on that job midway through the 1965-66 season.
So when it ended, the school started searching for a new coach.
Athletic director and head football coach Warren Woodson called
to make an offer to me and I quickly agreed. But when I visited
the basketball office at old Williams gym, I immediately had second
thoughts about the job.

The window was open and sand that had blown in from the
desert covered everything. The floor, the desk, the chair, the
typewriter, they all wore a coat of sand. McGregor and his staff had
used this room to change clothes, and his departure had been so
hasty that dirty jocks and clothes were hanging everywhere. It was
a dungeon down there. On top of that, I had agreed to try to rebuild
a program that had just gone 4-22, while its biggest rivals had
flourished. Up in Albuquerque, at the University of New Mexico,
Bob King's established program featuring Ira (Large) Harge was
nationally ranked. And the newly crowned national champions
were just thirty-five miles south of Las Cruces at Texas Western
(now the University of Texas-El Paso).

It all seemed a bit much for the $10,000 salary I would be
getting, and so from the dungeon I picked up the phone and called
Mary. "Look," I quickly asked, "would you consider staying at
Hardin-Simmons? After all, we hate leaving our friends, we have
four starters returning, and we'll probably have another good year.
Besides, the flies and mosquitoes are a problem only in the summer!"

She talked me out of reneging on the deal, and when I
returned to Abilene and told the people there I was leaving, the big-
money guys suddenly became very interested in my needs. "Let's
have lunch," some offered.

"What do you want?" others asked.

"What can we give you to make you stay?" still others wondered.

But at that point, it didn't make any difference. I had only wanted my screen door fixed.

Charlie Horton and Joe Lopez, two assistants, and several of my players, including Dick Nagy, dropped by on moving day to help us pack up. Mary prepared a meat loaf she planned to serve them at noon. Right before lunch, without us noticing, they loaded the stove, meat loaf and all, onto the luggage rack of the Rambler wagon (there was no room left for it in the U-Haul truck). We did manage to retrieve the largest pieces of the meat loaf and made sandwiches for everybody, but the remnants remained in the oven until we were settled.

We headed west, looking every bit like one of those Dust Bowl families portrayed in John Steinbeck's *The Grapes of Wrath*.

# 4

## Pecking Away

**B**oot camp. That's what our players call their experience between October 15 and the beginning of the season. But I know from my own experience that those six weeks are really not much time, so that's the way it has to be. Like a boot camp.

After the generalities of the first day, we start right in on our search for perfection. We want the players there on time. If one isn't, it's a ten-minute lecture. "Hey," I say, "you could cost us three, four games this year. Now we have to waste all this time talking to you when we could be working out. Those three or four games, aren't they more important than your coming in late?"

It's brainwashing, the little things. We want them all to rebound, and if one isn't, I blow the whistle. "You're going to be a small team this year," I say. Then I turn toward Anderson: "Nick, you told me we're going to win the Big Ten this year. Now how are we going to do that without some good rebounding?"

"You can't walk," I scream.

"You can't turn the ball over," I yell.

"You must play defense," I exhort.

We're creatures of habit, and if you fool around and loaf in practice, you're going to do the same thing in games. So we keep statistics on everything and demand that every play in every practice be as important as the last play of a close game. We want our practices to be more difficult than the games, so we make the situation highly competitive. We want them locked into the job at hand, so we demand that they concentrate. "Look," I tell them often, "you're better off if you work five minutes a day with good concentration than if you work out three hours a day while thinking about your date tonight."

Long ago, when I was in high school, I took a typing course. At first I practiced at home while listening to the radio. I made a lot of mistakes, mistakes that stopped once I started practicing in silence. And that's the way it has to be here. The coaches are on the floor when the players come out to jog a bit, stretch a bit. Then the players are handed jump ropes. We time them, challenge them to see how many skips they can make in thirty seconds or sixty seconds. Now comes some concentrated stretching, and after that, a short five-minute period we call free shooting. A little free shooting isn't bad, but it's not competitive. So we have trainers in the stands charting the performance of selected players. The players don't know whether they're being charted or not, and that makes them concentrate more.

They shoot foul shots, we record it. They go one-on-one, we record it. Running laps, we record it. It's total structure, just like a game situation. We're looking for quality, not quantity. When Jens Kujawa started here, his work ethic was not very good. But before he returned to Germany, he had become a hard worker. On a trip back from Germany, he told me, "Coach, in our practices with my club, we don't work as hard. It's an entirely different philosophy."

Here he is playing professionally, and that makes me feel good, because I know just how important good, tough practices are. It's perfection we're after. And my yelling, my insisting that they don't travel, my constant stressing of the fundamentals all serve to toughen them. If I get after a player and it still upsets him a great deal after his first year, I don't want him. That means he's not tough, and I want guys who are mentally tough.

It's like a muscle. The more you peck on a muscle, the bigger it gets, and pretty soon you've got yourself a tough muscle. Mentally it's the same thing. I keep pecking at their minds. If they're the right kind of people, pretty soon they're as tough as they need to be. "If I'm going to war," I tell them, "I want tough, highly capable people with me."

That's why they have boot camp in the Army, and that's why these six weeks have to be the same. You see, it's very rare for a tough individual to emerge from a soft environment. It happens, but it's rare. That's why we put players in an environment more conducive to creating people who are tough mentally.

We're not unique. Our program is like a lot of other programs, with some exceptions. During games, I'm not pulling off my sportcoat and throwing it and running up and down the sidelines. That causes fans to say, "Boy, that coach is tough, so his team must be tough." That has nothing to do with toughness.

But some people think you're soft because you try to be a decent guy and treat people right and don't go crazy during a game. Don't you think John Wooden's great UCLA teams were tough? Did John Wooden tear off his sportcoat and throw it around and do all that? No. There are a lot of ways to be tough, and what goes on behind the scenes, that's what counts the most.

The scene was depressing when I took over at New Mexico State that April of 1966, and the coach's dungeon was only part of it. The university had no arena, and the team played its home games at the Las Cruces High School gym. I had no full-time assistant and inherited only the part-timer, Bill Martinsen, who had aided McGregor. I had few promising players returning. During the previous year one player had bought himself a cola, gone into the stands during a game, and sat down to watch the game. Our closest rival geographically, the newly crowned champs in El Paso, had beaten us nine times in a row, often by embarrassing scores. Our in-state rival, the Lobos up in Albuquerque, had done almost the same, eight times consecutively. And the Aggies had gone five seasons without breaking .500.

I did have numerous scholarships to award to players whom I had hoped would turn this around, but there was little recruiting money to spend. So I was forced to devise a plan that was not only aimed at athletic success, but economic as well. I wondered if my old contacts in Texas and Mississippi would help me in New Mexico. In hopes of widening my recruiting base to the East Coast, I put in a call to Ed Murphy, a former Hardin-Simmons player.

He had spent the last two years coaching at a Class B high school in the tiny town of Avoca, Texas. But now he was home and spending the summer with his family in Syracuse. Years earlier, when I was still at Hardin-Simmons and he was playing for me, I had called him in before he'd left for another summer vacation and said, "Ed, we really need a forward next season."

"Coach," he told me, "I know where there's a great forward. A big strong kid."

"Why wasn't he recruited?" I wondered.

"He's poor," Ed said. "Had to go to work. He drives a commercial milk truck at 4:00 in the morning. But he's a terrific player. I tried to get him to come to junior college with me, but he wouldn't come."

"Try to get him," I ordered.

Ed and that prospect were then playing together in a summer league. After a game one evening, Ed told him, "I have to talk to you." The prospect agreed, and they went off to a place called Byrne's Tavern in an area of Syracuse that was then known as Skunk City. It was a poor, rowdy, Irish neighborhood, and there over beers, Ed talked to the prospect about Hardin-Simmons. He told him he could have a scholarship if he came down to play for us.

"OK," the prospect readily agreed.

"What changed your mind?" Ed asked him.

"I'm getting married, and figure I better do something with my life," he replied.

Minutes later Ed got up from the table and from a pay phone in Byrne's Tavern, he called to tell me he had gotten my forward. I then talked to the player and chatted with Ed a bit more. After he hung up, Ed returned to the table. There my newest forward looked up and asked, "Ed, where's Abilene?"

That forward turned out to be Dick Nagy, who is now my assistant. From the moment he joined me in Abilene, he was impressive. He was a grown man from a rough part of town, and when we scrimmaged against our freshmen, who were mostly nice walk-ons from West Texas, he literally knocked them around. He would start every game during his career at Hardin-Simmons, and by the time he graduated, he was a scholar athlete.

I never forgot Ed's eye for talent, and so now, in a new job and with limited resources, I was calling to ask him to be my assistant at New Mexico State. He would be a good man to have around, I felt. And during the summers, he could recruit the East Coast for me while living at home in Syracuse for free.

Three days before my call, as he was watching television, he had seen my face pop up on the screen and learned about my move. He had turned to his wife Shelley and said, "Coach has snapped. Here he won twenty games, and now he's going to a desert school where they won four. I have to talk to him."

He and his dad had already tried talking me into taking another Syracuse player, and so when I finally reached him, he thought I was calling about that prospect. Immediately he said, "I know why you called, and I'll do what I can to get him to New Mexico State. My loyalty's to you, coach, not Hardin-Simmons."

"No, Ed," I told him, "I want to hire you."

He accepted immediately, and then we began to talk about that prospect from Syracuse. "He's pretty good, scoring about 20 points a game. He's somebody you should recruit," Ed's dad had told me months ago. But I was then still at Hardin-Simmons, and so I had replied, "I've got four starters coming back. I don't have a place for him no matter how good he is." But now, with all kinds of places open, I said, "Ed, your dad told me about a guy up there. He's a 6-foot-2 forward, thin, probably not very good. But you're up there anyway, so why don't you watch him play?"

It turned out Ed was playing with him in a summer league, and just days later he called me back. "Coach," he said, "you've got to have this guy. He can really play."

"OK," I said, and after rejecting him once, I agreed to give Jimmy Collins a scholarship without seeing him play. Four years later, in 1970, he was an All-American and the Chicago Bulls' first-round, number-ten draft choice. Now he too is one of my assistants.

Ed stayed East for five weeks that summer, and after corralling Collins he decided to take a look at Nate Archibald, a terrific little guard who was headed to Texas-El Paso. But his train down to Yonkers was delayed and he arrived too late to see Nate play, so he dropped in to visit an aunt.

She was a high school history teacher who knew nothing about basketball. But during their conversation she told him, "I've got a kid in class. He's small, but everyone says he's real good. Maybe you should see him."

"What the heck," said Ed, "I've got nothing else to do."

His aunt then put Ed in touch with the player's coach, John Volpe. After they talked for a while, Ed asked him if he could arrange a meeting with the player. "If you want to come over and watch him play, I'll get some kids and set up a game," Volpe replied. "But if you just want to come over and measure him, forget it."

"I'll watch him play," Ed said.

"This kid's great, coach, but he's only 5-foot-7," he told me after watching him play.

"Really. Only 5-foot-7?" But I didn't give him a hard time. I've never been prejudiced about small players.

"You've got to believe me," Ed went on. "The kid's a great athlete, a great player. We don't have anyone who can play like him."

"OK," I said and agreed to give Charlie Criss a scholarship without ever having seen him play. He was a great player who helped us get to the Final Four in 1970. Although I highly recommended him to the pro scouts, he wasn't selected on any of the teams for the first five years. At the end of that time period, I talked to Charlie and advised him to give it up, that he'd never make the pros. But Charlie had a burning desire to play pro ball and continued working hard to make it. When he was twenty-eight years old, he tried out with Ted Turner's Atlanta Hawks coached by Hubie Brown, and he made the cut. He was the oldest and shortest rookie ever to play in the NBA at that time, and he went on to enjoy a fine pro career.

While Ed worked his part of the country, I worked mine. But we were poor, so poor I had to convince recruits to make their official visits to New Mexico State on their own. Paul Landis, a junior college player from California, was driven to Las Cruces for his visit by his mom and dad. Rob Evans, an All-American junior college player from Hobbs, New Mexico, drove himself to campus.

I couldn't afford to fly anywhere, so I drove more than 1,000 miles to Mississippi, where black athletes were still performing in anonymity, and where you could still find good players that no one had heard about.

"There's a tall, skinny kid down in Indianola who people think is a pretty good player," an old friend told me. So I went down there, found the player, and talked to him. I was the first white coach to show an interest in recruiting him, and he quickly agreed to come to New Mexico State without ever having visited the school. I had never seen him play either, but that summer I got him a campus job at $1.25 an hour. Four years later the Cincinnati Royals (now the Sacramento Kings) would make Sam Lacey their first-round, number-six draft choice, and head coach Bob Cousy and general manager Joe Axelson would fly to Las Cruces and sign Sam to a multiyear, no-cut, million-dollar contract. He too went on to complete a brilliant thirteen-year pro career.

We also got a 6-foot-7 forward named Tom Las from the East, who was built like a football player. And out of El Paso came a good ball-handling forward by the name of John Burgess. Somehow, some way, we got nine players to enroll at New Mexico State that spring and summer of 1966. Alhough Charlie Criss would be spending the year at New Mexico Junior College, he was headed our way as well.

When practice opened that fall, the freshmen were the talk of the school. They wouldn't be playing on the varsity for a year since frosh were not eligible for the varsity back then. But so little was expected of the varsity that the freshmen got all the attention.

Recruiting was very simple back then. You took chances on players you knew little about. Now it's a very specialized pursuit, and you never take a player without knowing about him in great detail. You had some twenty-five scholarships to give out, and you didn't worry about your mistake if one of your players didn't work out. Now the scholarship limit is down to fifteen, and you just can't afford to make many mistakes.

Dick Nagy and Jimmy Collins, my two remarkable recruiters, have both known me for over twenty-five years, and they're very aware of the type of player I like. We haven't always recruited that type, but they know if they bring in a guy who's going to be a problem . . . well, that player's going to have trouble because I'm not going to change. So we want a good person, a person I define as someone who attempts to do the right things. Now he doesn't always manage that, but he tries, he sees the need for it. Some guys just don't care, and if they really don't, they're not going to fit in here.

So we always check on a player's character, but the first reason we come in contact with a guy is his physical ability. His fundamentals, his ability to play the game—it doesn't do any good to start all this other work until we determine just how good a guy is. So when we find a guy who's scoring 25 points a game, for example, then we look at his skills. The most important skill in my mind is ball handling. If you can't handle the ball, you're going to hurt your team. If you can't beat the pressure, if you're throwing the ball away all the time, you won't help your team win close games. A lot of people have trouble catching and passing the ball. Even some of the pros have trouble passing it.

So ball handling is one, and two is shooting. If the guy's on the perimeter and he doesn't want to shoot, then we don't want him. Now sometimes you find a guy who's weak on shooting but is otherwise a great athlete; you take a chance on him. Nick Anderson didn't have to shoot from beyond fifteen feet because he had the ability to beat his man and get his shots. Other guys might not be great shooters, but they're great scorers. Kenny Battle became a better shooter when he was here, but he was more of a scorer. He just scored, and we take those types too.

We've lost a lot of games here over the years because of our bad shooting that I've basically told my assistants, "Don't even talk to me about a guy who can't shoot the ball. I don't want to talk to him." They don't always agree with me on that, and that's OK. I don't want "yes people" around me, but I feel shooting is so necessary, and it's important to convey that to them. Ten years ago I couldn't have told them, "Don't bring in a guy unless he's an excellent shooter." They might not have brought in anyone! But our program is at such a level now that we can afford to do that. With the 3-point line, everyone knows how important shooting is, and you can't ever bring in a guy thinking you're going to make a shooter out of him if he's not already. He won't last long.

The next thing I'm interested in is a guy's vertical jump, and not only because I want to know how high he can go. It's because a lot of people say the vertical jump is the best way to determine how athletic a person is, and I agree. After that, physically, we want to know if he can *create*, if he can beat his man one-on-one. If you find one of those, then you have a chance at an All-American.

That's what Nick did, that's why he was so good, even though he wasn't the greatest shooter. Jimmy Collins could beat his man one-on-one, averaged 25 a game his senior year, and made first-team All-American.    Michael Jordan, Isiah Thomas, Magic Johnson—when you have someone who can create, that's what you're dealing with, and those kinds of players aren't made. It's like this. You can take an aspiring artist and teach him how to draw the lines and where to put the colors, and you can make him a pretty good painter. But unless inspiration comes from within, he'll never become a master. To be a master, to be a creator like all those guys I mentioned—that has to be inborn.

But no matter the individual talents of the guys we recruit. They all have to have one major, innate characteristic. Without it, all these other things mean nothing. They all have to have the will to play hard.

It's a sad state of affairs when the coaching staff is more interested in a player graduating than the player is himself, so my major concern is trying to get some guys to go to class. It's not recruiting. It's not winning. It's going to class. One of my major concerns in coaching is trying to get guys to realize the importance of getting degrees, and I'm not the only one who has this problem. Among all coaches, it probably tops the list as one of the most difficult perplexities we have to deal with: convincing young athletes that they're in school to get their degrees. It's not just an Illinois problem. It's a national one.

A lot of them have aspirations to play pro ball, and you don't want to discourage that. But there comes a time when they have to face reality: only 1 percent of all college players ever make it in the NBA. If they don't face that, if a degree doesn't mean anything to them, then it's a really tough situation. Then they don't see a need to go to class, then all they want to do is stay eligible and get out. This is a problem that's been around for a long time now, and it used to be worse. Degrees mean more now than they did back then.

The public and the media are also now more aware of which guys are graduating, and it's important for all institutions to make sure their players get their degrees. I can't walk into our administration and say, "This guy's a great player and I'd like to have him, but I don't think he'll graduate." If I did that, I'd be in trouble. Now you can't judge for sure, and that doesn't mean we're automatically opposed to taking nonqualifiers. Sometimes nonqualifiers really have more academic ability than some qualifiers. But we like to believe everyone we bring in has a chance to graduate.

So after we determine that a player has the skills we're looking for, we want to know about his grades. Can he make it? If there's a weakness in his record, that's fine as long as I know about it. I just don't want to be surprised. I don't want a player to come here and then find out something about him that I didn't know. I get very upset with my assistants when it happens. That's why I'm always pushing them to learn more about their recruits. Not only their grades, but their character as well. I want to know everything. "But, coach, how do you expect me to—" they might start to say.

"Look," I tell them. "There's a way to do it. I don't know what you have to do, but it can be done. You can find out about that kid."

Now you may not find out about a kid because you don't want

to find out. You may not find out about a kid because you think he's a pretty good player and you have a chance to recruit him and you overlook some shortcomings. But if you really want to find out about his character, find out if he's a good person, you can. You talk to his coach. You talk to the faculty at his school. You talk to people in town. There have been times when we've found out things about players from people around their towns, and they made us think they weren't quite as good as we thought. You watch them play—that can tell you a lot about attitude too.

How does he react when he's pulled from a game? Does he stay in the game, or does he go to the bench and pout? Does he listen to the coach during timeouts, or is he looking around? If a foul is called on him and the referee blew it, how does he react? If you've been around the game for a while, it doesn't take long to find out about a guy's attitude.

Like I said, I want to know everything. I don't think you can have too much knowledge about a prospect. I know I've bugged my assistants some of the time because I want to know so much, but basketball's bigger now, more specialized now than it's ever been. And another thing: In the last ten years, we've had some pretty good clubs. At times we've been close to being *really* good, and it doesn't take much to make the difference.

I still don't know how good this, my fourteenth Illinois team, is going to be. But as they work their way through my six-week boot camp, I see things that encourage me. The players are a year older, a year more mature, and it looks as if they're more familiar with each other and like each other better. I sense they are a little bit closer. They have always played hard, they played hard the year before. But now they know what's expected of them, and I see them doing that more emphatically. I sense that all have accepted the system.

I had been apprehensive about our many personnel losses, and in our first practices I still wondered whether we were going to be able to cover big post men. When Lowell was playing for Tom Shields at Providence St. Mel, he'd had foul problems. I knew he'd had some difficult years and had a history of getting into foul trouble. But now I can see how much better he is. He's playing great, just great, and I can see how hard he has worked on those areas we talked about last spring.

Players generally just listen to our instructions and then spend their summers in our intramural building playing what I call recreation ball against such stellar competition as Professor Jim Anderson, Tony Clements, director of campus recreation, and Hakim Muhammad, a former NMSU player of mine. Craig Stinson, associate director, reports that at least one of them is in good shape! It is obvious that not only Lowell, but all of them have worked on improving. Steve Bardo is shooting better and is just stronger fundamentally. Nick is improved defensively and is working harder to improve his entire make-up. He's playing with more optimism. He spent some time on the bench the previous year and like all players, he got his head down when he wasn't playing. That's commonplace, but now we see a greater desire on his part, a desire to be a much better player.

Larry Smith—we've been waiting and waiting for him. When he was a star for Stan McAfoos at Alton High, he showed great promise. Now he's finally looking good, playing well, and that's what we need. We need his type of player. We see great improvement in Kendall Gill; there's no comparison between last year and this. Here we see a guy who has been on weights, who's much stronger, who's more confident, who's releasing the ball like he's supposed to. We have Kenny Battle on the perimeter so he can't be jammed like he was last year, and he's shooting and scoring. We like what we see in him. Ervin Small is also a much stronger, more confident player who's tougher on defense. Three returnees, Mike McDonald, Mark Shapland, and Eddie Manzke, are working as hard as ever. These guys earned scholarships their senior year because of their personal sacrifices and dedication to helping us become a better team. These players do all that we ask of them while receiving little or no recognition. Enthusiastic newcomers are Marcus Liberty, Andy Kaufman, and P.J. Bowman. We like all of this, and when I talk to my assistants I say, "This ball club's doing a pretty good job. I feel pretty encouraged about it."

I can see it in their eyes, they really want to do well. And when we start scrimmaging, they play well too. But I don't get too excited yet. Your teams always look pretty good when they're playing against each other. Then we go to Rockford for an intrasquad game played before a packed house. It's a great game that's won on a last-second shot. The fans there are impressed and enjoy watching this team play. Battle? Hey, who wouldn't want to watch Ken Battle play? Nick? Same thing. They're all small and about the same size, and the way they play makes them interesting to watch.

Harold Buck, Sr., from Savanna, Illinois, and his sons Scott, Lowell, and Harold, Jr., and cousin Gary, along with Bill and Joe Wilkinson are present for the contest. This group falls into a single category: gymrats. I've never seen people go to more games, scrimmages, or pick-up games. If there's anything going on anywhere, in any gym, you can count on seeing one or more of the Bucks or Wilkinsons there.

Almost the entire Brantner clan is in attendance. They had gathered in force, close to thirty of them, to have a pregame party at our niece Nancy's residence, a few blocks from the gym. It's just like holding a media conference when I'm around Mary's family, especially preseason. There are always hundreds of questions with thirty different opinions on how they should be answered.

"Great team you've got there, Lou," they tell me after this game, and I'm impressed too. Not to the extent they are, but I'm impressed by our execution. Players can jump and holler, do this and that. But the basic fundamentals of the game are what impress me, and I know now we're better in those areas than we were a year ago. But I'm still hesitant to think too optimistically.

I learned long ago not to judge a team in the summer or fall. In the fall of 1966, as I prepared my first New Mexico State team, there was very little to be optimistic about. We were woefully undersized, even for those days. And then one Saturday morning, I took them over to Mayfield High School to scrimmage all those freshmen I had recruited. The freshmen won.

Right then Ed Murphy and I started looking forward to the next season and coaching those youngsters. Yet we knew the present could not be ignored in favor of the future. So that afternoon, that same Saturday afternoon, we took our bedraggled varsity back to Mayfield High for a long and tough practice.

Out there, on the court, they didn't look like much. There was the 6-foot-5 Wesley Morehead, a forward who would play the center position all year. There was 6-foot-1 Ernie Turner, our most experienced player, whom I had recruited with the help of Buddy Travis, his junior college coach, at 1:00 in the morning. There was 6-foot-1 John Gamble, a veteran Marine paratrooper, who weighed about 220 pounds and was one of the toughest guys who ever lived.

There was 6-foot-1 Rob Evans, a native of Hobbs, New Mexico, who had been coached by my old friend, the incomparable Ralph Tasker, winner of close to a dozen state titles. Rob was at Lubbock Christian College when I began recruiting him for Hardin-Simmons. I had convinced him to come there and become a Baptist preacher. But when I took the job at New Mexico State, formerly New Mexico A & M, he decided he'd rather be a farmer than a preacher. Incidentally he became an outstanding basketball coach who is presently first assistant to the very successful Gerald Myers at Texas Tech. Paul Landis, the guy who had driven in from California, was our fifth starter; he played the point guard position to perfection. Behind them were 6-foot-6 Richard Collins and 5-foot-10 Willie Ford, a couple of guys I'd recruited from Mississippi. Both of these fellows, as well as the remaining team members, contributed greatly to the success of the season.

They did not have the ability of the freshmen, but after that Saturday and that extra practice, they never lost to them again. They just beat them up. They were tough, they were willing to work, and when the season started they caught fire. Evans gave us great leadership and became one of the most complete guards who has played for me. We won most of our close games with our defense and by taking as long as two minutes before taking a shot.

The public focus, which had been on the recruits, switched to the varsity. Ed Murphy and I, who had looked forward to coaching those recruits, forgot all about them. No one could believe what was happening.

We were far into that first season at New Mexico State, months past the discouraging fall, and now we were set to face the defending national champions from Texas Western and their defensive-minded coach, Don Haskins. Five games, maybe six, that's how many people thought my undersized team would win that year. But now, as we prepared for our trip to El Paso, we were riding along on the crest of a 10-7 record, while wading through the nation's third-toughest schedule.

Haskins, the Bear, was not quite the legend then that he is today. But he did have four players back from the team that had shocked favored Kentucky to win the NCAA title the previous March. There were 6-foot-8 Nevil Shed and 6-foot-7 David (Big Daddy) Lattin, tiny Willie Worsley, and the bigger Willie Cager. Their fans immediately jumped me when they saw me down there to scout them before our game. "Hey, Henson," they yelled. "You down here to learn some defense from the Bear?"

"Just a great place to come," I kidded back. "Great place to learn about defense."

But what they didn't know, even if they had bothered to look at our record, was that we played great defense too, that we were a great defensive team. We were also tough and able to control the tempo. Yet even I wasn't convinced we were good enough to take on what we would be facing in the Miners. "Mary," I said to her before we left for the game, "I just hope we can stay within 15 or 20 points of them."

"I can't believe it," I thought when there were three minutes left in that game. Here we were on Texas Western's home court and with just that much time remaining, we had them down by 18 and were on our way to a 13-point win. The fans there couldn't understand it, none of the people in that part of the country could understand it. They all thought it was a fluke. But then, just a couple of weeks later, they came up to our place, and we held them to 11 points in the first half and just killed them.

They had been ranked as high as fourth in the country, so we proved something with those wins, just as we had earlier when we hosted New Mexico, our in-state rival, when they were ranked fifth in the polls. We got them just a couple of nights after they, too, had defeated Texas Western, and we were pressing them, pressing them—and down a point with time running out.

"The biggest trophy we're going to give at the end of the year is the Purple Heart Trophy. It's going to be the biggest because it's a symbol of courage, it's a sign that the winner has taken a charge and sacrificed his body so this team could win," we had told our team at the beginning of this year. Now the Lobos, coached by consistent winner Bob King, threw the ball in. Their player caught it, took a few dribbles, and then picked it up and made a pass. As he did, Ernie Turner, a great defensive player, stepped in front of him, and while the ball was in the air he drew a charge.

We were down 1, he had a one-and-one, and there was no time showing on the clock. King, who would later coach Larry Bird at Indiana State, raged that he had been cheated, that the clock in this high school gym had broken, and that the time keeper was on our side. But his arguing was to no avail. With nerves of steel Turner made both his free throws to give us a 62-61 win over one of the top-ranked teams in the country.

We would finish our regular season at 15-11 and earn an invitation to the NCAA tourney. There we were matched in the first round against Elvin Hayes, Don Chaney, and a terrific Guy Lewis-coached Houston team that would go on to lose to UCLA in the national semifinals. They shouldn't have made it that far. We should have defeated them. We had them down 4 with a couple of minutes to go. Then Cheney made some quick steals, and a controversial call went against us. Evans, our great guard, drove and put in the basket that would have won it for us. But he was whistled for charging Chaney, and we lost, 59-58.

I will never forget that season, it was an amazing one. It was my season with a team that came to be known as "The Miracle Midgets."

"Does this team remind you of your Miracle Midgets?" I hear that question often as my 1988-89 Illinois season nears its start, and the reason is as obvious as the size of my players. Our tallest is the 6-foot-6 Lowell Hamilton, who is diminutive for a post player in this time. Around him are Nick, Kenny, and Steve Bardo, all 6-foot-6, and the 6-foot-4 Kendall Gill.

These guys, I had decided long ago, were better athletes and a better team than my Midgets of a dozen years earlier. But during our preseason camp, I came to realize just how alike they are—they and my first team back at Las Cruces High in 1959. They are all so alike I find it uncanny.

I can see that this team believes in itself and possesses a lot of heart, which were characteristics of the other two. This team is going to be smaller than most of those it faces, which was true of those others. And this team, like those others, is going to play without a dominating post man.

But most of all, I can see now that this team is willing to work, that it is going to work hard enough to join the other two as the hardest working teams I ever coached.

My first batch of recruits, virtually ignored during our Miracle season, proved to be as good as anticipated. Sam Lacey was a great rebounder and shot blocker. Charlie Criss was a great ball handler

My fifth grade mini Lou-Do

A senior at New Mexico State

On one of my first dates with Mary- 1954

Coaching at New Mexico State

**My first trophy as a coach- Junior Varsity District Tournament 1957**

**With my mentor and college coach, Presley Askew**

**1959 State Champs - Las Cruces High School (25-6)**

L to R: Front: Mgr. J. Medina, E.W. Wright, G. Fielder, D. Mullins, D. Rierson, Mgr. J. Maag. Back: L. Henson, D. Vargas, B. Banegas, L. Pickett, J. Singleton, J. Lopez, S. Green, Coach W. Holmberg.

**1960 State Champs - Las Cruces High School (27-3)**

L to R: Front: Mgr. J. Medina, Mgr. W. Mechem. Back: Coach W. Holmberg, Coach L. Henson, B. Cox, T. Yanez, B. Garcia, D. Rierson, D. Olsen, D. Weise, J. Singleton, L. Pickett, B. Banegas, B. Fielder, M. Nelson, D. Vargas, Coach E. Boykin.

**1961 State Champs - Las Cruces High School (28-1)**

L to R: 1st Row: Coach L. Henson, B. Banegas, B. Little, B. Fielder, D. Vargas, Coach E. Boykin. 2nd Row: Mgr. B. Garrett, J. Medina, M. Sandell. 3rd Row: M. Fielder, M. Padilla, E. Rosas, A. Wright, S. Bullard, D. Olsen, C. Cleek, J. Valles, P. Vargas, R. Nunez, Coach K. Colson.

**1948-1949
Illinois Final
Four Team
(21-4)**

L to R: 1st Row: W. Kersulis, B. Thurlby, Capt. D. Eddleman,
W. Osterkorn, F. Green, B. Erickson 2nd Row: Coach H.
Combes, D. Foley, J. Marks, V. Anderson, D. Sunderlage,
Asst. Coach Roettger 3rd Row: Mgr. J. Nelson, G. Trugillo, B.
Odum, R. Gatewood, T. Beach, J. Cottrell

**1950-1951
Illinois Final
Four Team
(22-5)**

L to R: Front: T. Beach, Capt. D. Sunderlage, Coach H. Combes, I.
Bemoras, C. Follmer Back: B. Peterson, R. Fletcher

**1951-1952
Illinois Final
Four Team
(22-4)**

L to R: Front: I. Bemoras, J. Kerr, Capt. R.Fletcher, Coach H.
Combes, B. Peterson. Back: J. Schuldt, C. Follmer, M. Baumgardner,
J. Bredar, M. Hooper, H. Gerecke

## My Family

L to R: Seated 1st row: daughter Leigh Anne, Lori Henson Wojciehowski holding granddaughter Catie, Lou Jr. holding granddaughter Lindsey. Seated 2nd row: Leigh Anne's fiancé, Coit Edison, daughter-in-law, Laurie Nast Henson, granddaughter Lacey. Standing: Lisa, Mary, and me.

**1942 Illinois "Whiz Kids" (17-1)**

L to R: A. Phillip, K. Menke, A. Mathisen, J. Smiley, G. Vance

**1963-64 Hardin-Simmons (20-6)**

L to R: Front: M. Meriney, D. Seamster, R. Turnbow, L. Henson, D. Pospeich, J. Martin, Coach M. Cunningham. Back: S. Rust, C. McHenry, D. Nagy, D. Hales, M. Foreman, C. Rappard, E. Murphy, D. Turnbow, H. Peacock, P. Fortin, C. Dishman, N. Madkins.

**1966-67 "Miracle Midgets" (15-11)**

L to R: 1st Row: T. Palmer. 2nd Row: B. Harris, C. Tafoya, P. Landis, R. Evans, J. Gambill, R. Roybal, R. Phillips, L. Bates, W. Ford, E. Murphy. 3rd Row: E. Turner, R. Franco, W. Morehead, C. Leggett, R. Collins, D. Dabich

L to R: T. Yates, R. Kirby, R. Judson, R. Leighty. A. Matthews, N. Bresnahan, K. Ferdinand, R. Adams, L. Cobb, T. Gerhardt, T. Bushell, S. Lanter, J. Berry, L. Lubin, L. Wothke

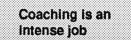

Coaching is an intense job

L to R: Bob Hull, Dick Nagy, me, Tony Yates, James Griffin

**1969-70 New Mexico Final Four Team (27-3)**

L to R: 1st Row:E. Huff, M. Horne, K. Colson, L. Henson, C. Criss, T. McCarthy,J. Collins 2nd Row: R. Franco, J. Burgess, C. Reyes, J. Smith, S. Lacey, L. LeFevre, R. Neal, B. Moore.

**1979-80 Illinois NIT Final Four Team (22-13)**

L to R: 1st Row: C. Stoelting, G. Galen, K. Tomlinson, S. Lewis, S. Horvath 2nd Row: L. Lubin, D. Nagy, L. Henson, T. Yates, B. Hull 3rd K. Bontemps, R. Judson, P. Range, N. Bresnahan, E. Johnson, J. Griffin, D. Holcomb, B. Leonard, M. Smith, L. Cobb, R. Gray, K. Westervelt, Q. Richardson

**1983-84 Illinois Team (26-5) finished 6th In Nation**

L to R: 1st Row: R. Woodward, S. Meents, A. Welch, D. Klusendorf, Q. Richardson, G. Montgomery, D. Maras 2nd Row: B. Hull, J. Collins, T. Wysinger, D. Altenberger, E. Winters, T. Schafer, B. Douglas, L. Henson, D. Nagy

# Illini Spirit...

Photo by Mark Jones

...the Cheerleaders

...the Illinettes

...Gary Smith's
Basketball Band

...and the
Orange Crush

Photo by Michael K. Smeltzer

Loren Tate *left*, Executive Sports Editor, Champaign-Urbana News Gazette and Jim Turpin *right*, WDWS Station Manager, Champaign, calling the plays for the Illini Sports Network

## *The Media...*

Dan Roan, WGN and Dick Martin, Illini Sports Network

Illinois press interview room after a game

Photo by *Mark Jones*

**Derek Harper-Dallas Mavericks**

**Nick Anderson- Orlando Magic**

**Ken Norman-LA Clippers**

# *Illini in the NBA...*

**Eddie Johnson-Phoenix Suns**

**Kenny Battle-Phoenix Suns**

*Photo by Brian Moore*

L to R: Bob Todd, Associate Athletic Director of Administration; John Mackovic, Athletic Director and Football Coach; Dana Brenner, Associate Athletic Director of Revenue

*Photo by Brian Moore*

L to R: 1st Row: Jane Hayes Rader, Hester Suggs, Alumni Association Executive Director Lou Liay, Mary Liay  2nd Row: Chuck Flynn, Sam Rebecca, Terry Cole, Bob Evans

*Photo by Brian Moore*

L to R: 1st Row: George Shapland, Bill Small, Dave Downey, Deon Flessner 2nd Row: Howie Braun, Jim Wright, Dick Paterson, Joe Hallbeck, Doug Mills, Bob Shapland, Tom Harrington, Dick Petry

**Receiving my 400th win trophy from Chancellor John Cribbet**

**Assistant coaches and I celebrate our secretary, Dorothy Damewood's 30 years of service.**

L to R: Mark Coomes, Dorothy Damewood, Dick Nagy, Jimmy Collins, and me

**Accepting my
500th Win Trophy
from Chancellor
Morton Weir**

**Champaign-Urbana
congratulates me on
my 500th win**

**Lowell Hamilton slam dunks in the Assembly Hall**

**U of I president, Stanley Ikenberry congratulates the Final Four team at the Seattle homecoming. Lowell Hamilton, Mike McDonald, and Kenny Battle are seated.**

*Photo by Mark Jones*

**Nick, Kenny, and I celebrate winning the Regional Championship**

and shooter. Jimmy Collins was a terrific scorer. And together they were good for 40 points a game. John Burgess, Jeff Smith, and Bill Moore were our dedicated blue-collar players, and our super sixth man, Chito Reyes, was a great shooter. Neither they nor any of their teammates had a problem with arrogance, and they were always willing to practice and play hard.

In their first season on the varsity together, they led us to a 23-6 record and a return to the NCAA tournament. There we lost by 9 in the first round to UCLA, which was led by a junior center then called Lew Alcindor, now known as Kareem Abdul-Jabbar. The next season we were even better. We finished 24-5, but again we were pitted against UCLA in the NCAA's opening round, and they routed us by 15 behind Alcindor's 16.

Once more we improved, this time to 27-3. Then in the spring of 1970, we were at last placed in a tourney bracket that did not include the dominant Bruins. Rice, the Southwest Conference champ, would be our first-round victims here. We toyed with them, had them buried by halftime, and won by 24. Next came Kansas State, the Big Eight winner, coached by Cotton Fitzsimmons, now Eddie Johnson's excellent mentor of the NBA Phoenix Suns; we nipped them by 4. Then we faced Drake, coached by the late, great Maury John. We got them down by 18 early and eventually defeated them by 9.

That put us into the Final Four, and we were that good, we deserved to be there. Collins and Lacey and Criss were all on their way to the NBA. But in the semifinals at the University of Maryland's Cole Fieldhouse, where Lefty Driesell's Terrapins had begun to move, we got unlucky again. We got matched in the semifinals against a UCLA team that started five future pros. Steve Patterson was now its center, and he was a fine player but hardly

Alcindor; on the wings were Sidney Wicks and Curtis Rowe, and in the backcourt were Henry Bibby and John Vallely. We were unlucky too with Sam Lacey, who went into that game with a sprained ankle. Yet we trailed the Bruins by only 7 at halftime before losing 93-77. Jimmy Collins had a tremendous game and scored 28. Lacey, hampered by his bad ankle, turned in a gutsy performance by hauling in sixteen boards and scoring a subpar 8 points.

Their college careers were then over, without the national championship they had the talent to win. There was but one team in the country that could line up with them on a neutral court and have better than an even chance of coming out on top. That one team was UCLA, and in those days no one was beating the Bruins.

I remained at New Mexico State for another five years, and at the end of that time had won 175, lost 70, and received a total of six NCAA tournament bids. I had been appointed athletic director after my first season and had overseen the construction of the Pan American Center, where I insisted on a parquet floor, since I was so fond of the one in the old Boston Garden. My program was established. I was friends with many on the Board of Regents. University President Gerald Thomas and Vice President and assistant Carl Hall, Academic Vice President Don Roush, and Vice President of Finance Bob Kirkpatrick were all great to work with. I was set there as coach, or administrator, or both for as long as I desired.

I was comfortable and I wasn't planning to leave, but I could see problems emerging on the horizon. As the athletic director, I could see that NMSU desperately needed a new football stadium. As good a head coach as Jim Bradley was, his recruiting efforts were hampered when prospects came to campus and saw our vintage stadium. He could not perform miracles with the meager talent assembled. The lack of football success translated into dwindling attendance and lost revenue, thereby, hurting the entire athletic program. Women's athletics were then coming on strong, and they also needed money that we did not have. Our only salvation as I saw it was to build a new football stadium in an all-out effort to stimulate support throughout the community and the state. Additional monies would be slated for the football recruiting budget in order to gain success and respectability in that program.

We drafted key people to aid us in the attempt to pass a bond issue to construct the stadium. Prominent among these were Clay Fiske of El Paso, Texas, NMSU foundation board member and staunch alumnus; Howard Klein, twenty-five-year veteran Aggie booster club president; Dr. Jim Tucker and his politically astute wife Mary; colorful native son Ernest Harris and his industrious wife, Joan, representing the agricultural community; Byron Darden, well respected attorney and civic leader; Frank Papen, successful banker and politician; civic-minded former college coach Bud Richards and his wife Jackie; and many others who worked tirelessly to promote the passage of the bond issue. My own staff, associate director Keith Colson and assistant athletic director Joe Lopez, and their wives Evelyn and Sherry worked diligently as well. But all efforts were for naught and the issue was soundly defeated. The failure was a disappointment to all, but it merely meant that we'd have to come up with a new game plan.

I still had no desire to leave NMSU even though I had received some feelers from a few colleges and one or two pro teams. When I didn't interview for any of them, people assumed I would remain at NMSU indefinitely.

But my ninth season in Las Cruces had been an enlightening one for me. Our team, picked by most to finish last in the conference, had gone on to win twenty games and make the NCAAs. This last surprising Aggie team, composed of Jim Bostic, Bill Allen, Rusell Letz, Richard Robinson, Dexter Hawkins, and Alan Graham, was matched in the first round against one of Dean Smith's great North Carolina squads. It had future pros Mitch Kupchak, Tom LaGarde, Walter Davis, and Phil Ford. Yet our guys, as out-manned and as out-gunned as they were, managed to lead them into the second half. But then, slowly, mercilessly, the Tar Heels' talent asserted itself, and they ran away to a convincing 24-point win.

Later Mary and I sat down to talk. "Lou," she said, "it's been a tough eight years for you doing both jobs."

"I don't want to do both forever," I assured her.

"Which one do you want to do?" she asked.

"I want to coach," I said without much hesitation.

"That's getting more difficult to do here," she said, and she was right. In the early years, for one example, since Southern schools were not yet recruiting blacks, I could count on my connections in Mississippi to get some good, unknown players. But that was all changed now. All college teams were integrated by now, so it was getting more and more difficult to recruit, and the odds on us ever returning to the Final Four were getting longer and longer.

So being a realist, I looked at Mary and said, "You're right. I spread myself pretty thin these days. Let's see what develops." I didn't want to leave my alma mater, and all of our great friends and supporters. But I knew that if I was going to continue to coach, and be fair to my family and myself, I would probably have to.

Shortly after Mary and I talked, I received a call from Oklahoma athletic director Wade Walker. I had grown up in that state, been to the Final Four, given clinics, and received publicity back there. Now he wondered if I was interested in his school's vacant basketball job. I told him I was. A day after Wade and I talked, I received a call from Illinois Athletic Director Cecil Coleman. We had been athletic directors together in the same conference when he had been at Wichita State. We had gotten to know each other really well, had stayed in touch, and talked often since he moved to Champaign. Now he wondered if I was interested in his school's suddenly vacant basketball coaching job. "What the heck," I thought after Cecil's call. "I'll just visit both at the same time."

Mary and I talked some more after that, and then without her, I set out to make my visits. My first stop was in Tulsa, where the Oklahoma interviews were being held. I met with Wade, and then with his committee, and then again with Wade. "Now Lou, " he said to me. "I'll tell you what. I'll do everything I can, but I can't pay you more than Barry. I'll give you the same salary as Barry."

Barry Switzer, who resigned as the Oklahoma football coach in June of 1989, was making $30,000 at that time. Switzer was a bright young coach who had already won one national title and would go on to win two more. But Wade was insistent, and he kept repeating, "I just can't pay you more than Barry. I just can't."

"Wade," I finally told him. "Let's see. Let me go to Illinois and see what they have to say."

We left it at that and I headed for Champaign. When I landed at the not-yet-remodeled Willard Airport, I was immediately disappointed. "Not much," I thought. I was not too sophisticated, but my first thought was, "You know, this may be a big university, but it's a little airport."

There I was greeted by Bill Sticklen, then the Athletic Association's business manager, and he drove me around Assembly Hall, which I had seen before and thought was beautiful. He then took me to Cecil's house, where Cecil's wife Margaret served me some lunch. After that there was nothing to do but wait behind closed doors.

Cecil wasn't there, but he had ordered me to keep my presence in Champaign secret and to maintain a determinedly low profile. For right then, as I sat in his living room, he was interviewing Virginia Tech coach Don DeVoe about the job he wanted to discuss with me.

Mary had grown up in Illinois, and so before I set off on my pair of job interviews, we sat down and spread a map of her home state on the table in front of us. I had long considered it an area of untapped potential, an area with talent enough to support a program. Often in our private talks, I had told her, "If I ever leave NMSU, Illinois is one of the places where I'd be willing to go."

Now, with that move a possibility, we studied the map. I picked up a pencil and circled Champaign, Chicago, Indianapolis, Springfield, Decatur, Danville, the Quad Cities, and Rantoul. I hadn't even heard of Rantoul before, but it was close to the University, so I included it among those places I perceived as my recruiting base if I signed on at that school.

So I had done some investigating before I arrived in Champaign and had some knowledge of the situation when Sticklen finally drove me to the Varsity Room for my 3:00 meeting with the Illinois Athletic Board. Years later I would be talking with a retired professor, and he would say to me, "Lou, I was on the committee that hired you. And you know what impressed me and a lot of other guys at the table? You were the only candidate that stood when you talked to us. The rest of them sat down."

I usually stand when I'm in a situation like that; I wasn't doing it to impress anyone, but sometimes it's amazing when you find out just what *does* impress people. When I finished my hour-and-a-half interview, I thanked the members, headed back to Cecil's house, and again waited. Some ninety minutes later, right around 6:00, he returned and immediately he said, "Lou, you're the guy. You're the new coach."

"Cecil, I really appreciate that. That's great." And then I stopped to think. "I've accepted the job," but I wasn't sure I wanted it yet. I thought I wanted it, but my plan had been to consider it for a night and to discuss the possible move with Mary again before accepting. But here was Cecil, a good friend, and I wanted to make him feel good, which is human nature. So instinctively I continued and said, "Cecil, it's a great job."

Later, after talking further about the situation with Cecil over dinner, I did call Mary and told her, "The job's mine if I want it. In fact, Cecil already thinks I'm his new head coach." Before I had left Las Cruces, our family had agreed to go along with me if I accepted either position, and so Mary didn't say much. "You do what you want to," is all she said, though I knew she would certainly like to return to her home state. But she did not want to push me into officially accepting, she did not want her feelings to influence my decision. She did ask if she could call her Illinois relatives, though, and tell them the offer had been made. "So long as they keep the information to themselves," I told her.

While she made her calls, I continued my conversations with Cecil, and eventually we got around to Tony Yates, one of the

University's assistant basketball coaches. He had applied for the job I had just been offered, and that morning a headline story in the Champaign paper had said it should be given to him. "Tony's a good one," Cecil told me. "If you want to keep him, I think it'd work out real well."

"That'd be fine," I replied. "I just want to talk to him."

Cecil then called and asked Tony to come over, and after he arrived, Cecil excused himself and went to bed. Then I sat down with Tony, who naturally was disappointed. I understood that, and I felt sorry for him. But I was extremely impressed after talking to him for a short time. I knew I wanted him on my staff and offered him the job as my top assistant with an increased salary.

I didn't want to have to talk him into accepting, sometimes you have to compromise later on if you do that. But Tony was nothing but class that night. The next day he accepted my offer. That turned out to be a very important moment in my career at the University of Illinois.

"Illini Pick DeVoe Basketball Coach." That was the headline in the sports section of the *Chicago Tribune* on the morning of April 5, 1975. Later that morning I was going to be introduced as the successor to Gene Bartow, who had left the school after one season for UCLA. My name was never mentioned in the article that recapped the career of the thirty-three-year-old DeVoe.

I was amused by that mistake, but back home in Las Cruces, our phone started ringing off the hook. Mary was getting bombarded by calls from those relatives she had talked to just hours earlier. "Lou didn't get the job," they told her. "The newspapers say DeVoe's the new coach."

"Believe me, Lou was offered the job, and he accepted it," she countered. But just in case of some bizarre slip-up, Mary called to reconfirm with me that I was indeed accepting the job offer.

"Yes," I assured her, "it'll be announced at an 11:00 news conference."

Later that day the following telegram arrived at our Las Cruces home. *Congratulations, Lou! For twenty-one years we have been under the impression that the only one who would hire you in the state of Illinois was the Jolly Green Giant!* It was signed by Mary's entire family.

The mistake in the news media proclaiming Don DeVoe as the new coach occurred because everyone knew he was in Champaign and staying with Associate Athletic Director Dick Tamburo. He had also interviewed for this same job just twelve months earlier, when it had gone to Bartow. So he was the leading candidate this time around. And lined up behind him were Tony, Syracuse's Roy Danforth, and any number of in-state high school coaches. Since the University then had such poor relations with the high schools, many even felt one of the latter should get the job. Among the names being pushed was that of Quincy High's Sherrill Hanks.

Like DeVoe, he had been a candidate before Bartow was hired, and his candidacy had been pushed by the state's high school coaches association. "I'm sure they're still behind me," he said after Bartow's resignation. "I'm sure the coaches in Illinois would like to see one of their own get the job."

"It is time for the University of Illinois to hire an Illinois high school coach to be head basketball coach at the University," a Chicago columnist chimed in that Friday I was offered the job, the same Friday a Champaign columnist pushed for Yates. "The practical side is that if Illinois high school coaches are mad at the Illini, they're going to steer their best players to other schools. If one of their own is coach, they're going to help their man in recruiting."

My name, in contrast, had never been mentioned in the same sentence as the vacant Illinois job, and it was unlikely that anyone associated with the school ever heard of me on that Saturday morning in 1975. I was a hot item in the West and Southwest, but in the Midwest, I was somewhat of a stranger.

I read the papers while having breakfast with the Colemans, and then at precisely 10:50 a.m. Cecil and I climbed into his car inside the closed garage. We drove directly to the Varsity Room parking lot and walked into a room full of people expecting Don DeVoe.

Only one person other than those individuals who had been involved in the hiring process recognized me, and that was Professor A.L. Neumann of the Illinois Animal Science Department. Neumann had formerly taught at NMSU and there we became acquainted. AA board member Professor Frank Hinds, who was cognizant of that fact, had invited him to attend. When the announcement was made, I was greeted by quizzical stares. Loren Tate, the sports editor and columnist for the Champaign *News-Gazette*, has since become a good friend, but his reaction that afternoon pretty much captured the mood of the moment. After Cecil introduced me, Loren looked up and blurted out: "Lou who?"

"We'd like to have a great team in a year or two, but that's not my primary goal. I have no plans of coaching anywhere else, so we'll build step by step," I informed the press.

"For the next few days, I'm going to contact as many players as I can. I want to spend all of the time recruiting," I told them.

"I'll recruit outside of Illinois, but basically I want to sell the home players on Illinois. That worked for me in New Mexico, even though we didn't have the talent that's available here. These coaches in Illinois produce a lot of good players, and I hope our biggest problem will be explaining why we can't give scholarships to all of them."

I told the press what I believed, but the harsh reality of my new situation was driven home in the following hours. I talked briefly at the Assembly Hall with my new aide Tony Yates, Bartow assistant Lee Hunt, and volunteer assistant Ron Jones; then I drove over to Vine Street to meet with Bartow himself. He was a longtime acquaintance, and while sipping iced tea in his back yard, he told me of the difficulties he had encountered here at Illinois. He told me that he had been considering leaving the job even if he hadn't been picked to succeed John Wooden at UCLA.

I finally returned to Cecil's home to prepare the remarks I would make at that night's All-State Banquet, and there I learned firsthand just how far the Illinois program had fallen. There I discovered that almost all of the fifteen players being honored had already committed to play for colleges outside their home state.

And that wasn't all. It was evident that very few of them were even interested in talking to me.

# 5

## First Signs of Respect

**M**y fourteenth season in Champaign officially opens on November 26, 1988, with an easy 83-59 win over Bob Hallberg's Flames of the University of Illinois at Chicago. It's one of those games in which the starters don't have to play much more than twenty minutes each, and its result is determined when we run off to a 44-18 halftime lead. The win, while gratifying, is expected. Yet one of the more interesting statistics of the evening is virtually ignored in the first blush of the new year. Later, as our victories accumulate and we rise in the rankings, the fact will be referred to often. But few notice yet that this entire Illinois team is made up of players from within the state.

When I took the Illinois job in that April of 1975, I was aware that the University was blessed with a grand basketball tradition and claimed a litany of great basketball names. In 1915 the school, led by All-Americans Ray Woods and Chuck Alwood, went undefeated and was declared the mythical national champ. Two more All-Americans were produced in 1918 and 1920 respectively: Earl Anderson and Chuck Carney. In 1937 it won the Big Ten title behind "Pick" Dehner and Harry Combes, who became highly successful coaches, and  Lou Boudreau, who would go on to become the Hall of Fame manager, shortstop for the Cleveland Indians, and then a long-time announcer for the Cubs.

There were the renowned Whiz Kids of the early Forties, whose mentor was the outstanding Doug Mills, later to become Illinois athletic director. This sensational group was composed of Andy Phillip, Jack Smiley, Art Mathisen, Ken Menke, and Gene Vance. In 1949 came a third-place finish in the NCAA tourney behind the legendary Dike Eddleman and first-team All-American Bill Erickson. There were other third-place finishes in 1951 and 1952. And Harry Combes, the coach of those teams, would himself become a legend by winning more basketball games than any other University of Illinois coach during his twenty seasons on the Illini bench. Johnny "Red" Kerr, now the Bulls' excellent announcer, was among the great players he guided, as were Erickson and Don Sunderlage, Jack Burmaster, Ted Beach, Rod Fletcher, Irv Bemoras, Jim Bredar, Bill Ridley, the Judson twins Paul and Phil, George BonSalle, Bruce Brothers, Mannie Jackson, Govoner Vaughn, Harv Schmidt, Don Ohl, Dave Downey, Skip Thoren, Bogie Redmon, Bill Small, Tal Brody, Don Freeman, Rich Jones, and Jim Dawson.

Four members of the aforementioned group still hold all-time individual records. Skip Thoren continues to hold the all-time single game rebound record that was established in 1963, an amazing 24. While Dave Downey was leading his team in scoring and rebounding from 1961-63, he was setting the record for the most field goals in a single game (twenty-two), and scoring the most points in one game (53) against Indiana in 1963. Don Freeman possesses the single-season scoring average record (27.8ppg), which was set in 1966. Don Sunderlage established the record for the most free throws attempted and made in a single season (171-218).

Harv Schmidt would succeed Combes before the 1967-68 season began.   He would go on to coach All-Americans Dave Scholz, Greg Jackson, Randy Crews, Jodie Harrison, Mike Price, Jeff Dawson, Rick Schmidt, and Nick Weatherspoon, who continues with the best career rebound average (11.4) in history, which he accomplished in 1971-73.  Schmidt never managed to enjoy the success of his old mentor.   His team fell to eighth in the Big Ten in 1972 and after pulling them up to third a year later, they dropped to ninth in 1974 with a 2-12 conference record and 5-18 overall.  He resigned during that season, and after it ended he was replaced by Bartow.

I have known Harv since he was an assistant at the University of New Mexico, and I was head coach at NMSU.  It is my opinion that Harv was an excellent basketball coach whose tenure here at Illinois was made more difficult because of the times.   Ironically, Harv gave my family and me the first tour we ever had of the Assembly Hall during the summer of 1968 when we passed through Champaign-Urbana.

Gene Bartow, former head coach at Memphis State, signed a five-year contract and then left Illinois after a single season—a season in which his team went 8-18 and finished ninth in the Big Ten with a 4-14 conference record. In his short stay Gene had made important contributions to the program through his hiring of Tony Yates and the recruitment of Audie Matthews of Bloom High School.

When I arrived the program was in need of a major overhaul and was suffering in comparison to many of its successful conference rivals. Bob Knight had quickly established himself at Indiana and handily defeated Illinois in its last six games.  And Purdue's winning streak against the Illini was up to thirteen and stretched back to 1967. Attendance in Assembly Hall was down to around 7,000 per game, and contributions to the school's grants-in-aid program were also down sharply. Television coverage was almost nonexistent, and only a few radio stations carried the team's games. There was no coach's basketball camp in place, and when I announced my first one for that summer to be held at Jim Phillips's Bromley Hall near campus, only forty-seven boys signed up. And on top of it all, we were on NCAA probation and limited to giving just three scholarships that year and the next.

"If there are any unemployed saviors out there," Gary Stein wrote in the *Rockford Morning Star* just before I was hired, "the job opportunities are great in Champaign." I didn't view myself as a savior, but I never dreamed that I wouldn't be successful. I thought that way because even with setbacks, I had been successful in high school, at Hardin-Simmons, and at New Mexico State. I knew I had a great facility at Illinois, was part of a premier conference, and in the middle of a fertile recruiting area. At Las Cruces High I inherited a team that hadn't begun to realize its potential. At Hardin-Simmons, our gym was little more than an airplane hangar. It was worse yet at New Mexico State, where our first home court was the same gym in which I had coached my high school teams—and they had gone 4-22 the previous year. But now, I thought, *now* I'm finally going to a good job.

Then very quickly, my thinking would change. I realized this job was going to be the most difficult of them all because that fertile recruiting area turned out to be far more fallow than fertile. In fact, the program was at rock bottom, a perfect situation for out-of-state recruiters.

The Monday after I was named to take over, I met Dorothy Damewood, the basketball secretary who stayed on with me and has proved to be an invaluable asset. Then I settled into my office to plot recruiting strategy and answer calls. One call came from long-time friend Ken Hayes, outstanding Tulsa University basketball coach, who was calling not only to congratulate me on my new position but to inquire about my former job at NMSU, which incidentally, he obtained. Another led to a meeting with a couple of alumni, Jim Wright and Deane Stewart, who knew many of the inner workings of the University and some of the problems surrounding its basketball program. Wright had assisted both Harry Combes and Harv Schmidt for a combined total of twelve years. He and Stewart offered their revelations over lunch. They told me that I had serious problems recruiting in Chicago or, for that matter, anywhere in the state. "I've seen it," Wright told me. "I've seen what happened to Harv Schmidt and Bartow. You're going to have some real difficulties."

Now I knew the situation was bad, but I still didn't know to what extent or for how long it had been that way. The year before, the state's top prospect, Audie Matthews, who had been coached by Wes Mason at Bloom High School in Chicago, had signed on with Illinois. But I would learn that he was an exception, the one outstanding in-state player who did not snub his own state university. Others like him had fled in droves, and they included any number of All-Stars and All-Americans.

Quinn Buckner had gone to Indiana and was about to lead the Hoosiers to the national title. Bo Ellis had gone to Marquette to play for the colorful Al McGuire, and he too would end up with a national championship ring. Jim Brewer had gone to Minnesota and Larry Williams to Louisville. C.J. Kupec had gone to Johnny Orr's Michigan, and Norman Cook to Kansas to play for the time-tested Ted Owens. Steve Puidokas joined George Raveling at

Washington State, and Bob Guyette went to Kentucky. I found the list staggering, and it did not even include that year's top high school seniors who had already decided to defect.

East Leyden's Glen Grunwald was on his way to Indiana, as was one of the state's top big men, Derek Holcomb. Lawrenceville's Jay Shidler was on his way to Kentucky, and Steve Krafcisin was headed to North Carolina. Our cupboard was bare, we just could not recruit in this state. That was why it was so important that personable Tony Yates agreed to be part of my staff.

Tony had made a breakthrough by getting Matthews, who could have gone to almost any college in the country, and four other in-state players as well, namely Tom Gerhardt, Mike Washington, Rick Leighty, and Nate Williams. It was a start, something to build on, but I had no idea how rough the road ahead would be. At the beginning, I couldn't even get Illinois high school players to come and visit the campus.

Those defections were our major concern, but they were hardly the only ones that then confronted us. There was a general apathy about basketball, which was reflected in the small attendance at Assembly Hall. There was squabbling within the athletic department, which led some to rename the school the "In-Fighting Illini." There was some bitterness among Bartow's recruits, who felt abandoned by his sudden defection and move to UCLA. There was even criticism of our schedule, which did not include Bradley or DePaul or any of the major state universities, although it did have us playing at Nebraska, at Southern Cal, and in South Carolina against Furman. "It would be bad for our recruiting if we lost to other schools in Illinois," Cecil said in defense of that schedule, unintentionally showing how low our program had fallen.

"Is it asking too much," *Chicago Tribune* columnist Dave Condon wrote on the day I was handed that program, "to ask the University of Illinois to give us a basketball team that will finish at least as close to the Big Ten championship as Republican John Hoellen was to Mayor [Richard J.] Daley [in an election where the city's longtime Boss was a runaway winner]?"

In 1973-74, Harv Schmidt's final season as the Illinois basketball coach, his team had no black players, and charges of racism were leveled against him. He heatedly rejected those charges and pointed out that three years earlier, he had had six blacks on his team, and he had since tried to recruit others, such as Norman Cook and Jim Brewer. "I've always had great rapport with blacks as a player and coach," he declared.

That was the atmosphere that had greeted Bartow when he came to Illinois from Memphis State, where his starting lineup was once made up entirely of blacks. He also had the reputation of having great rapport with blacks, and he furthered his case when, a day after getting the job, he set out for Chicago's Bloom High in pursuit of the highly touted Matthews. But the state's high school coaches were still in open rebellion. They wondered why the University had hired him rather than adopt a plan proposed by Quincy's Sherrill Hanks. He had suggested that Illinois hire three high school coaches from different parts of the state to guide its team. When the proposal was rejected in favor of Bartow, the new coach was on the spot to quiet them by winning big and winning quickly.

When Gene didn't, the mood of those coaches only hardened. When Hanks was passed over once again after Bartow left, their attitudes hardly improved. But this time the person they were wondering about was me.

Tony was set as one of my assistants, but I took a little longer in hiring my second. I now knew the atmosphere was charged and immediately after I took the job, representatives of the state's high school coaching association came to me about hiring one or two of its members.

They put tremendous pressure on me, and although no coach likes to be told what to do, I did listen to them. But I had certain feelings on the matter. First of all, I felt I needed two guys who were experienced in recruiting, and I knew if I hired someone without that background, it was going to take at least two years for him to learn to do it right. Another consideration was this: Let's say I did hire a high school coach from a certain conference. Do you think the other coaches in that conference would rush to send their kids to him? They're competitors too, they've had their battles, and it just doesn't work that way. In fact, it usually works against you since each of the high school coaches you didn't hire feels he should have been the one selected.

So we hired Les Wothke, the well-respected coach from Winona State in Minnesota. Les is now the head man at Army, but he had earlier been a high school coach in Bloomington, Illinois, and at Rich East in suburban Chicago. That satisfied some of the people who had come to see me, and some it didn't. But I felt we had done the right thing.

We had hired someone who had been a high school coach in the state, someone who had worked on the college level and knew about recruiting, and someone who was also a nice person and an outstanding coach. So I was happy. I had Tony Yates, Les Wothke, and Mark Coomes. I also got Bill Molinari, whose brother Jim is head basketball coach at Northern Illinois University, as my graduate assistant. I thought we had an excellent staff.

We had problems, and there was only one thing to do. Apply the work ethic. "Get into the high schools. Talk to the coaches. Find out what they're thinking," I told my assistants. And just minutes after I returned from my lunch with Jim Wright and Deane Stewart, Tony and I headed up Interstate-57 on my first recruiting trip to Chicago.

I was still reeling from all that they had told me, and here I was staggered further by Tony's depressed state. He was disappointed over not getting the head coaching job; that was definitely part of the reason for it. But a larger part was caused by the experiences he had already had attempting to recruit players to Illinois. He spoke of those trying times as we drove, spoke too of how pessimistic he was about future recruiting. And finally, with the mood of this moment so pervasive, I chose to escape. "Wake me when we get to Chicago," I told Tony, and then I fell into a nightmarish slumber.

We were greeted by few friendly faces on that first trip to Chicago. It proved such a disaster that we cut it short and returned to Champaign early. Back there, ironically, I started receiving calls from any number of high school coaches who wanted to recommend players to me. They felt our program was at such a low ebb that we would accept anybody.

My assistants and I must have visited 400 high schools in my first year at Illinois. We dropped by, found the coaches, visited, and moved on. With some of them, we discussed specific problems, and during this time some of them told me point-blank, "I'm never going to send a player to Illinois." But most of the time we just had general conversations. I was only trying to get to know the coaches so I would have a chance to recruit one of their players if ever they had one I was interested in. It's often best to make contact with a coach when he doesn't have someone to recruit so he remembers you later on when he finds a prospect on his hands.

The first player we signed that year was Larry Lubin out of the Chicago suburb of Evanston, coached by former Illini great Jack Burmaster. Larry was a good player, and his leadership qualities were invaluable to our program. Tremendous shooting forward, Urbana native Ken Ferdinand signed next, much to the delight of his fine coach, Dave Casstevens. A big breakthrough came the following year when we got Levi Cobb, coached by the outstanding Bill Worden, from state champion Morgan Park High and the Chicago Public League.

Cobb was the bigger key of the two recruiting classes, for that talent-laden league hadn't sent a player directly to Illinois for at least five years. But we worked on him, and Tony worked on him, and when he picked us it was front-page headline news. "Levi is everything you could want in a player, that's why he's so valuable. There's no question this is a big help for us," I said at the time. Then I added an even more important postscript. "This," I said, "is a big psychological lift for us."

The situation was very similar to what would occur at DePaul two years later. They successfully recruited Mark Aguirre, coached by former Illini football player Frank Lollino, at Chicago's Westinghouse High. That made the school, which is set hard by the city's El tracks, an acceptable choice for other great high school players in the area. Levi did that for us, and now other great players in the Public League, players who just a year ago would have ignored us, started taking a look at Illinois.

When other players see a top player go to a school, play, and be successful, they get interested in that school. I felt that was going to happen, and that's why I said Levi was such a big psychological boost for us. With the addition of Neil Bresnahan from Oak Park Fenwick; Rob Judson, whose dad Phil coached him at Zion Benton; and Steve Lanter from Mascoutah, Illinois, we felt we had the nucleus of a fairly competitive team.

It's hard for us to go into another state and recruit a player, especially if he's in a state that includes a top Big Ten basketball school. Indiana controls their state. Purdue gets a few, but Indiana is in control there, and it is very unlikely that we will recruit a player that they want. Ohio State, if they're going to continue being competitive, must control that state. Michigan does a good job there; that's why it's so hard for Jud Heathcote at Michigan State. Iowa, no question there. So if we go into any of those states, into any state really, and the player shows an interest in his own state school, we don't pursue him. Sometimes the grass seems greener to a youngster, and if a player's interest is real, we take advantage of that. But we're not going to beat many state universities on a player, and I think that's as it should be. It should be next to impossible to beat the state university.

Conversely, I don't think anyone should be able to come into Illinois and beat us on a player we're recruiting. *With all things being equal,* seldom should another university be able to come into Illinois and recruit a player we want. It's not because I consider myself a great recruiter; I'm pretty good because I work at it and because my assistants do an excellent job. It's because of the many advantages we have to offer a young man at our University.

From an academic standpoint, the University of Illinois at Urbana-Champaign ranks in the top five among our nation's public institutions of higher learning, and over a recent ten-year period, Illinois has ranked in the top twelve of both public and private universities. If those rankings are not impressive enough to a potential student-athlete, other information may get his attention. According to Kenneth W. Perry, emeritus professor of accountancy, a survey published by *Public Accounting Report* with interviews of nearly 400 department of accountancy chairmen at U.S. colleges and universities, ranks the University of Illinois undergraduate program of accountancy number one in the nation for the ninth consecutive year. The Graduate School of Library and Information Science also has a number-one ranking, followed by the Colleges of Engineering and Education, also ranked in the top three in the nation, just to mention a few of our leading programs.

Not only do we have a top-ranked university from an academic standpoint; we have a class basketball program that's regularly in the top twenty and receives high visibility now with all of our recent success. Last year we had twelve nationally televised games, and most of the others were on regional or statewide television. We are covered extensively by radio and the press as well, so a player knows that he will get exposure second to none if he joins us. He must understand that the Illinois media will consistently cover his career, at times on a daily basis. But never will he receive this type of coverage if he leaves our state. A player's parents can come on a Saturday afternoon, watch him play in a great game in beautiful Assembly Hall, take him out to dinner afterwards, and be home at a reasonable hour. Then there is the attraction of playing in the highly prestigious Big Ten conference, which in recent years has produced more professional players than any league in the country.

We also sell the idea that a player can make a name for himself in the state. "Do you want to live in Ohio after you graduate?" I ask him.

"No."

"Michigan?"

"No."

"Where are you going to live?"

He usually says Illinois, and then I tell him, " We have a state population between eleven and twelve million. About twenty-five of our games will be on TV in the state. You'll make a name for yourself, and people will get to know you. They'll identify with you. Then, when you get out of school your job or business opportunities are unlimited if you don't happen to make the pros. Our alumni are either chairmen of the board or the presidents of approximately thirty-five major corporations in America. Do you think it won't help if you're from Illinois, and you and some out-of-state guy both apply for the same job? Who do you think's going to get it? Just look what it'll do for you."

Now about the only thing other schools can do in the face of all that is negatively recruit. We don't like to do that here. We like to point out all of our many positives, for we believe that will sell our program. We believe in our product, and we're going to sell it. We're not going to get down in the gutter and talk about the negatives in programs, like some others do.

But on occasion, opposing coaches tell prospects, "Don't go to Illinois, they're loaded. They've got too many players." Whether we're loaded or not, they'll say that, and then the young man might think, "Well, yeah, that's right. I remember seeing write-ups about all those kids going to Illinois. They were stars in high school, and now they're there." Those players might not be stars at Illinois now, but that's the way this young man remembers them, and they become magnified in his eyes.

"You can play immediately here, and at Illinois you'll have to sit." That's another one they use all the time. They say, "If you go to Illinois and you make a defensive mistake, you get pulled out of the game." Or, "Illinois has pretty good teams, but they just can't seem to win the NCAA title." That's true of something like 250 other schools as well, but that's grasping for straws.

Negative recruiters may knock me as a coach and talk about how I can't win the big one. They may say I'm not personable, that I don't let my teams run, that I substitute too frequently. When it gets close to the signing date, it's like being in a game. If they're up 20 with fifteen minutes to go, they're going to stick to their game plan. But if they're down 20 with fifteen minutes to go, then they're going to scrap that plan and try something different. Opposing schools get desperate and will take drastic action to try to beat us on a recruit. Innuendo is a powerful weapon.

Occasionally at the Big Ten coaches' meetings, negative recruiting appears on the agenda, and we discuss it. Sometimes the head coach doesn't even know it's been occurring. Generally speaking, I feel that there's less negative recruiting going on today than there was five years ago.

One year we were all set with an in-state player, a player who had been to our camp and had been recruited by us for three years. But then just a week before the signing date, he went to visit another school. Before he left he told us he was definitely coming to Illinois. But when he returned he called and said, "I'm not so sure any more." Well, that other school had just treated him to an unbelievable weekend, a royal weekend that had nothing to do with the reality he would face if he went there, and he was impressed.

He came back wearing a sweatsuit from the school, talking about how great the school was, and Jimmy Collins really had to work on him for the next few days. "How was your visit?" he asked the player.

"Coach, I had a great time," he told him.

"Don't tell me that," Jimmy said.

"But, coach, I really did have a great time. I really like it there."

"Do you want to fly all the way up there to go to school?"

"Yeah, it is pretty far."

"And the school, it's in the snow capital of the world."

"Well, yeah, I guess you're right about that."

The novelty of the weekend finally did wear off, and the player signed with us a few days later. But that shows just how slick some recruiters are and how one big weekend can influence a player's decision. That school hasn't forgiven us though, and the next time we played, their assistants refused to speak to Jimmy. They claimed we snatched the player away from them. Although he grew up in our state, and their school is about 1,000 miles across the country, they claim we sneaked in on them to claim the recruit. Just the opposite was true, but some people think that a good offense makes a good defense.

In view of our recent experiences in dealing with Illinois high school players and out-of-state recruiters, we made a decision that is a reversal of our previous practice. If we suspect that illegal recruiting is occurring with these in-state athletes,we will report our findings and the schools that are engaging in such practices.When this type of problem occurred in the past, we only confronted the individuals whom we supposed were involved in the irregularities.

We try to keep our recruiting fairly basic. We like to see our guys visit the campus with mom and dad. We want to get to know them, we want them to get to know us. It really bothers us when the parents can't come, so we encourage that. Parents are a vital part of the recruiting process; we want them to be totally involved in it.

Over the years, Mary and I have established some great relationships with many wonderful parents; it's one of the most rewarding aspects of the coaching profession.

We request that the recruit and his parents come together and arrive on campus somewhere between 5:00 and 6:00 p.m. on a Friday evening. When they get here, we check them into a hotel, preferably one with a view of Assembly Hall. That night we take them to dinner between 7:30 and 10:00 p.m., usually at the University Inn. I like that because the nighttime view of the campus from there is just beautiful. After dinner the recruits go out for the evening with some of our players, and Mary and I have the parents come over to our home for coffee and dessert.

The next morning, we have an academic meeting that includes people like the associate dean of the College of Liberal Arts and Sciences, Robert Copeland; associate dean of the College of Applied Life Studies, Jerry Burnam; assistant dean of the College of Mechanical Engineering, Carl Larson; associate dean of the College of Commerce and Business Administration, Larry Johnson; or assistant dean of the College of Agriculture, Warren Wessels. Then too, we may have a professor or two from the recruit's field of interest. Terry Cole, the athletic department's director of academic services, is always available to make his excellent presentation, as well as his outstanding assistant Mike Hatfield. If the recruit wants to sit in on a class, we arrange that too. But in this morning meeting, we go over everything. I stress for mom and dad how important I feel it is that their son truly *wants* his degree. "Look," I've said many times, "we like guys who want to get degrees because if they don't see a need for one, then we have a difficult time getting them to class. And if we have a hard time doing that, then we're just going to have all kinds of problems."

After the presentation one of my assistants, either Jimmy Collins, Dick Nagy, or his son, Scott, a terrific graduate assistant, shows the young man and his parents around campus, and then they usually attend a football game. When it ends, we either have them over to our house for dinner, or take them to a restaurant. The next morning we have a reception for the recruit and his parents in the Varsity Room. We invite some faculty and staff members, such as Professor Charles Henderson from the School of Social Work; Mrs. Pat Askew from the Admissions Office; Sister Marie Golla, Political Science; Professor Maria Keen, English; Mrs. Willeta Donaldson, Admissions; Professor Phillip Bowman, Psychology; Mr. Lonnie Clark and Mr. Bruce Nesbitt, Administration; and Professor Dick Arnould, Economics. These campus representatives can answer many questions that players and their parents may have, while we all have a continental breakfast. Then they go back to their hotels, pack their suitcases, and leave. It's all very simple, but I think we cover what needs to be covered.

Later we ask our players what they thought of the recruit, but we don't make any big deal of that. I know that some schools are always bragging about not recruiting anyone without the approval of their players. Most schools routinely get their players' approval on recruits as we do, but we don't go around advertising the fact on a billboard; that's the phoniest thing I ever heard of.

Many players choose schools for the wrong reasons. People laugh when I tell them some of these, but believe me, I've heard them all.

He met a girl he liked on campus—that's the most common one. There was a hamburger joint close to the campus, and he felt it served the best hamburgers he'd ever eaten. He liked the fight song. He liked the color of the uniform. He can get a certain uniform number. Some schools get a jersey, put the recruit's name on it, hang it in the locker room, and then tell him, "Here's your locker. There's your jersey." That impresses a lot of them. Other schools will walk the recruit into their completely dark arena and then, just as he reaches halfcourt, an assistant will flip on a spotlight and their fight song will start playing. Believe it or not, that sometimes works. That's the sad part about it.

Now we want our players to pick the University of Illinois for the right reasons: because it's solid, it's sound, it's good for them. I believe the institution should be the most important thing in a player's decision, even more important than the coach. That's why I don't believe a player should be free to leave a school even if he signs a letter of intent and the coach then departs. Now I know that's contrary to what many people think, and I understand that it makes it tough on the young man.

But many of them go to a school because of the assistant coach who recruited them. If the assistant leaves, should they be free to go as well? What I'm saying is if the recruit did it right in the first place, he selected the institution. He selected it because it had a top twenty program, because it was in a good location, because he liked its math department, because this whole umbrella met his approval.

Sure, sometimes a coach leaves quickly, and the player can't control that. Well, you can't control everything. And with this rule in effect, the recruit should come close to choosing a school for the right reasons.

The Illinois program grew during my first years at the school, but it was a slow, one-step-at-a-time process. I never considered leaving, I always thought we'd get the job done. But there were definitely times when I wondered whether we'd ever break into the top echelon of the Big Ten.

The strength of the conference was one big reason the job was just so much tougher to accomplish. It is a help to us now, now that we're on top. But back then, at that particular time, it was just the opposite. Back then, our Big Ten opponents would tell our recruits, "They're down. They're at the bottom. They're never going to get out of the second division." It was a tough thing to fight, a tough thing to overcome. But we improved, even though it wasn't always obvious to the people watching.

We did surprise those people by opening with five straight wins in my first season. But after going 7-2 in the nonconference part of our schedule, we fell to 7-11 against Big Ten opponents and finished in seventh place. That next recruiting year we landed Cobb, Bresnahan, Judson, and Lanter, but then we sang a familiar song. We went 8-4 outside the conference and 8-10 within it. That off-season, Reno Gray joined us from junior college. Derek Holcomb, originally from Peoria Richwoods where he was coached by consistent winner, Wayne Hammerton, transferred to Illinois from Indiana. But with Derek sitting out his required season, we again played what was a maddeningly familiar tune. We were respectable outside the Big Ten, where we went 6-3; but no better than a second-division team in the conference, where we ended up 7-11.

We had lost six straight times to Michigan State; and against Michigan, Ohio State, Indiana, and Purdue, we had done no better than 2-6. But at least we'd broken our losing streaks against the latter two and gained some respectability. We hoped to build on that as we set out to recruit in the spring of 1978.

We traveled up to Chicago, where we were being greeted more warmly now, and landed a terrific player named Eddie Johnson, Mark Aguirre's teammate at Westinghouse High. The now legendary Bob Hughes, who coaches at Dunbar High in Fort Worth, Texas, called. Years ago, when I had integrated Hardin-Simmons, I had recruited two of his fine players, Clarence McHenry and Bill Robinzine. Now he tipped me to an inside finesse player he had by the name of James Griffin, and we signed him too. We signed Perry Range, coached by well-regarded Larry Coots out of South Beloit, Illinois. And up at Rich East, Les Wothke's old school, we took a hard look at a fine guard, Craig Hodges. He had a young, unknown coach by the name of Steve Fisher. But since we already had Range, who would do an excellent job for us, we passed on Hodges, and he went on to a fine NBA career.

Over at Indiana State, a guy named Larry Bird was getting set to start his senior year. Up in Chicago, the venerable Ray Meyer was blending Aguirre and four other iron men into a team that would gain him the national recognition long his due. Further up, in East Lansing, Michigan, Jud Heathcote welcomed an exciting kid they called Magic onto his Michigan State team. They would all end up in the Final Four.

We would not. But down in Champaign, with our new recruits and with Derek Holcomb now eligible, we were finally ready. We were finally ready to make a breakthrough.

Larry Lubin, my first recruit, was the captain of our 1978-79 team. We opened the season with two easy wins at home and with two more at Tulane and at Missouri. Four more victories later, we traveled down to Lexington for a tournament at the University of Kentucky. There we defeated Syracuse, which was in the top twenty, and then we just really drubbed Texas A&M, which had upset a heck of a Kentucky ball club. Then it was up to Anchorage for the Great Alaska Shootout, where we won the title without too much trouble. Now we were ready for the real thing, the Big Ten portion of our schedule.

We were 12-0 and highly ranked. We felt good about that, but we really questioned just how good a team we were. We were pretty good, we knew that. But we had had to struggle against teams that weren't as well-known as we, and that was cause for concern. But now we beat Indiana, which was a nice win for us, and Northwestern, another good win. Suddenly we were set to go up against Michigan State, and the number-one ranking was in sight.

Presley Askew, my old college coach, came in for the game, and so did Byron Darden, who'd been my attorney; J.W. Yates, my brother-in-law from Tulsa; and Jim and Mary Tucker, our dentist and his wife from Las Cruces all came. We had a houseful! They saw one of the greatest games ever played at Assembly Hall. Magic was there, and we were on a roll. With the game tied, we called timeout and set up a play that ended up working to perfection. Steve Lanter, our point guard, penetrated, and as the defense collapsed around him he kicked the ball out to Eddie Johnson. At the buzzer Eddie made the shot that gave us a big victory.

Now we face Ohio State with Kelvin Ransey and Herb Williams, super players on a great team. If we beat them and get our sixteenth straight win, we're number one. With 40 seconds to go, we're poised to do just that. We're up by 2, and after a timeout we're ready to run an out-of-bounds play that our scouting has told us should work. Eddie faked a screen and took off. When we got the ball to him, he was wide open. He caught it and drove to the basket. But there he tried to lay it in off the backboard, and Carter Scott blocked his shot. Ohio State immediately came back to score, which sent the game into overtime. They ended up defeating us, 69-66.

We had lost our chance to be number one in just my fourth year at Illinois. We all felt great about beating Michigan State and disappointed when we lost to Ohio State. But the toughest part about the weekend was the blizzard that halted air and ground transportation out of Champaign. We were trapped until the following Wednesday with our five extra guests. When things loosened up, we sent the biggest eaters out first!

The number-one ranking is far from my mind as my fourteenth year at Illinois unfolds. That spot is firmly held by Duke, and we are still trying to find out just how good we are.

I feel that Mississippi, coached by my former assistant Ed Murphy, will give us a good test. Ed is a heck of a coach. He's knowledgeable about the game, has great team discipline, and he is a super recruiter. I know that based on experience. Ed has a great player in Gerald Glass. Nevertheless, we come out, get them down 24-6, and coast to our third straight win. Florida is next. They're going to be our real test because they have great size, a great inside game, and a lot of people think they're a top twenty team. But their guards are inexperienced and not as seasoned as their front line. If you can get to a team's guards, you can get to a team.

That's what we do here: our pressure defense affects them and hurts them. Nick and Kendall make three steals each, Kenny and Larry Smith make a pair apiece, and altogether we make fourteen to their one. We force them into twenty-six turnovers, make only five ourselves, throw up 48 points in the first half and 49 more in the second, and handle them, 97-67.

We're happy with the win, but I still don't see anything that makes me think this team is great or special. To me, it's just another victory in which we played pretty well. Our practices early in the season still reflect the character of those we held in our preseason boot camp. That will change later and deeper into the year. Here I want the players to be thinking about goals and those important fundamentals.

We have what we call an "efficiency rating procedure," and it is what we use to evaluate each player's performance. It's not simply points scored or rebounds collected; it's more complicated than that and involves any number of formulas that give a truer picture of a player's all-around game.

There are eight categories altogether, and only one of them is judged subjectively: the coaches' evaluation of a player's intensity and defense. The rest are by the numbers, which are adjusted to give what we feel is an accurate measure of a player's effort in those areas that are important to us. One category is rebounds and steals, and there we give a bonus point for each one that he gets in excess of five. For charges, you multiply the number he picks up by five, since we feel they're so valuable. Bonus points are also awarded for every assist in excess of three, and points are subtracted for turnovers and personal fouls. In other words, we're judging him on rebounds, assists, defense, drawing the charge—we're trying to make him aware of his total game.

So if a player scores 20 points in a game, he walks into practice the next day with his shoulders back and his head high. He feels like he's done everything and that he's the king. But after looking at our efficiency chart, maybe we see that he was just an average player in that game, that maybe all he did was score. We are not happy with him; that's just one phase, and we're looking for the total package. Then I get after him.

I ask him, "OK, who do you think was our best player in the game?"

He usually doesn't choose himself. A lot of times he selects the top rebounder, because he's heard me talk about that so much. So then I check the top rebounder. "Hey, on the efficiency chart, he was only our fifth best player."

It all goes back to indoctrination, to brainwashing. We run off copies of the chart and give one to each player. We hit this hard during our six weeks of fall practice and early in the year. But when we get into the Big Ten season, we just mention it and don't make a big deal out of it. By then we should have done what we set out to do, which is to brainwash them on teamwork, on getting assists, on drawing charges, on doing all those little things that go into winning ballgames.

Everything we do is based on that, on teamwork and playing hard. And this just reinforces that thought in the players' minds. It gives them goals to shoot for.

I was once talking to Jim Claunch, an insurance executive, and he told me, "Lou, you know what I've found out. Dollars aren't going to motivate people. Goals are worth more than dollars." Pro players are a good example. You can pay a guy $2 million, and he still may dog it up and down the court. So money doesn't do it.

"What does it, Lou, are short- and long-range goals." Jim handled that by setting up contests. Whoever sold the most insurance over a two-week period would get, for example, a $30 clock radio. Now the radio itself was worth very little, but he found that people would go out and extend themselves to win it. They didn't care about the money; they wanted the prize. It was an incentive. Others respond to a long-range goal like a trip or a bonus at the end of the year.

So goals are the best ways to motivate people, and I'm not talking here about the goal most players have, which is to play pro basketball. That's a long way off, and there are too many variables between here and there. And if that is their only goal, I've got a problem. They're not going to be receptive to my teaching because they're already thinking beyond Illinois. So they're not going to listen; they're not going to be willing to devote time to the classroom and study hall; they're not willing to do any of that because they feel they have an alternative: pro ball.

So again, we have to break them down and build a solid basketball foundation. Some goals we share with them. We all want to win the Big Ten every year; we all want to win the battle of the boards every year; we all want to shoot over 50 percent as a team during the year. Other goals are individualistic. I may pull Kenny aside and say, "Ken, you shot 60 percent last year, and this year you're going to do just as well." We talk to them about who our top rebounder should be, who our top assist man should be. And at the end of every year we give out eight or nine awards for things like assists, field goal percentages, and free-throw shooting.

Now you would think, "That should do it, that should motivate them all to do the right things." It doesn't. It doesn't because even those goals are too far away, so far away that they mean nothing early in the season. So we have our own version of that $30 clock radio. We have shirts that say "Chairman of the Boards," or "Mr. Provider," or "Secretary of Defense." We have four or five of them, and at the end of practices, we award them.

At the end of a practice I might look and see that Steve has fifteen rebounds, and his shirt is wringing wet. I call Steve out and say, "You know, we're really proud of Steve. Fifteen rebounds, a fantastic rebounder." Then I pull his shirt off for him, wring it out, let the perspiration drip on the floor, and say, "Steve, you really worked hard. Why don't you go over there and sit down and rest." Sometimes I send a manager to go get a soft drink for him, or maybe a chair so Steve can put his feet up. Then I ask him, "Now, Steve, how many sprints do you think these guys should run today?"

Or I turn to Marcus and say, "Hey, Marcus, Steve had fifteen rebounds today and you had seven. Now, Marcus, is Steve really twice as good as you are?"

"Oh no, coach."

"Well, Marcus. It's right here. He got fifteen rebounds and you only had seven. Now I don't think he's twice as good as you are either; but sometimes you just have to look at the results and they show he is."

Now, if he's the kind of player I think he is, Marcus is getting a little mad. So now I say, "Tomorrow when we come out, let's see if you can come closer to him than that."

The next day in practice, you don't think that Marcus is going to come out and fight hard over that shirt? The players may act like it doesn't mean anything. But if you're wearing that shirt, that's individual recognition, and guys like that. It's something they all want.

So daily goals, I think you have to have them. You can't have too many of them. And some of them will change depending on what we're emphasizing in a particular season. But no matter what they are, they're there, and they serve to motivate.

We take our Illini Classic tournament with easy wins over Duquesne and Arkansas-Little Rock, and then break 100 points for the third straight time while routing Tennessee Tech. We are now 7-0 and rising in the rankings. But now for the first time, we are set to face a team that truly has a chance to defeat us. We are set to face the highly successful Norm Stewart and his Missouri Tigers.

They are our regional rival, a rival we've defeated four straight years. But now they're loaded. Dave Dorr, excellent veteran *St. Louis Post Dispatch* sportswriter, tells me that this Missouri team is one of the best he's seen. In the preseason National Invitational Tournament, they had proven themselves by losing to Syracuse in the championship game only in overtime. And they will be coming at us with the kind of size that could give our small team trouble. My players don't know it, but I'm so concerned about this game that I drill them on Missouri defenses while they think we're practicing for Tennessee Tech.

The Tigers are a tough team, a hard-nosed team, a brutal team on the boards. They jump right on us at the start of the game. Midway through the first half, we're already down by 11, and when they stretch their lead to 18 doubts start dancing through my mind. They come and go in a flash, in just seconds, but they do appear. We're not shooting very well, and they're making some great shots over our defense. We're not playing very well and can't do anything against their size. Most depressing, we are reverting to all those same mistakes that cost us so much a season earlier.

I'm really tough on the players during this stretch and make all kinds of substitutions. They're playing hard, but I tell them they're not. My job is to push them beyond the level at which they're performing. I tell them they're undefeated and that if they want to stay that way, they have to execute better and start running their patterns. "You guys deserve this," I tell them during one timeout. "Look at that score! You deserve it because you're doing too much free-lancing. You got away with it against weaker opponents. We warned you it would catch up to you, and you didn't listen. You've got to run the offense. Run the offense and we'll be OK."

While my Illini were taking a beating on the floor, immediately behind our bench some of our fans and family members were also taking abuse. Chuck Keller, Illini fan from Effingham, was having beer poured down his back as his wife Doris and my wife Mary were taking verbal abuse. In fact, toward the end of the game, one of the Missouri fans shoved Mary, causing Arnold and Mary Lynn Perl, who had flown in from Memphis for the game, to enlist protection from a nearby police officer for the duration.

We finally do start running the offense and close to within 7 by halftime. In the locker room, I go to work building on that. "Guys," I say, "I just couldn't believe some of the things that were happening to our ball club. You just wouldn't listen. Then you start running patterns and look what happens. You score 11 straight points. Hey, we're in the ballgame. If you just go out and do a decent job, you're going to win it." I use those words intentionally because I don't ever want them thinking they have to play a great game in order to win. I want them to feel they can win if they just do the things they're supposed to do. And that's what they do in the second half. Finally, with 13:30 remaining, we tie Missouri at 47. Then Ken Battle, our leader, just explodes. He scores 7 of our next

12 points, 12 of our next 23, 17 of our last 40, and we go to 8-0 with an 87-84 win.

Twenty years ago I would have been elated with this win, no question about it. But now my emotions are much more restrained. I didn't like the way the game was played, and I didn't like our poor execution in the first half. But in the locker room I don't say much about that. I want the players to feel good because they have managed to win when they weren't at the top of their game. So I tell them, "Hey, you guys didn't play well, you know that. But you showed great courage. You pulled together, helped each other, out-fought them, and won a great game."

I mean that. They have shown great courage, and right then I know this team is a little bit special. But I have seen other games like this one before, and so I still don't know just how special it is. I still don't know if they will sustain this great courage, game in and game out.

"We could be in trouble in this game," I say to my assistants. We are standing in Louisiana State's Assembly Hall, and there are any number of things concerning me. I didn't like our poor fundamental performance against Missouri, and now we have to go up against a good LSU team that features superfrosh Chris Jackson. We are on the road in front of a tough and hostile crowd, and set to referee the game are three officials from the Southeastern Conference, of which LSU is a member.

Then we go out and play poor defense. I scream and yell about our defense, but our rebounding is the best I've ever seen, and we're scoring at an unbelievable rate. It's a press-and-run type of game, and LSU is just playing great. But when the first half ends, we're up 61-51, and I can barely believe the stat sheet as I read it outside our locker room door. Lowell has shot eight of ten. Kendall and Kenny have shot six of eight. Nick has shot four of six, and off the bench, Marcus has shot three of four. As a team we've hit an amazing 73 percent of our shots. But our lead isn't any bigger because LSU has hit 65 percent of theirs.

We have played a fantastic first half, just unbelievable. We're executing well, and I'm pretty encouraged. But we are making defensive mistakes that LSU is taking advantage of. "You guys are doing a lot of things right," I say after I finally go into the locker room. "But you haven't played a lick of defense tonight. Now if you can't play the defense the way it's supposed to be played, then we're going to change it for you. You've convinced me you're not going to do it the way we planned, so we're going to forget about that. We're going to play straight man-to-man. We told you to rotate defensively, to help each other out. But you're not doing that, so we can't use that defense anymore. Battle, he's doing it, but no one else is, so it's over. Don't do it anymore. Play them head-up, man-for-man, and double on Jackson when you can. But other than that, just get after them."

They do, and over the next twenty minutes, they play what may be the best half I have seen in all my years of coaching. We make 3-point shots and slam dunks, we dominate the boards and run off baskets by the bushel full. We score 13 points to their 4 in this half's first 2:30. Then, just a minute and a half later, we get a streak in which we put up thirteen to their three. We're up by 29 now with nearly twelve minutes remaining in the game. Already I'm beginning to substitute. I've known the colorful Dale Brown, the excellent motivator and coach of LSU, ever since he was an assistant back at Utah State, and I don't want to embarrass him. I don't want to embarrass anybody. But he's been around this game a long time and suffered a lot of knocks, and I certainly don't want to put him through this.

But our substitutes are playing great too, and finally even the LSU fans are fascinated by what we are doing. "People kept coming by and complimenting Joey Lord and me about the team," Mary will tell me later. She and Joey, a girlfriend with whom she had been sitting during the game, were overwhelmed by the gracious manner in which they were treated. I'm not surprised that even their fans were saying nice things about our players. We're putting on a clinic out there, playing as close to the perfect game as you can get. On the bench, I'm a bit embarrassed as I watch. "We don't want to beat them that badly," I think. But I also feel good. I feel good seeing all those things we talked about in practice, all those things we worked on in practice, finally coming together. I feel good because they're doing those things the way they should be done, and because they're improving.

Finally, with nine seconds to go, P.J. Bowman hits a twelve-foot jumper to give us a school record of 127 points. When the clock runs out, we have ourselves a 127-100 win. It has been a very unusual game. As I walk to shake hands with Dale, I'm not sure what I will say or how he will react. "Lou," he says before I can open my mouth, "I really appreciate your not running up the score and taking it easy on us." I believe he's sincere, I don't think he's putting me on. That's something no one but the two coaches involved can understand. He was on his bench, I was on mine, and we both know exactly what took place.

If someone else had said that under those conditions, it may have bothered me. I would have felt that it was his way of telling me he thought I had run it up. But I know what Dale means, and

I react that way. I just tell him it was one of those unusual nights when everything went right for us.

The ease with which our Illini handled LSU that evening was a huge and pleasant surprise, only surpassed by the much bigger shocker of the night that was delivered to me by *Decatur Herald and Review* crack sports editor Steve Cameron. He quietly revealed to me that late that afternoon, the University of Illinois administration had selected head football coach John Mackovic as the successor to departed athletic director Neale Stoner. Mary and I were as surprised as everyone else, for I had traveled with John to grants-in-aid outings all spring, and not once had he indicated any interest in the position.

Those trips had given me ample opportunity to become acquainted with John and to observe him in action. I liked what I had learned about John; he's intelligent, innovative, and extremely well organized. This leads me to believe that our athletic department is in very capable hands.

# 6

# Up To Number One,
# Back to Square Two

**I**t's a Wednesday night in mid-January, and we're at a motel in suburban Chicago. We are 15-0, ranked second in the nation. The following evening we're scheduled to meet Northwestern in its Welsh-Ryan Arena. Behind us now is the everdangerous Rainbow Classic in Hawaii, where strange things happen and many great teams get beat. It's also a trip that costs you money, maybe $25,000. But you make it because it's good for recruiting, because it's a chance for your players to have a great experience, and because it gives us three games that don't count against the twenty-eight-game schedule limit. We managed to win the championship there in a good game with Georgia Tech. Then we returned home and opened our Big Ten schedule with victories over Michigan State, Wisconsin, and Michigan. Before that last game (which Michigan entered ranked number six), Wolverine coach Bill Frieder jokingly said, "I'll bet Lou $500 that his team wins."

"I've been in this league sixteen years, and they may be the best team I've seen," he said after we won 96-84. "Maybe the '76 Indiana team was better, but Illinois is a hell of a team."

"Bill's very nice. Very nice," was all I said. See, you just don't know what a coach is thinking when he says something like that. You can read it two ways. Maybe he really did believe that. But maybe, since we'd just beaten him, he was trying to prepare his team psychologically for our next encounter by building us up. It certainly was an unusual statement, though, and I didn't particularly like to hear it. I knew all of our alumni would see it and remember it, and that put us at risk of disappointing them. It could also hurt our players, who can't help but be affected when they keep hearing how great they are.

But now, as they mill around our hotel outside Chicago, our players aren't interested in that. They're interested only in that night's game between number-one Duke and North Carolina. The Blue Devils, who have held that top spot since the beginning of the season, will be facing their first true test of the year, and I'm interested in it too. But my reasons are different from my players'. They're interested because they know a Carolina win opens the way for them to become number one, which is something I don't care about at all. But I'm a basketball junkie, a guy who just likes to watch good games, so I want to see it as well.

Our hotel, however, isn't hooked up to the cable network that will be carrying it. So after a few quick phone calls, we rent a room in another one four blocks away. Jim Turpin, Loren Tate, Mary, and I drive over along with the team, and there we are, all in this room. Duke falls behind, and our guys start cheering. "Hey, guys," I tell them. "Forget about this game. Enjoy it, but don't get emotionally involved. We've got a game ourselves tomorrow night."

They settle down a bit then, but this is the first time I realize how much being number one means to them. They have been thinking about it all the time.

After my fourth Illinois team failed in its attempt to become number one, we traveled to Madison for a game with Wisconsin. We played well there and defeated the Badgers, but after hitting five of six shots, Steve Lanter, our excellent play-making guard and shooter, tore up his knee.

He was our point guard, and although a lot of people didn't realize it at the time, that left us without a true point guard to play that most important of positions. The rest of our guards were second guards. We were now like a football team without a quarterback, and suddenly people started to press us. Now we had trouble getting the ball up the court; and in close games, at the end, we had no one to handle the ball, to take care of the ball. Our losses started to mount.

We lost to Purdue by 8, to Iowa by 6, and to Michigan by 2 before rebounding briefly to defeat Minnesota. But then came losses to Michigan and Purdue, a pair of victories, and then five more losses that ended our season on a distinctly sour note. Most of the time my teams win at the end, and that's the way it should be. You should improve as the season goes on and be better at the end than you were at the beginning. So after we had won fifteen straight and been close to number one in the country, this was embarrassing. This was very distasteful from a coaching point of view. But I couldn't do anything about it.

More than that, I couldn't explain to everyone just how much Steve meant to us and how his injury really hurt us. I would have sounded like a coach making excuses, and we're not excuse-oriented here. It would have fallen on deaf ears anyway because at that point, people didn't care. They just knew that we had won our first fifteen games and then lost our last five. They didn't care that we played them without Steve. Good coaches win at the end, that was the only thing they thought about.

So that season, which had once seemed like such a break-through, actually ended up hurting us. We had made progress, but now people were again saying, "You guys can't get it done. You guys can't get it done." We had gradually gotten better and been moving along pretty well, and the fans had gotten optimistic and all fired up. Then we had trouble winning a game. I had built up some credibility, but now much of it was gone.

I wasn't back to square one, but I certainly wasn't much further along than square two. I was virtually back to starting all over again.


There was no real pressure on me entering my fifth season at Illinois. My original five-year contract had been extended, and that practice has continued throughout my time at the school.

There was also no lack of enthusiasm among me and my coaches. We knew what had happened to us, and we were looking forward to the challenge of rebounding. But with a lot of other people the cloud lingered, and they approached that year with little enthusiasm and a definite sense of apprehension.

But Levi Cobb and Neil Bresnahan were back as my co-captains, and there were Eddie Johnson, Derek Holcomb, Mark Smith, Kevin Bontemps, Brian Leonard, and Reno Gray, among others. We opened that year with an excellent win at Brigham Young. Neale Stoner, who had just been appointed athletic director, stopped by to watch that game while on his way back to California to wrap up some personal business. We then lost to Missouri by a point, but followed with wins in nine of our last ten games before our conference schedule began.

We would end up finishing sixth in the conference with an 8-

10 record. But combined with our early-season success, that was enough to get us into the National Invitational Tournament. It was the first time since 1963 that Illinois had been involved in post-season play, and that stirred the campus with excitement. There was unbelievable interest, and Assembly Hall was sold out as we beat Loyola of Chicago, then Illinois State, and finally Murray State to qualify for the semifinals in New York against Minnesota.

Those Gophers included current pros Kevin McHale, Trent Tucker, and Randy Breuer, and during the year we had split with the Gophers. They had beaten us first by 4, and we won the second by 2. Breuer would be the one who killed us in Madison Square Garden, where we again lost to Minnesota by 2. But then we came back with a gutsy performance to beat Nevada-Las Vegas in the consolation game, a game no one really felt like playing.

But we had to win it. We had to win it because we're competitors, and it doesn't matter if we're playing a consolation game or the national championship. So we fought and fought and won, and we were feeling pretty good. We'd overcome our early struggles, and now we'd rebounded from the big disappointment of last year.

Levi Cobb and the fifteen-game winning streak, both of them were breakthroughs for us. But making the NIT, just getting into post-season play, that was another breakthrough, and it was as big as those others. It let us hold our heads up again.

"Winning attitude." You hear that phrase all the time, but here's the thing about it: a winning attitude comes from winning, but you don't win without a winning attitude. It's the old problem—which came first the chicken or the egg. It's a very difficult one to solve. If you get lucky and get two or three great players right away, you can solve it overnight. But I didn't get that lucky at Illinois, and that made those first years very hard on me. At age twenty-six at  Las Cruces High School, my first head coaching job, we won the state title. Everybody was talking, the ball was bouncing right, and two more state titles followed quickly. Then Hardin-Simmons, two twenty-win seasons in four years after starting with nothing.  New Mexico State, four wins the year before I got there, the NCAA tournament my first year there,  then three straight twenty-win seasons, and then the Final Four.

But here, here we go four, five years and the progress is slow. After the success I'd experienced, that was really hard, very difficult to take.  The frustrations just kept mounting during those early years.  Second-division finishes, no players selected to the All-Big Ten teams.  Things like that bothered me, and I was forced to look for little things to hang onto.  For instance in the 1978-79 season, we led the nation in field-goal defense by holding our opponents to 40.4 percent shooting.

That kind of thing kept me going, and then in 1980 we led the conference in scoring,  had the best free-throw shooting percentage,  and got selected for the NIT.  Boy, were we feeling good.  We felt like we were somebody again.


It all started with that first NIT appearance, which I'm convinced put us into the NCAA tournament the next year.  That next year, too, Eddie Johnson would become the first of my players to make All-Big Ten during the five years I'd been at Illinois. He would later be drafted by the Sacramento Kings and then traded to the Phoenix Suns.  This past year he scored 21 points per game and was voted the NBA's Best Sixth Man of the Year.

But Eddie wasn't the only player on that 1980-81 team.  We

also had Derek Holcomb and Mark Smith, Perry Range and James Griffin, and a pair of fine new guards, Derek Harper and Craig Tucker. We blew away a pretty good Texas Christian team, killed a Missouri team that would go on to win the Big Eight, destroyed Oklahoma by 30, and entered our Big Ten schedule with only one loss in nine games. The only thing wrong with our team was our youth. We were a bit young at guard, but we were still good enough to finish third in our conference and only two games behind champion Indiana with a 12-6 record.

That was finally enough to let us make the big move, the move into the NCAA tourney. We were sent out West to UCLA and Pauley Pavilion. When I was at New Mexico State, that had been the site of one of my first-round disappointments against an Alcindor-led UCLA team. But here Mark Smith hit two free throws with two seconds to go, and we won our opener over Wyoming by 2. The victory matched us against Kansas State, and many people favored us to defeat them. But they had a great guard in Rolando Blackmon—he would soon be a first-round pick of the Dallas Mavericks—and they beat us by 5.

We lost Derek, we lost Eddie, we lost a ton that year. But even though we almost had to start over again, we have been winning some, and a tradition has been put in place. That helped our 1981-82 team led by George Montgomery, Brian Leonard, Perry Range, Derek Harper, and Craig Tucker win. Although we did drop back a bit, we were still good enough to make it into the NIT. During the first round we set a school single-game record for most points scored against Long Island University, with a prolific 126.

Terry Cummings and Teddy Grubbs, who had succeeded Mark Aguirre as the top prep players in Chicago, had gone on to

DePaul, and we have still barely scratched the surface in that talent-rich city. A year earlier we had gotten George Montgomery, coached by the exceptional Don Young, out of the Public League's Corliss High School. But he was not then a star, and we were still looking to recruit another big name like Levi Cobb.

We did that now in the spring of 1982 when we signed King High's Efrem Winters, who had been coached by the widely acclaimed Landon "Sonny" Cox. Winters was a former Public League opponent of George Montgomery, and he was generally considered one of that year's top two high school talents in Illinois. Bruce Douglas, who was coached by the wily Jerry Leggett and led his Quincy team to the state championship, was the other. And astute coach Wayne Hammerton's star, Doug Altenberger out of Peoria Richwoods, was rated just behind them. And then came Scott Meents out of tiny Hersher High near Kankakee, whose coach had been the highly successful Ed Sennett. They were a very good group of freshmen. They blended well with our awesome rebounder and post defensive specialist, George Montgomery: with highly skilled Derek Harper and flashy Craig Tucker. Together they got us back into the NCAA tournament.

That year we were sent West again, this time to Boise, Idaho, to face one of Jerry Pimms's patient Utah clubs. We were followed by two charter planes filled with boosters. They landed there just hours before the game; and one of them, Wayne Norrick, president of our booster club, went to their hotel to check in. "I'm sorry. We just don't have a room for you," he was told. "But you may want to check back again after the game."

Our game was late, the second of the evening, so many of our boosters went off to get something to eat—only to learn that their hotel had no restaurant. OK, they figured, we'll just have a hot dog when we get to the arena. But by the time they reached it, the arena had sold out all its dogs, and they were forced to dine on popcorn and candy bars.

The game, which we were expected to win, didn't go much better. Jerry Pimms's club, a poised senior club, just worked the ball and worked the ball and beat us by 3. We went back to the hotel then, but not many of us, players and coaches alike, felt like staying. So we arranged to have one of our charters fly immediately back to Champaign. As she left the hotel to catch that flight, my secretary Dorothy Damewood, grabbed an orange and blue flower arrangement off the front desk and said, "You don't need this anymore." She thought it had been made up for us, and didn't know that they were also the colors of Boise State.

Our flight was in keeping with the evening. We were overweight and had to dump fuel, which did not leave us enough to make the trip without a refueling stop. That prolonged our journey until 8:00 in the morning, and we were served nothing more than tiny sandwiches. When we finally got home, we were a bunch of hungry travelers.

One other thing happened that bizarre night as well. Wayne Norrick, unaware of our sudden departure, had decided to stay on in Boise. He went back to our hotel's front desk after the game to see if he could get a room now. "Take your choice," the receptionist told him. "We have 150 of them."

I got concerned about the Northwestern game as soon as I saw how emotionally involved my players were in their quest for number one. That tells me a lot; that tells me they're not in the right emotional frame of mind to win a game like this. They're not thinking of Northwestern, they're thinking of the polls. I'm not the only one who's concerned—my assistants feel it's going to be a rough night as well.

But we don't know how rough it's going to be until we go out for our warm-ups. The Northwestern student section, a section that calls itself the "Zoo Crew," swings into action. "Two, four, six, eight, Proposition 48," they chant in reference to the three players on our team who are saddled with that label.

When our players are introduced, they shower the court with ice and quarters and rolled-up diplomas, and the missles continue flying throughout the game. Nick will be hit once by ice, another time by a quarter as he prepares to take foul shots. Steve Bardo will be hit by a quarter while going for a rebound. My turn is next. When I'm introduced the Crew critiques the Lou Do by throwing rug fragments at me. Finally, as we are gathered around the bench just before the tip-off, a couple of them dash from the stands and douse us with tubs full of confetti.

I have never been through anything like this before. I know it's not Northwestern or anything their coach Bill Foster wants to support. I know it's just some of their students being a bit over-zealous, going beyond the bounds of good taste. But I'm upset, and my players are angry.

Still, when the game begins, Northwestern runs off the first 7 points, and now I can't be concerned about the Zoo Crew or any of its taunts and antics. I don't ordinarily hear much during games anyway. Everything here is pointing toward a loss, and I know I must get my players' minds off the polls and back on Northwestern. We finally do pull even midway through the first half, but we are still only up 2 when halftime comes and we go to our locker room.

There I sense that our players are still mad about the treatment they are receiving. Although they don't say anything to me, I see them talking about it among themselves. They're upset, I can tell, and although Northwestern stays close to us right until the end, there is no way they are going to let themselves lose this game.

We are certainly in a position to lose, but our players are mad, and they go out and fight—and win. So the Northwestern students actually helped us. Without them, we wouldn't win this game. Without them, we would not be going into a Sunday game with Georgia Tech, the only win we need to be number one.

You always expect a certain amount of taunting when you're on the road, especially when you're on the road in the Big Ten. None of our arenas is what you would call a real pit. But all of them, all of them are loud.

Start with our own Assembly Hall. When we arrived, if we weren't playing a big game, a fan could drop a dime, and we could hear it on the bench. We wanted to do something about that, so we started the Orange Crush, a student cheering section whose first president was former manager Alan Solow. Al did a great job drumming up vociferous support, and after he became a Bronze Tablet graduate, he was accepted into Harvard Law School and became a highly successful Chicago attorney. The Orange Crush put chairs along the sidelines and wore specially marked orange t-shirts in hopes of creating a home-court advantage. Before we came, you'd hear the opposing fans say, "Assembly Hall is a great place to play because it's a neutral floor." Well, we worked on that, and it's no longer a neutral floor. Our fans really get into it, and I think it's a fairly difficult place to play.

Purdue's Mackey Arena, you think acoustics. We have good acoustics in our building because it's used for so many other functions. But the acoustics over at Purdue are not very good. You bounce the ball on the court, and the noise bounces back at you from the ceiling. That's one reason the place is so loud. The other is the way the building is constructed. So they definitely have a home-court advantage there. It's a very tough place to play.

Indiana's also a tough place to play, although we usually do pretty well there. Even though it's loud and we've lost games there, most of the games go down to the wire. Ohio State, we play great there. Michigan, the arena there is very similar to our own. Iowa's just like Purdue—the acoustics are bad, and it's usually too hot. They always have the heat turned up too high, and the way it's constructed, it's probably the loudest arena in the conference. You always have problems yelling out instructions to players when you're there; but that's something that's a bit of a problem at all these places.

But arenas, they just don't mean that much to me. A building is not going to defeat you. What will defeat you is the quality of the team you have to play in that building.

I think what's called the home-court advantage has more to do with the disadvantages opponents face while playing away from home. First of all, when you're on the road, you're eating different foods and sleeping in a different bed and just generally out of your normal environment. Secondly, when you're on the road, maybe your incentive to win is not as high as it is at home. It has a little to do with not playing in front of your fans. But there's more to it than that, there's a third element: On the road, maybe you're not willing to do those things you *have* to do to win.

I'm convinced that you have to prepare yourself to win ball games. But on the road, I'm not so sure players are willing to go through the self-discipline they need to get ready to play. For example, we win a big game easily at Michigan on a Thursday night and then have to go to Michigan State for another one on Saturday afternoon. In the locker room after that first game, we're going to tell our players, "OK, look. You've got to start getting ready for Michigan State." But it has been a tremendous victory, and it's hard for them to go back to their hotel rooms and start getting their game faces on again. They don't want to think about it, they just want to relax and have a good time. Well, you can't do that either at home or on the road. But on the road it's even harder for a player because he has to do it by himself. At home, he has his friends and fans to help him.

Now, conversely, all those things are working in favor of the home team. And you can't stop there—you have to think of officiating. I think officials in general do a pretty good job on the road, but I also think subconsciously that the home team often gets the advantage. It's the same principle that's at work with the players. They're cheered at home, and they love it; they don't love being booed. You're an official and you make a call: the home crowd is going to cheer you if it goes their way and boo you if it goes the other way. I think our league is an exceptional one for getting the same treatment on the road and at home.

I know some people say, "Officiating isn't that important a part of the game." I know some people say, "Hey, the better team's going to win anyway, and the officiating won't have anything to do with it." Forget that. Don't believe it. How a game is called has a lot to do with its outcome. Some coaches have raised the working of officials to an art form. They plan what they're going to do, refine their plans, and then put them into action during a game. One tactic is to go after them early, to go out when the game starts and begin complaining immediately about everything. That way you hope an official overlooks a call he could make against your team just to keep you from complaining more. Another tactic is to wait until they make a mistake—and they're all going to make one—and then complain bitterly. Since you've been such a nice guy until then, the official may indeed think he blew it, and on the next judgment call, it'll go your way. Another coach might wait until the end of a game when they have a substantial lead and then go out and get a technical. Some people can't understand why he'd do that, but it's easy: he's setting up that official for the next game.

Here's the way it works. You're up 20, and you know you're going to win. But rather than letting a bad call go, you look down the road and try to get an advantage. You get a technical. When an official calls a technical, he has to file a report with his conference office, and chances are the coach is going to file his own complaint as well. By doing that, he has put the official on the defensive. So the next time he's officiating and it's a tough game, this referee starts thinking, "Hey, I had trouble with that coach the last time. I don't want to go through that again."

It's all intimidation. Each one of those tactics is based on intimidation and I do think officials, especially young ones, get intimidated some of the time. Now there are some coaches who just go along and let the game be played, and honestly, I do try to be that way. I remember when I was a Division I college official in two different conferences in the Southwest. When you do a good job, you like to be treated with some respect. I try to respect their efforts.

But I expect them to do a good job. I'm not going to ride them all the time, but they better treat me right or they're going to hear from me.   We have a rule on our team that our players are *never* supposed to complain to an official about a call.   But if our team is being taken advantage of, I'm not going to sit there and take it. I'm going to stand up for my players and tell them right out what a lousy call they just made or complain about the poor job I think they're doing.

On January 22, 1952, an Illinois basketball team coached by Harry Combes and led by All-American Rod Fletcher and a big redhead named Johnny Kerr was elevated to number one in the nation. An interesting sidelight is that Harry Combes took his Illini team to the Final Four three out of the first five years that he coached. But for the last fifteen years of his career, they did not return. Now, exactly thirty-seven years after that last appearance, we have a chance to return there for the first time since.

Assembly Hall is jammed.   ABC, with the colorful duo of Keith Jackson and Dick Vitale, is on hand, and our opponent is Georgia Tech, whom we defeated just a month ago in Hawaii. They were tough there, and they are even tougher here.  We play an absolutely lousy first half.  They score the game's first 4 points, and they're up by 8 six minutes into it.  After we close to within 3, they outscore us 18-7 in the last seven minutes of the half.  That sends us into the locker room down by 14.

They push their margin to 16 by scoring the first basket of the second half, and then, only then, do we rouse ourselves to life.  "I knew Illinois would come back," Tech coach Bobby Cremins will say later, and we are spurred on by one of our most exciting weapons.  First Kenny slams home an alley-oop pass from Steve Bardo, and then Lowell does the same on an alley-oop from Nick. Now our team is alive and our crowd is rocking.

We finally take our first lead of this game on a Bardo 3-pointer with 3:21 remaining. But Tech comes charging back to tie us at 70, to tie us at 72, to tie us at 74, and send the game into overtime. Those five minutes end with us tied again, this time at 82. But then we outscore Tech 15-2 at the start of the second overtime in a living display of the teamwork that we talk about so much. Larry Smith starts the run with two free throws. Then Tech ties us with two of their own. Nick hits a 3-pointer, Bardo hits a jumper, Lowell and then Larry hit two free throws each. Then Kenny makes a steal, hits a reverse layup, and buries a dunk on a pass from Larry.

A little over a minute later we are 103-92 winners and certain to be the nation's number-one team when the rankings come out twenty-four hours later. Again, just as against Missouri, we have shown great courage while coming from far behind. We expended an incredible amount of energy and emotion on the way to our victory. Our players, every one of them, have pushed themselves hard to attain this goal and now, through their extraordinary effort, they have achieved what has long been on their minds.

Each of those factors is reason enough for at least some celebration, but our feelings are dampened. Kendall Gill, our finest outside shooter, limped off in the final regulation seconds of this game with an injured left ankle. Now we are waiting to hear how seriously he has been injured. I think I know the answer to that question, and at 7:00 that night my worst fear is confirmed. His foot is fractured, and he's out for seven weeks.

In the first week, in the first game of our 1983-84 season, we partially avenged our tournament loss to Utah by just destroying them in the Rosemont Horizon in suburban Chicago. We went on to beat Gene Sullivan's Ramblers of Loyola-Chicago in the championship game.   But our spirits were dampened when our starting forward, 6-foot-8 Anthony Welch, went down early in the game with a broken foot.   Our impressive freshmen were now experienced sophomores. George Montgomery was developing into a real force; and little Quinn Richardson, the least publicized of the lot, was proving to be an unheralded key. If you watched him play in physical education class, he probably wouldn't be that impressive. But when he played for us, while shooting a record-breakng 59 percent from the perimeter, all he did was win  games.

We roared to eight straight wins, lost by 2 to Kentucky, then defeated Missouri and opened our Big Ten season with victories over Minnesota and Wisconsin. We would go on to run up a 15-3 conference record and tie for the title with Purdue. Then we sat down to watch the NCAA pairings that would tell us where we were bracketed in the tourney. We had a team that was capable of making the Final Four, we knew that by then. But after seeing that television show, we knew the odds of our reaching that plateau had been lengthened considerably. For we had been placed in the Mideast Region, the same region as Kentucky, which just happened to be its host.

It was a policy that has since been corrected: letting a team play on its home court in the regionals as it tried to make its way through the tournament. Here was Illinois, struggling to get to the Final Four, hoping to get to the Final Four for the first time in more than three decades.  To reach that goal, we faced the prospect of having to beat tradition-rich and powerful Kentucky on its own floor.  Kentucky would be going for its seventh Final Four in history, would be going for it at home with a team that included future pros Sam Bowie, Mel Turpin, and Kenny Walker. I thought it was unfair.  Our players had worked hard all year long, and I didn't think we should have to encounter such a thing.

"I just want to say that it does give them an advantage playing at home," I said at the time, and I left it at that. I left it at that because I didn't want to look past our first-round opponent, Rollie Massimino's excellent Villanova team, which had defeated eventual national champion Georgetown earlier that year. The Wildcats were a good team and we started off nervously against them. They were a strong inside team, and we shot poorly against them. But eventually we packed the middle on them and advanced with a 64-56 win. The exceptional play at both ends of the floor by our fine power forward, Efrem Winters, sparked this victory.

That game in Milwaukee got us to the semifinals in Lexington, where we were scheduled to meet Atlantic Coast Conference tournament champ Maryland. They were then one of the hottest teams in the country. But with 6:18 remaining, we were up by 6 and scrambling for a loose ball that would give us a shot to widen our margin even further. But there in the melee, Efrem Winters stepped on George Montgomery's foot and limped off with a badly sprained ankle. Although Scott Meents played well in relief, both he and Altenberger would eventually foul out, and we would be forced to hang on for a 2-point win. One of the keys to this victory was the tremendous defensive play by Doug Altenberger as he guarded the great Len Bias. The second key was the sensational defense of Bruce Douglas, which continued throughout the tournament.

Now we were matched against Kentucky in their home court, a home where they'd been undefeated that season. We were hobbled by Efrem's injury, smaller by an average of three inches per man, and playing in front of more than 20,000 wild-eyed Wildcat fans. Yet there we were, down only by 2 with 27 seconds remaining after a twenty-footer by Quinn Richardson. Quinn and Bruce Douglas pinned Kentucky guard Dicky Beal in front of the scorers' table—pinned him good and for numerous ticks of the clock. Beal shuffled his feet, and we screamed that he was traveling. It was traveling or a five-second violation, that was what we were screaming. But the officials were not going to call that on Kentucky at Kentucky. Instead they called a foul on Bruce, Beal hit his shots, and we lost by 3.

I have always believed that you make your own luck, that you make your own breaks. But that afternoon, I wasn't so sure. I couldn't be sure after watching the officials' calls go the way they did in the second half. "I'm not going to cry about the officials," I said. "But how can we come to Kentucky, play on their floor, and have the fouls go eleven or twelve to two until right at the end?"

In fact, with fourteen seconds to go in the game, we had had ten second-half fouls called on us, and Kentucky got only two. But that was enough to have me at a low boil after this game. Yet I was composed enough to write a message to my players on our locker room blackboard. I wrote: "26-5. Big Ten Co-champions. Be proud."

We were a talented team that season, but not a team of talents that people raved about. Yet the fans saw how hard we worked and appreciated our efforts. They saw the good things now happening to our program and started rallying around it. Those early days, those days when we aroused only tepid interest, were long behind us now. That was obvious even though the disappointment of that defeat only continued to grow. My summer camp, which is housed in Jim Phillips's Bromley Hall, had drawn only forty-seven boys the first year it was held; now it attracts close to 1,200 youngsters. Our Rebounders Club has grown through the years. President Orville Holman has seen its membership grow to nearly 500. Our radio coverage, which was confined to a single station back in 1975, now goes out over a forty-six station network; and Loren Tate and Jim Turpin now do the excellent job once performed by that living legend, Larry Stewart. I have a weekly radio call-in show, originating with local station WDWS and co-hosted by station manager Jim Turpin. There's also a weekly television show, also handled by Jim Turpin on our local station WCIA, and fed through our state hook-up. I have another fifteen-minute weekly radio show in-season with Mike Haile on local station K104. During the season, most of our games are on the Illini network with the play-by-play and color skillfully performed by that dynamic duo of Roan and Martin, Dan and Dick.

The entire community has embraced Mary and me. And most importantly, we feel their warmth and return it to the degree that we wish to retire here and remain in the Champaign-Urbana area. But I refuse to discuss when that day will come!

The frustrations we felt in Lexington suddenly began to grow and seemed to feed on themselves. We lost Quinn Richardson from that unlucky team, but we had a good nucleus remaining, and they went on to have a fine year. Then in an NCAA regional semifinal in Providence, we ran into a Georgia Tech team that had the future pro trio of Mark Price, John Salley, and a freshman named Tom Hammonds. They defeated us, 61-53.

That made us failures in the eyes of some people. We were failures because we had lost to a great team. Then the next season, with our outstanding freshman class suddenly seniors, we lost by 2 to Alabama in our second game of the NCAA tourney. It was a tough defeat that Wimp Sanderson's Alabama Tide hung on us at the buzzer. Yet they weren't dogs either, they were a very good team. But our fans had high expectations for us, and so again that loss made us failures in the eyes of many.

The next year Lowell was a sophomore, Kendall and Steve were freshmen, and we thought we had a remarkable team. We had Ken Norman, Big Ten rebound champion, leading Illini rebounder and scorer for two consecutive years, and eventual first-round choice of the Los Angeles Clippers. We had determined veteran Doug Altenberger, who had an extra year of eligibility after blowing out his knee. Jens Kujawa was our 7-foot sophomore pivot man; he was a German exchange student from Taylorville, Illinois, where he had lived with the Bill Hopper family. Our outstanding guards, Tony Wysinger and Glynn Blackwell, were all on hand as well, and we rushed off to eight straight wins before being stopped by North Carolina. We bounced back to beat Missouri and then lost to Loyola of Chicago in a game we all felt we should have won. Then we ran off victories over Sean Elliott and Arizona, Colorado, Michigan, Michigan State, Wisconsin, and Northwestern.

But now, with our record 14-2, this season turned into the most frustrating I've ever encountered in all my years of coaching. It began against Iowa. We had them down by 22 at home, but they came roaring back to defeat us by 3 in a contest that could aptly be termed a "slugfest." Two games later we were at Purdue and up by 3 with four seconds remaining. During a timeout, I turned to my assistants and we discussed the decision we faced. "Guys, do you think we should foul them?" I asked.

"No. No. No." They were in agreement. They all agreed we should not foul and should instead take a chance on their hitting a 3-pointer that could send the game into overtime.

I agreed with them, and now I turned to the team. "Make it

tough on them to get the ball in, and when they do, cover Troy Lewis and Doug Lee," we instructed. Those two players were Purdue's two real 3-point threats. We failed to get the job done.

We lost in overtime and I was criticized for that decision, criticized severely. Then we went to Indiana, where we were down 3 late in the game. The situation mirrored the one we had faced in West Lafayette, and here Bob Knight refused to foul us. Instead, he let us get off a couple 3-point attempts. We didn't make them and lost by 3. His actions showed that he shared my philosophy on this aspect of the game.

We would later lose again to both Iowa and Purdue, but we finished with four straight wins to guarantee ourselves a spot in our fifth straight NCAA tournament. Our first-round opponent would be a tiny school from Clarksville, Tennessee, by the name of Austin Peay.

Dick Vitale declared it a mismatch, and promised to stand on his head on the air if Austin Peay defeated Illinois. Denny Crum, whose defending national champion Louisville Cardinals were shut out of the NCAAs, made the observation that the tourney should not give bids to conferences like the Ohio Valley, the conference that included Austin Peay. One of my players, upon hearing the name of our first-round opponent, turned to the man he was with and asked, "Who do we play next?" Many of his teammates shared his attitude, and all week long they got the same question in fraternity houses, in sorority houses, and as they walked across campus. "Who do we play next?"

I even heard that question, and that's why I'm always concerned when we play a team without a big name. Since they're not ranked, since they're not on television, since they're not written about in newspapers and magazines, people automatically think they're no good. Since players are people too, they are also susceptible to taking on that attitude, an attitude that is only reinforced by the talk going on around them.

But Austin Peay had beaten Minnesota at Minnesota and had played Kentucky very close at Kentucky. They were not a team to be dismissed so easily. "Now, look," I told my assistants after I saw the draw. "We have a tough game. It's going to be a tough one for us. I don't want to scare our team, but somehow we have to get them to understand that."

We entered the tourney ranked number twelve that year, but we were not a great team. We had played some outstanding games, but we were inconsistent and had finished only fourth in the Big Ten. I knew that we would have trouble unless we approached this game in the right frame of mind. So we spent the early part of the week trying to convince our players that Austin Peay could play, to alert them to the fact that Austin Peay was a good team. We talked of their defense, they played good pressure defense. And we talked of their speed, but we could never get through. We had just defeated Indiana and Michigan and Michigan State, consecutively. After defeating people like that, it was hard for us to get ready for one like this. We tried our best to scare them, but we could never quite do it.

I knew it was going to be rough. We were in a no-win situation. If we lost, we were dogs. If we won, it was expected. But I wasn't going to give them another scare speech here in the locker room. I felt it was too late now and that would only make the players ill at ease. So all I said was, "Look, guys, they're a good ball club. We know that, you know that, but they're not as good as we are. Now let's go out and play ball."

A week earlier, at Michigan and at Michigan State, we had played some of our best basketball of the season. But here, as feared, we were flat. We were flat early, in the middle, and through much of the second half—most of which we spent chasing Austin Peay.

Now, with 1:10 remaining and with us down by 1, the Governors' Darryl Bedord missed a 3-point attempt. We got the ball back, and Tony Wysinger buried a twelve-foot jumper with twelve seconds left to put us ahead. But Austin Peay got the ball upcourt quickly, and there we trapped Richie Armstrong in a double team. We had a good double team on, and he had no place to go. But his teammate Tony Raye slipped in behind us. Armstrong got him the ball, and he was fouled with two seconds on the clock. He was not an outstanding foul shooter, but he hit both of them. We got the ball to midcourt in one second and called time out. We set up a play, Steve got the ball to Ken Norman, and Ken squared up to the basket and took a fifteen-footer that bounced off the rim as the buzzer sounded.

I was almost embarrassed at my post-game press conference. "Look," I said. "Sure, it's frustrating to lose, but Austin Peay is a pretty good ball club." They were pretty good, but I got the feeling no one believed me. The media, I felt, scoffed at my words.

It was like a death in the family. You never get over it, but you finally push it out of your mind. It also helped that I was a realist, like most people who grow up on a farm: a drought wipes out your crops, so you just roll up your sleeves and start again.

But losing a game like that was a coach's nightmare. I don't subscribe to the theory that you've got to be a little lucky to win, but here I found myself thinking, "C'mon, give me a break. We gotta get a break along here someplace." It was unbelievable, just unbelievable. When I met the next morning with a group of writers who covered the team, I was still down. But that turned into one of the most memorable breakfasts I've ever had. Included in this group of sports scribes were Jim Ruppert of the *State Journal-Register*, Gary Childs from the *Peoria Journal Star*, Terry Boers from the *Chicago Sun Times*, Steve Cameron of the *Decatur Herald and Review*, Fowler Connell from the *Danville Commercial News*, and Reed Schreck of the *Rockford Morning Star*. We discussed the season, we discussed the game, and as we went along, they all seemed to understand what had happened. No one there was that critical of the game, and that was important. It could have been a disastrous time for me and the program. Later in the day, I talked with Dave Dorr of the *St. Louis Post Dispatch* and Loren Tate of our local paper, the *News-Gazette*. They shared the same sentiment of those with whom I'd had breakfast.

So I appreciated that, but it was still one of the worst breakfasts I've ever been through. We had had a pretty good year, but because of all those frustrations, it had also been the worst of my career. That game provided the perfect ending for the season. You couldn't have written a better script.

Losses hurt players momentarily, but they don't dwell on them like coaches and fans do. I've found we can lose a heartbreaker to a Big Ten opponent, and the players, if they're good people and conscientious, will be hurt that night. Then they're over it by practice the next day. They bounce back quickly.

So the Austin Peay game was just a gnawing memory when the next season started at the Maui Classic in Hawaii. There we defeated Baylor, lost to Villanova, and beat eventual national champion Kansas. That was a good indication of the type of season we would have. We would go on to win some big games, while losing others because of our poor shooting. A loss at Purdue followed by an important victory at Indiana; a loss at home to Iowa followed by wins over Michigan and Northwestern. That was the pattern, and that was how our regular season ended. But our twenty-three victories and fourth-place finish in the conference were enough to return us to the NCAA tourney.

We easily won our opening-round game against Ken Burmeister's Texas-San Antonio team. And in the next, against Villanova, we ran out to a 10-point halftime lead. Our lead was still 10 with just under three minutes remaining. But then it was nightmare redux, frustrations revisited. We had entered the NCAAs as a 67 percent free-throw shooting team, the worst free-throw shooting team in the Big Ten. Here our failures from the line finally caught up to us. Five times in the last 2:45 of this game, we went to the line in one-and-one situations. And five times we missed the front end of the attempt.

Nick missed, then Steve Bardo missed twice, Jens Kujawa missed, as did Kenny Battle. I've often said that free-throw shooting is contagious; if one player is hitting them, all his teammates seem to hit them. And if one player starts missing them, well . . . That happened to us here: we came down with the disease as Villanova nailed four 3-pointers to take the lead with twenty-five seconds remaining. A layup by Kenny nine seconds later put us back up by 1; and after getting hammered on the play, he went to the line with a chance to stretch it to 2. He missed.

He missed, but Villanova's Mark Plansky did not. With four seconds on the clock, his two free throws ended our season. Again we had failed to live up to everyone's expectations, and the way the game was lost contributed to a nightmarish spring and summer.

Until I got to Illinois, I was always considered to be an outstanding coach. All those years at Las Cruces High School, Hardin-Simmons, and New Mexico State, we never got any negative publicity; it was never insinuated that maybe I should have done something differently. I didn't become a bad coach until I arrived here. So when that criticism started, it came as a shock to my system and to my entire family. It was something we all had to adjust to.

It started, I guess, after that season we opened with fifteen straight wins and ended with five straight losses. Sure, I bled a little bit then, and it bothered me somewhat. Since then I've learned to go on, just to go on. If I let that get to me, really, then I'm not a strong person. And I must be strong enough not to let it bother me, or it can affect my team. But criticism, especially criticism that's not justified, bothers anybody.

After our losses in the NCAA tournament, suddenly there was a lot of criticism. "Lou can't coach in the NCAAs. I don't know what it is, Lou just has trouble in the NCAAs."

"Lou can't win the big one."

"Lou's a great recruiter, but not a good bench coach."

"Lou's kids aren't disciplined enough."

"Lou's offense is too disciplined."

"Lou puts too much pressure on his kids."

"Lou's kids are too tight."

All these questions and criticisms surfaced, and I could understand part of it. We hadn't been that successful in post-season play, and maybe we had disappointed some people. But to say we were failures because we lost a ball game, that's wrong, that's completely wrong. I don't consider any team that gets to the playoffs a failure; somewhere along the way they had to win some big games. People don't care about that though. All they see is that you didn't make the Final Four, and that makes you a failure.

It's funny how coaches pick up labels, but it happens to a lot of us. Mark Coomes, my assistant, was in Chapel Hill, North Carolina, one time when a guy next to him in a restaurant says, "We have the best defensive coach in the country down here."

"I know Dean Smith is good and everything," Mark replied, "but we have a real good defensive coach too."

"No, we have the best," the man insisted. "How many guys in the country do you know who can hold Michael Jordan to 20 points a game?"

So here was this guy criticizing Dean Smith, one of the best coaches in the country, criticizing Dean for making his players perform within a system. He has been criticized too for not winning more than one national championship. After Indiana lost to Seton Hall in the 1989 regionals, people there started griping that Bob Knight hadn't played Jay Edwards enough.

National television and its announcers have the most to do with coaches picking up labels. They say something, that this one's a great young coach, that one's a poor bench coach, and then writers and fans pick up on it. Often what comes out is ridiculous, just ridiculous. Back when Gary Williams, the new Maryland coach, was still at Boston College, his team was getting ready to play Syracuse, which was and still is coached by Jim Boeheim. A newspaper writer wrote a column comparing the two teams, something like the "Tale of the Tape" that they use before big boxing matches.

You know how it goes: at forward the nod goes to Syracuse; at guard, a check to Boston College. He got down to the coaches, and he gave the advantage to Gary Williams, which was just crazy.

Jim beat Gary seven of the ten times they played while Gary was at Boston College. If the writer had done a little research, he could have found that out. But Jim has been unfairly labeled in some circles as an average coach, and the writer just went along with that. Check his record.

It didn't make any sense; just like I don't think a lot of the things said about me make any sense. But the worst thing you can do is react. You just can't react to adversity or bad publicity. If you try to explain facts, then you look like you're making excuses. If you get mad, you make yourself look bad and probably hurt your team.

Now I must say that most of the people around our program have been just great. The Board of Regents, the administration, faculty, staff, students, our hard-core fans, and the media that regularly covers us;—they've all been very fair. But the labels that have been put on me, hey, there are probably people outside our program who think, "Oh, poor Lou. He's just barely hanging on."

# 7

# Benji's Legacy

**D**uring the lunch hour just prior to our departure for Minneapolis, I make a brief hospital visit to a long-time Rebounders Club board member, Bill Gaston, who has just had cancer surgery. I want to get a few words of advice from him on how to beat the Gophers, so I am pleased to find him alert and quite willing to share his thoughts on the game. His lovely wife Sean was also present. The three of us talked about our number-one ranking and the challenge of retaining it now without Kendall's talents.

Upon our arrival in Golden Gopher country, we try to phone our good friends, the former outstanding basketball coach Jim Dutcher and his wife Marilyn, to have our customary enjoyable evening with them at dinner. On this occasion, however, we discover that they are vacationing in Florida, and so we settle in for the evening with Joey and Dick Lord, friends and fans who have accompanied us on this trip. We all order dinner from the room service menu, switch on the television, and watch Michigan State cruise by Purdue.

"You know, they don't look ready to play." Our team is warming up to play Minnesota, our first game after being ranked number one in the country, and I overhear a radio announcer say that into his microphone.

I don't think anything of it at the time. Our players are going about their business as usual. But as soon as the game begins, I realize he had been right. We are playing without emotion, without any emotion at all. We repeat what is almost a trend, our now-familiar second-half rush. But this time it's different. This time something is missing. This time we end up losing by 7.

We shoot only 40 percent for the game, and we're out-rebounded. We commit more turnovers than Minnesota, and they get eleven steals to our six. We play horribly, we play badly. And just like that, our seventeen-game winning streak and our reign atop the polls is over.

Kendall's injury is part of the reason, but Steve Bardo comes closer to the truth. In the locker room he tells a reporter, "We might be getting a little lax and not taking care of business."

We're competitors, and we wanted to beat Georgia Tech. But saying that, I will also say that it wouldn't have been all bad had we lost. I had mixed emotions about being ranked number one. I think being ranked number one has both advantages and disadvantages. One of the advantages is the publicity you receive, and what that means to your players and for your program. Another advantage is that being number one gives your players added confidence. The disadvantages, first of all, are that everybody is out to get you, and they're probably going to play their best against you. Then if you get beat, you're in danger of dropping two or three more in a row since you pushed yourself so hard to become number one. But the big problem is getting your players to listen to you.

TV announcers are saying nice things about them, newspapers are writing flattering articles, their friends in the fraternities and sororities are telling them how great they are. It's very difficult to communicate with them in this situation and correct them. You tell them they're doing something wrong, and they don't want to listen. They think, "Hey, we've won seventeen in a row, this guy's impossible to satisfy."

Mike Krzyzewski, the Duke coach whose team spent much of the early season ranked number one, felt his team reacted the same way, and he used a good analogy to illustrate the point. When he corrected his players during their time atop the polls, he said he was much like a parent on Chicago's luxurious Gold Coast telling his kids to be sure to turn out the lights. Since there was no sense of urgency, the parent was going to have a hard time getting the kid to listen.

It's the same thing with a team. You see the mistakes they're making in practice; but since they're undefeated and ranked number one, they don't feel any sense of urgency to correct the mistakes. They have a tendency not to listen. But that attitude's not unique to college basketball players. That's just human nature.

When Steve Lanter went down in early 1979, I don't think we realized how important he was to the team. When Kendall Gill went down in early 1989, we didn't realize his full importance either. But we quickly found out.

Now we knew we had lost a very valuable player, but we felt at first that we had enough talent to overcome Kendall's injury. We could move someone into his spot and that we would be OK. We weren't, and what happened was this: First, his loss disrupted our substitution pattern. Next, we missed Kendall's outside shooting— he was a 53 percent, 3-point shooter when he fractured his foot. People started playing zone against us, giving us the outside shot, and jamming our people inside. Finally, it affected our defense drastically.

When Kendall was in there, we matched him up with our opponent's point guard, and he was tremendous. He disrupted other teams' attacks and made all kinds of steals. That freed up Steve Bardo, selected by the Big Ten coaches as the best defensive player in the conference, against the shooting guard, against the shooting forward, to go up against anybody. But now, with Marcus in as Kendall's replacement, we had to switch Steve over to the point guard. We couldn't let Marcus try to do that job as a forward. So while Kendall's injury certainly hurt our offense, it probably impacted us even more defensively. That's why it was so devastating for us, more devastating than we thought it would be originally.

On Friday evening before our Indiana game at home, I had dinner with the Indiana contingent of Bob Knight, Ron Felling, Tates Locke, Dan Dakich, Chuck Farrington, and Bob Hammel, outstanding sports editor of the *Bloomington Herald-Times*, as well as with local attorney Bob Auler. Bob Hammel summed it up when he told me, "Lou, you have one of the best teams in the country with Kendall Gill in the line-up." "Yes," I agreed, "but without him we're hurting both offensively and defensively."

The first half of the Indiana game on Saturday was our worst first half of the season up to that point. We have only 25 points when it ends, after averaging more than 90 per game for the year. But then we have a great second half, Jay Edwards misses some free throws, and we win by 10.

Then we travel to Purdue, where we play horribly again, but with time running out we can tie it up when Nick is fouled as he scores from underneath. But because the basket is disallowed by one of the worst officiating calls I have ever encountered in my entire career, we go on to lose by 4. Then we push on to Iowa, and again we lose by 4. "I don't think we'll win another road game all season," I tell my assistants after this defeat.

We are trying everything now to compensate for Kendall's injury, but we're like a football team without a passing quarterback. We have no true, good-shooting, two-guard to push into his spot, and none of the replacements proves to be the answer. Marcus is our first choice, but he's a forward playing at guard, and that hurts us both offensively and defensively. We try Larry Smith, then P.J. Bowman at the point, and make Steve the two-guard. But even though P.J. makes some big shots for us against Purdue and Iowa, just like he did for Tom Cooper and the local Parkland Junior College National Champs, we're just not the same cohesive unit.

It isn't Marcus's fault. It isn't P.J.'s fault. It isn't Larry's fault. It's the situation. We just don't have a two-guard to replace Kendall. After feeling so good about this team for so long, I am suddenly concerned. We are inconsistent up and down, and as the old saying goes, if you're inconsistent, you're in trouble. Now we're looking a little better in practice, but I still worry that we could slip into the Big Ten's second division.

I can't get a reading on this team now. I know we're still pretty good, but I also know we've gone from a top team to a very average team with one broken bone.

The surprise of this season, one of the reasons it progressed so remarkably, was our offensive improvement over the year before. I've always believed that players improve only so much offensively. But in thirty-three years I never had a group improve as much as this group did.

If you start out in the fifth grade, then polish your skills in junior high and high school and your first two years of college, well it just doesn't make sense that you're suddenly going to improve substantially on your skills. But that's what happened here. Kendall went from a 47 percent shooter to a 54 percent shooter, and his jump shot was even more remarkable from the 3-point range. There he improved from 30 percent to 46 percent. Our team average on 3-point shooting rose from 28 percent to 42 percent, and our free-throw shooting was substantially better too.

Now if I had my way, I would never, never discuss shooting percentages; I don't like to talk about shooting at all. It's such a delicate talent, I don't want to fool with my players' minds. I don't want to play mind games with them, and I don't want my assistants down on the floor talking to them about shooting. I don't want them saying, "Look, you've got to move your thumb over a bit," or "you've got to move your forefinger to the center of the ball."

So these guys improved on their own. These guys picked themselves up by their bootstraps and developed and mastered some skills. That's why it bothered me when people kept talking about our talent, kept saying that we were successful because we were this highly talented team. It was more than that. It was a team that had no center, that didn't have much size, that was working to refine its skills. Then they went out and won because they wanted to very badly.

Many of the preseason predictions about this team were based on Marcus joining us, and he helped. The guys on the bench, they did a heck of a job too. But a lot of the credit had to go to guys like Kendall, Lowell, Ervin, and Larry; guys who were subpar at something the year before and worked to make themselves better.

As we search in our effort to replace Kendall effectively, Marcus is one of the players caught in the middle. He starts one game, sits much of the next, and I learn later that he doubts whether he's good enough to play in the Big Ten.

But Marcus, who was forced to sit out the previous season, is enduring what almost any top recruit endures in his first season of college basketball. He was regarded by many as the country's top high school player during his senior year. But now he's on the bench, playing maybe twenty minutes a game, and he's frustrated. First of all, he wants to play; more than anything else in life right now he wants to play. On top of that, the team is doing really well. Then there's Nick, his old friend from Chicago, who's playing great. But it's even more than that, it's his family and friends, all these people watching on television and seeing the number-one player in the country sitting on the bench. These people keep asking him, "Marcus, what's wrong? What's wrong with you? Why aren't you playing more?" There's nothing wrong with Marcus, he's just growing up.

Now I've already seen an article on Marcus, an article in which he basically said he was starting to play again like he had in high school, that he just hoped he could get back to that level. Well, Marcus isn't playing like he did in high school. He's playing much better, but the competition here is on a completely different level. So he's taking shots now that he made in high school, and he's not making them here. That's frustrating too, but that's also part of maturing.

One of the most interesting courses I took in college was an education class in graduate school in which I read Rousseau's *Emile*. To put it simplistically, one of Rousseau's theories of education is never to do anything for a young person that he can do for himself. In the book, he creates an imaginary son, Emile, whom he sends out alone into the fields. He wants him to be alone so that after he experiences adversity, perhaps a fall, he has to get up on his own. It's part of growing up. And that same principle is at work here, only on a higher level. Marcus is falling and picking himself up, making mistakes and correcting them. It's all part of acquiring the discipline, the self-discipline he needs to be a top player at this level.

That's why we're pushing him, that's why he's spending time on the bench. That's why with younger players, I have a tendency to be realistic and to talk to them a lot about the level on which they're presently playing and the heights they could reach one day. Now when he gets older, he's going to take on more responsibility by himself, and then we'll back off a bit. But right now, Marcus is going through a lot of frustrations.

He's handling them pretty well, though, and because he's handling them well I think next year he's going to be a much improved player.

During his freshman year, the year he was forced to sit out, Marcus initially watched our games from an Assembly Hall seat that was near our bench. But then during the season, we were told he should probably sit further up in the stands. The rationale for that order was this: from his first seat, he might be able to hear what I was saying to the team during a timeout. This could be construed as coaching him, and the NCAA rule does not permit a student-athlete who falls under Proposition 48 to receive instruction.

Now isn't that amazing? But those kids, now commonly referred to as "Prop 48s," are excluded from almost all team activities, and that's just one reason I don't like the rule. Proposition 48 has established minimum grade and entrance exam requirements for Division I college athletes. I agree that there should be academic standards for athletes, and that proposition does cover their high school averages and college entrance exam scores. But like a lot of people, I think those entrance exams are unfair to minority and disadvantaged students. But they are held to that standard, and if they don't meet it they're told they can't play with their team, can't practice with their team, can't be part of their team in any way. And then to top that, they're stripped of a year of eligibility, which is one of the worst aspects of the rule.

Now if you want to learn about mechanical engineering, you talk to experts in that field, right? But coaches aren't given that much credit. This rule was established by people who don't understand athletics. If they did understand, they wouldn't have passed it. First of all, these kids are going to be in an intramural gym practicing anyway. Any coach could tell them that these guys are going to play against nonscholarship players who have nothing to lose; they're going to pick up bad playing habits and risk serious injury. They won't be utilizing any more of their leisure time for studying, so they may as well be participating in limited practices.

That's why I think they should be permitted a certain amount of practice time with the team. You have rules for everything else, so why not put in another one giving them an hour with the team a few times a week—at least that way they're in an organized situation and feel a part of the team. You have to understand, these guys have played basketball all their lives. They live for basketball. When you tell them they can't play or be part of the team, it's very difficult for them to handle. It can do nothing but hurt them.

Forcing a player to disassociate himself from the team can be harmful to him in several ways. A young man has played in a controlled environment in high school. But now, just as he's making one of the most important transitions in his life, the move to his college career, the support structure is withheld from him.

Every day our staff talks to our players about class attendance and academics in general. These five- to ten-minute talks occur before practice on an individual basis. During practice I admonish the group to attend classes regularly, study hard, meet tutors and study halls when they're scheduled, and so on. After practice we talk to individual players about their problems. A student-athlete who is governed by Prop 48 misses all of this beneficial academic counseling.

Academic services, headed by the highly efficient Terry Cole, is an  arm of the athletic department that exists solely to assist athletes in every phase of their academic lives. It is policy here at Illinois that athletic coaches are not permitted to discuss a student-athlete's progress or grades with any professor. So certain members of the academic services staff physically check each student-athlete's class attendance on a daily basis. If he has an unexcused absence, he is required to report to a two-hour supervised study hall at 6:00 a.m. Although these study halls are open to Prop 48 student-athletes, we don't have the leverage to encourage class attendance, such as by manipulating starting assignments, playing time, and withholding them from games.

The most damaging aspect of Proposition 48 is how a  player becomes stigmatized. He's a Prop 48, and ten years down the road, no matter how well he may have done in school, he's still going to be a Prop 48. That's why, in many ways, I think we'd be better off with freshman ineligibility  overall. At least that way you remove the stigma now attached to such an athlete.

I have mixed feelings on  freshman ineligibility, but anything is better than a guy not passing an exam and having newspapers and television label him for the next ten years. So if it takes freshmen ineligibility to get that stopped or corrected, then we probably should do it. That's how damaging I think Proposition 48 is to an athlete.

We play Ohio State at home after dropping those two on the road, and again we're horrible, even though we manage to win by 2. "We're just not playing well at all," I worriedly tell my assistants.

Kendall's injury, the mere loss of his physical ability, is what hurt us at first. But now our failure to execute or succeed is hurting us psychologically as well. Some players, seeing what is happening to us, are trying to over-compensate, and that only erodes the situation further. They're trying to do too much and forgetting just what it is they should be doing.

Without Kendall, our passing quarterback, our inside game is being jammed to death. We're like a football team facing a defense that has brought all eleven of its men up to the line of scrimmage. We need another shooting guard in there badly. You can see here why I reminded my assistants how important it is to recruit perimeter shooters. We had one in Andy Kaufmann, and he would help us now in our struggles, but he developed a blood clot in January and is sitting on the sidelines with Kendall.

That's our situation as we prepare to play Northwestern. But our players' attitudes before this game alleviate some of the concern that I'm feeling. "I haven't forgotten the treatment we got up there," Nick says, "and that's all I'm going to say about it." "We all will always remember the treatment we got there," says Kenny. "Hopefully, that will make us more fired up and ready to play."

We break out new orange uniforms to wear in this game,

which give us a psychological lift now and throughout the remainder of the season. The players wanted to wear the orange uniforms for what they consider special games. So the players are ready—especially Marcus. Since Kendall's injury, he has shot only four of twenty-five, but here he goes seven of twelve and scores a career high 20 points while leading us to an 86-69 win. That's more points than he scored in our previous seven games combined; and later I say, "Everybody has been pulling for Marcus. He needed this ball game. I can't foresee the future, but I'm sure he'll be a better player because of what he did tonight."

All of our players execute better in this game, and four nights later, at Michigan State, we just blow the Spartans off their floor, a floor upon which we will never again bounce a ball. For beginning with the 1989-90 season, a big new arena will replace old Jenison Fieldhouse as home of the basketball Spartans. We're up by 9 midway through the first half, up by 21 five minutes later, and win the game by a comfortable 19. Marcus, with 11, again plays well. But this game marks our return as a team—five guys end up in double figures.

Our players quite naturally feel good about themselves—we're on our way back. But in the locker room I caution them. "Guys, look. We're only half through this week; we have to get ready for Wisconsin. I know you want to celebrate this victory, but don't do it. Let's think about Wisconsin."

They can't do that. They have played their first really good game since Kendall's injury and feel relieved. They, like me, know that Illinois has defeated Wisconsin in sixteen straight games. So at Madison on Saturday, less than forty-eight hours after they feel they're on their way back, they're ready for a fall. That's just the way we play.

In the first half we shoot only 33 percent and score only 18 points, while allowing the Badgers to shoot 50 and score 32. Nick scores only a single field goal in these first twenty minutes; Kenny and Marcus, none at all. They are killing us on the boards as well; they out-rebound us here 32 to 18. In the second half it doesn't get much better, our play is atrocious. This evolves into one of those nightmare games, a game when a coach can do nothing at all.

Although Badger head man Steve Yoder has been an outstanding coach over the years and has produced many quality teams during his career, I've never seen one of them look sharper or play better than they do this afternoon.

Now I normally don't let one game affect me a great deal one way or the other, whether we play great or whether we play poorly. But after all we've been through, to have the bottom fall out now, this is our lowest ebb.

It's immediately dubbed "The Massacre in Madison," and the day after it occurs I have the players report to our film room at 8:30 in the morning. As they watch their terrible Saturday performance, I want them to see just how bad they were. But right after that we turn our attention to Purdue, whom we play at home in little more than thirty hours.

Between now and that game I am very positive. I believe that the worst thing you can do when your team is winning is to think that everything is great and to tell them it's great. That's when I prefer to be negative. That's when I'll point out their mistakes, that's when I'll mention some fundamentals that we have to work on so we can get even better. At those times we need something to keep going, to keep from getting complacent.

But here we're hurting, we're in bad shape, and I have to try to pick them up and get them going again. So I reassure them that they are still a good team. I tell them that it was only one game, that we shouldn't let it ruin our good season. I want them to see me taking the Massacre in stride so they in turn take it in stride.

Overcoaching. That is something you always have to fight, especially in situations like this. Overcoaching is one of the most common mistakes you can make, but we all have a tendency to do just that, especially young coaches.

Defensively, I think I've always done it right. We're going to use a basic man-to-man, extend it a little bit, do some trapping. But you're seldom going to see us in a zone or using four or five trick defenses. Our philosophy is not to out-trick the other team, but to out-execute them. Now offensively, over the years, I think I've sometimes tried to do too much. Most coaches invariably want to do too much offensively. It's always tempting to put in just one more play to take advantage of an opponent they're going to face.

Illinois head football coach John Mackovic gave me the best illustration with regard to overcoaching. He told me that the great Tom Landry, former coach of the Dallas Cowboys, was having a staff meeting when some of the assistant coaches complained about the simplicity of their offense on their twenty-yard line. The assistants indicated that the opposition always knew basically what they were going to run. Coach Landry stared at his assistants as only Landry can and said, "The important thing is that *we* know what we're going to do."

Everything looks good on paper, but if you're not careful, you wind up using too many plays. As they say, *too much thinking gives you slow feet.* So when I go to clinics now, I tell young coaches, "Spend sixteen hours a day studying the game, and you should never lose a game because you don't know what to do. Now you may lose a game because of poor judgment, but if you are suddenly confronted with a box and one, you should know what to do against it. So go out and learn everything, then teach only 2, 3, or 4 percent of what you know. Then you'll probably be successful."

And that's true, true enough that I've even heard some coaches say that the less they taught, the better coaches they became. What they meant by that was the same as what's meant by the old KISS philosophy, the one that says, "Keep it simple, stupid." You just have to have a sound philosophy, that's the key. And if you don't have a basic sound philosophy of the game, I don't think you're going to last very long unless you're in an ideal situation.

Remember the great Celtics teams under Red Auerbach? They used to run five, six plays; they didn't do anything fancy. John Mackovic, our excellent football coach at Illinois, has told me he does the same thing. He says his quarterbacks have options on which receiver to throw to but those receivers don't have options, they have to run certain routes.

Bob Knight just amazes me. In all the games I've coached against him, I've seen him draw up a special offensive play just once. Other than that, he just runs his passing game, consecutive picks, down picks, back picks. He just stays with it and stays with it and stays with it, and his teams do it better than most. That's his philosophy. And when you play him, you know exactly what you're going to get. *Beat!*

But people sit in the stands and think that coaches have made all kinds of changes in order to win that game. That's usually not the way it really is. Coaches who are winning, winning big, often just go along with it. Like Bear Bryant, the late great Alabama football coach, who lost his first game of the year and then said in a media conference, "I didn't have my guys ready to play. It's not their fault they lost. I didn't prepare them right."

Now he could afford to say that because he knew he'd probably win his next ten games and then go to a bowl and win that too. And do you think, in his own mind, that he felt he hadn't prepared his team? He had four weeks to prepare them, plenty of time; but that's all part of the indoctrination of the media and fans. Take credit for the one loss, and you're more likely to receive credit for the next ten wins. There are so many mind games being played.

For instance, after a game the media often want to hear what changes you made to turn it around. They're just crying to hear that—it gives them something to write about. But I don't like to discuss that, and a lot of coaches don't like to do it. But some coaches are more than willing to promote themsleves, to create a better image in the eyes of the public. Fellow coaches can see the subtle ways in which they handle those situations; and we chuckle about them.

That kind of stuff goes on all the time. Some coaches dress a certain way to call attention to themselves (would you believe a bright orange sportcoat?), but why would you put on a $600 suit to sweat in? Another coach, Billy Tubbs, the highly successful Oklahoman, a guy I've known for years, comes out and says, "The Big Ten? That league isn't that tough. They have a lot of dogs in there." That's instant national publicity, and suddenly he's being widely quoted in all of the major news outlets. By the way, Billy, I haven't heard any barking lately.

It happens on television too. You see some coaches hug their players for the benefit of the viewers; that's the kind of stuff the public likes to see. But I'm not sure I want to put my arms around those sweaty guys!  When coaches allow themselves to be hooked up with a live microphone for a particular game, they usually don't coach that game as they normally would.  Everything is positive. Everything is, "John, don't worry about missing shots, everybody misses shots."  They clean up their act.  They don't want to tarnish their "wholesome" images.

I don't say anything.  I don't need to say anything.  We're getting ready to play Purdue in our first game after the Massacre, and I can tell we're ready by just looking at our players.  I know we're going to win.

This Purdue team is a classic example of what I talked about previously: the fact that a team must have perimeter shooting. Purdue last year, in my opinion, had one of the top teams in the country.  Since then they lost some of their outside shooters, and this season they couldn't win half their games.

I know we're going to win, but I don't anticipate the performance we put on this Monday night.  Offensively, defensively, we roll right from the beginning.  Purdue, somehow, manages to stay close for eight minutes, and they trail us by only a point after Lowell goal tends on a layup by Kip Jones.  But then Lowell himself stretches that lead with a jumper.  Defensively, we start playing unbelievable, devastating defense.  Over the next eight minutes we hold them without a point and score 19 ourselves.  At halftime we lead by 22 after limiting them to nineteen shots and forcing them into a dozen turnovers.

Marcus is playing his best all-around game of the year for us. Nick, Kenny, and Lowell are making all those shots they missed on Saturday afternoon.  We win by 27, and it could have been 57. Afterwards the media want to know if we're back.  I'm noncommittal, since this was a home game and we've just lost badly on the road. But then we go to Ohio State, trail by a point at halftime, and run away from them with a 57-point second half. In that half we shoot 73 percent. And Nick scores 35 for the game, a super game.

Now it's back home for a rematch with Minnesota, the team that started us on our roller coaster ride. They hold the ball on us and keep the game slow. We don't look pretty, you never look pretty in a slow-down game. But we play fairly well and win by 5. We are now three games behind league-leading Indiana with three remaining. Our next date is a Sunday afternoon engagement at Assembly Hall in Bloomington.

Last year's Illini-Hoosier clash at Bloomington proved to be one of significance in my career: it was there that my 500th college win was registered with a gutsy, emotional performance by our team. Long before this contest Jimmy Phillips, one of our managers, had quietly contrived to gain possession of the game ball if it was indeed the 500th win, so that I could add it to my trophy collection. So there we were in one of the most unlikely arenas for this milestone to occur and at Indiana's end of the floor, Jay Edwards swishes a 3-pointer at the buzzer, but we won 75-65.

Jimmy darts like a madman past the scorer's table and TV cameras, scoops up the loose ball in full view of the entire Indiana bench, and starts to make off with it. He's immediately surrounded by three sturdily built Indiana managers who demand the return of said ball while turning deaf ears to his explanation of why he snatched it. Jimmy even offered to replace it with an Illinois ball or pay cash for it, but he gained no ground with this uncooperative trio.

While Jimmy's hanging on to the ball for dear life, and the

others are attempting to wrest it from his grasp, a stern-faced Bob Knight stops to demand, "What the hell's going on here?" Jimmy hurriedly explains his actions to Bob, who then glares into the unwitting faces of the three managers and orders, "Give him the goddam ball!" I proudly display that ball in my Illini office at home.

"Want to get together?" Bob Knight asks. He has called my office and is now wondering if I would like to go with him to watch his son Patrick play on Saturday night and have a late dinner.

"That would be fine," I tell him, and we make arrangements for him to pick me up that next Saturday evening at our Bloomington hotel.

I know that some people think we don't get along, but that isn't the case at all. We often meet for dinner before we play and at other times too. My relationship with Bob, in fact, is as strong as any I have with other coaches in the league. But people still think that we don't like each other.

Sure, there was a time when Bob and I shouted at each other. Right after that came the book *Season On the Brink*. In it Bob was quoted as saying some fairly negative things about me and Illinois. I read newspaper clips about it, and then Bob called and we discussed three or four things that appeared in the book.

We ended up with a situation in which the writer claimed that Bob said certain things, and Bob claimed that that's not the way it was. I respect Bob for calling me. He didn't have to, but he called.

Now I'm not going to defend him on everything, because I don't agree with everything he does, just as he doesn't agree with everything I do. But we're a lot more alike than most people might think. And except for that short time, we've had a good relationship ever since I came into the league. Bob is without a doubt one of the outstanding coaches of any sport of all time.

There's no question, either, that Bob's opinion carries a lot of weight in the league, that his presence is felt throughout the league. That may make a few coaches nervous. But it doesn't bother me. Anybody with his personality, with three national titles, and with all the wins he has is going to be controversial. If he doesn't like something, he's going to voice his opinion. That's the way it should be.

It bothers some of the other coaches when Bob doesn't show up at the preseason media day that we're all told to attend, but I think nothing of it. I know I'm going to show up, and if he doesn't show up, he doesn't show up. That's between Bob Knight and the Big Ten office. Besides, how can you predict when illness will strike?

I've been asked if it bothers me that Bob's been a guest speaker on various occasions in Champaign-Urbana. In fact, a local group once called to ask if I would mind their inviting Bob, and I told them, "Fine, go ahead if you can afford him!" Of course, I was only kidding about the expense, because he charged nothing to speak for a local charity. Bob was even considerate enough to call before he came over. I think he felt that if I didn't want him here, he wouldn't come. But I told him I thought it was a great idea, and if I hadn't been out of town that day I would have been there to listen to him.

Bob and a couple of his friends from Ohio come to my motel in Bloomington to pick me up, and we drive on to Martinsville to watch Patrick in a playoff game. On the way over Bob turns to me and says, "I'd rather have Patrick's team win this game tonight than for my team to beat yours." Then in the same breath he says, "But I could change my mind about that tomorrow."

I know how competitive he is, and I know from experience that watching your son is tougher than coaching a big game. That's the way it was with me when my son was growing up. Lou, Jr., played on two state championship high school teams in New Mexico, and so I know what Bob goes through. He's just so intense.

When we're a little late getting there, Bob just wheels up to the front door and parks in a tow-away zone. Not one of us utters a word, but I'm sure one common thought is running through all our minds: "When we come out of here, his car is gonna be gone." Well, not only is his car still sitting there when we emerge, but what we think is a ticket shoved under his windshield wiper is merely a handwritten note, "Thanks for coming!" If I would park in a no-parking zone like that in Peoria, for instance, my car would be ticketed and towed—and they'd probably trash it on the way to the pound!

Soon after the opening tip, one of Patrick's teammates takes a shot when he should be passing. After hearing Bob's reaction, I take a slow sip of my cola, lean back, and brace myself for a long night. I'm starving since I haven't eaten since breakfast that morning. So periodically during the game I intercede with silent prayers for victory on behalf of Patrick's team for I know that the bright promise of a late-night dinner might quickly be lost amid the gloom of defeat.

It's an exciting, down-to-the-wire game with Patrick playing well, making key free throws, and helping his team pull out a well deserved victory. As a matter of fact, I'm thinking I might even try to recruit Patrick . . . providing I don't have to make a home visit!

Later outside the locker room, Bob talks briefly to Patrick. I wave to him, since I've known him for a long time, and then we head back to Bloomington for the long-awaited dinner.


The first glimpse of Bob's face just prior to the start of the game tells it all. He has indeed changed his mind. Nick hits an eight-foot turnaround 45 seconds into the game, and the war, the battle is on. This is not going to be a sight for the faint-hearted; it's going to be filled with stray elbows and pawing hands, with clawing defenses and bodies bouncing off bodies.

That is the style of both teams, and both teams are doing a great job of playing their styles. Neither side is giving away anything easily or for free. We resemble a pair of heavyweights trading their best shots in the center of the ring. We go up by 4 early, but with 8:57 remaining in the first half, Jay Edwards drives for a layup, and Indiana takes an 11-10 lead. We take it right back as Kenny dunks on a pass from Steve Bardo, but only 1:21 has passed. That's how tough the defenses are playing.

They tie us at 12, and we're tied again at 14, 16, 18, 20, and 23. But at the half Indiana leads by 2, 27-25. "I don't think," Bob says to me as we pass on our way to our locker rooms, "that I've ever seen a harder played first half." I agree with him. I don't think I've ever witnessed two teams play more intensely than the two we have just seen.


People talked about our talent throughout this year, yet I never believed we were quite as talented as everyone said. But our toughness, our discipline, our willingness to work were underrated all year. They kept saying we were a bunch of great athletes who just went out and played. Again it was a matter of image.

Back when I was at Hardin-Simmons, we regularly played another Abilene school, McMurry College, that is still coached by the highly successful Hershel Kimbrell. They used a patterned offense. They'd pass the ball, pass the ball, pass the ball ten times before they shot it. Even though they didn't beat us, afterwards people would say, "Boy, did you see McMurry move the ball? That's a really disciplined team."

We shot quicker than they did, so we didn't look as disciplined; that's a perception that came to surround this Illinois team. To people who didn't understand, we may have looked undisciplined. But to a man, each of those guys was extremely disciplined and willing to play a role that took advantage of his talents. It would have been easy, with all the quickness we had, to put them on tracks and let them run. But we disciplined them enough and they had enough self-control to press and play defense and do all those little, difficult things that are needed to win games.

Each year they were in school this group became tougher and more disciplined. Those were our strengths. That was the foundation of this team.

Our foundation is tested immediately as Indiana runs off 8 straight points on us to open the second half. Then they push their margin up to 13 with 11:31 remaining in the game. "It doesn't look good. How many teams come back at Indiana after being 13 down?" I momentarily think. But less than two minutes later, P.J. Bowman makes some tough shots, and we're back to within 8.

"We've got a chance," I think now. We're playing hard, we're playing tough, we're playing pretty good defense. And just as we have all year long, we're hanging in there and proving to everyone our belief in the work ethic.

Still, with 8:21 left, a Joe Hillman 3-pointer puts the Hoosiers back up by 11. Our defense tightens, and we score 9 straight points. When Indiana stops our run with a timeout, we're only 2 down. All year we took pride in our endurance, and here we call on it again as we claw and scratch and scrap—and finally take our first lead of the second half with only 1:38 remaining.

It's now 67-65, and there it stands when Indiana calls timeout with the clock down to seventeen seconds. On our bench we all know what's going to come, we all know the ball is going to Jay Edwards. We tell our players to deny him, to front him, to work to keep him from getting the pass. But he pops free and gets the ball, gets it and penetrates to the left baseline. There, from eighteen feet, he falls out of bounds and puts up a jumper over Nick and Lowell and the backboard too. "It doesn't have a chance," I think, but it drops through cleanly.

It's an unbelievable shot, and the Indiana players start to celebrate. They have tied up a game that they now believe they will win. But heady Steve Bardo has already called timeout, and two seconds still show on the clock.

We draw up the play quickly. Steve will throw the in-bounds pass, and Larry Smith will be stationed along the baseline to screen if Indiana chooses to contest that pass. We think of putting Nick under our basket and trying to pop him free behind another screen, but decide against it since Indiana switches so well. So we line up Nick, Lowell, and Kenny low in our offensive set. From there, Nick will break back toward Steve, and Steve will throw the ball to a spot. "Now, Nick," I say, "I don't care what they do, you've got to get to this spot. Even if they have a man there, we expect you to go and get the ball, because that's where Steve's going to throw it."

I emphasize that point, that he *must* get the ball, and then I add one final instruction. I know Nick is a good stationary shooter, but even better on the move. So now I tell him, "After you catch it, take one bounce before you shoot. You've got two seconds, that's enough time, so take a dribble before you shoot."

Then we go out, and Steve throws a perfect "strike" to Nick, who dribbles once around Edwards and then puts up a thirty-footer that's in the air as the buzzer sounds. It too rips through the net and is immediately immortalized as "The Shot." And now we're celebrating a most implausible 3-point win.

"That's the work of Ben Wilson," some of our players are yelling at Nick. "That's the work of Ben Wilson. He's still with you guys in spirit."

"Yeah," Ervin Small is thinking. "He's still with us."

Ben Wilson was a senior at Chicago's Simeon High School in 1984 and was considered one of the finest prep players in the country. We were among many who were recruiting him, and although it was by no means certain that we were going to be successful, he seemed to have narrowed his choices to us and DePaul.

If he had selected Illinois, he would have been a senior on this team. But in November of 1984, he was killed in a random shooting one block from his school. The morning after that shooting, the morning he actually died, our team had a lengthy layover at Chicago's O'Hare Airport enroute to Alaska. Mary and I caught a cab to go visit his mother. Those thirty-five minutes we spent in the cab were some of the longest minutes of our lives; Mary and I didn't say much to each other.

I had often talked to Benji, as everyone called him, and I had visited him in his home. But never, until this morning, did I see his bedroom. Mrs. Wilson was one of the most courageous persons I've ever seen, and she was handling the situation much better than we. She took us to that room, and there I saw the numerous sayings Benji had hanging on his wall. I'll never forget one of them. It ironically read "Think before you act."

Many of the players on our team have never forgotten Benji either, and that is especially true of Nick and Ervin. Ervin had been his teammate at Simeon, and Nick had been his buddy on the playgrounds; and both thought often of their old friend. Nick, who wore uniform number 25 for us, had asked for that number because that had been Benji's number at Simeon. "Every time I bounce the ball," Nick said during this season, "I think of him. Now when I bounce the ball, sometimes I even revert and try to play like him."

"After that great win at Indiana," Ervin said at the same time, "I just laid in bed and thought: In high school one time, Nick won a game exactly like that—against Hyde Park. That was the same year Ben got killed. So every time I see a shot like that, it reminds me of him. Sometimes I just lay in bed and feel him saying, 'Keep playing. Keep playing.'"

A lot of us on this team were somehow involved with Ben Wilson, and none of us will ever forget him. Especially Jimmy Collins, who became his friend while recruiting him; to this day a picture of him hangs in his office.

Kendall dresses for our next game, a home game against Iowa. Even though his recovery has been just short of miraculous, we don't start him. Any player coming back from an injury should do so gradually, both physically and mentally; pace himself as he readjusts to the game.

But with him on the bench, you can sense that our team is more confident, that it has gotten a long-awaited shot in the arm. We play a marvelous game against the Hawkeyes and win 118-94. Three days later, in Ann Arbor, we get off a 22-2 run early in the second half and just overwhelm Michigan on the way to an easy 89-73 win. It's so bad that their own fans boo Glen Rice and the other Wolverines on what for them is a sad Senior Day.

A note of sadness is also struck for Mary and me on this day. For just behind our bench sits a courageous friend and Illini fan extraordinaire, who is witnessing in person his last sporting event. Bob Donahue, a three-time honorary coach with a perfect 3-0 record has been driven from Toledo for this Michigan-Illinois showdown by his loving wife Kathy and their handsome twenty-one-year-old son Jeff. Bob's face is beaming with joy after the game; the painful and tiring trip has been worth it. The Illini's battle to the Final Four over the next few weekends keeps Bob interested, keeps him going. One short day after the Final Four championship game, Bob lost his hard-fought battle to cancer.

On Sunday, March 12, having concluded our regular season, we hold a media conference that is also attended by our athletic association personnel, Rebounders board members, our basketball staff and families, and others close to the program. We gather in the Varsity Room to watch some of the Big East tourney final. But more importantly, to see the NCAA tournament selection show that will let us know who and where we will be playing the following week. I am not nervous at all, although I know Indiana is the Big Ten champ. I even think there is a slight possibility we will be named the number-one seed in the Midwest. We have beaten both Indiana and Michigan twice, and more significantly, we have Kendall back—and we're undefeated with him in our lineup.

"I know our nice win over Michigan really helped us," I say after we learn that we do get that top seed. "But under normal circumstances, the conference champion would get it. This is unusual."

We learn one other thing that afternoon. We learn that our first-round opponent in the Indianapolis Hoosier Dome will be a small school from Lake Charles, Louisiana, coached by Steve Welch: McNeese State.

I am at the point now where I'm calloused. Hey, we win or lose another NCAA game? I'm not going to let that bother me one way or the other. A few years ago it might have affected me, but I don't even let those trivial things go through my mind anymore. I'm calloused because I know the NCAA tournament is a crap shoot. If you go in and you're healthy and your guys happen to hit, you advance. But if you have a good team and they play badly, it's over and you go home. It's not like the NBA, where you get seven games. If you base success on whether you win one or two or three or four games in the tournament, you're going to have some very miserable years.

But I know the talk, and I know that our playoff history is going to be brought up, so I want to do my best to take the pressure off my players. I have heard them talk during the year about redeeming themselves in the playoffs, so I tell them, "You don't have anything to prove. Just go out and do your jobs. We've had a good year, you don't have to prove anything to anybody." I feel they'll do pretty well since all of them were around for Austin Peay and involved in what happened against Villanova. They'll remember that, but at the same time I want to be sure. So on Monday and Tuesday, I talk to them about how they underrated Austin Peay. I remind them  how they gave the game away to Villanova.  It is important for them to face reality, to know what can happen.  But I don't want to pound it into their heads to the point that they're thinking about getting beat.  So we touch on that, we alert them. It's like a tornado alert.  We just let them know that this is the way it is.  But we're going to be OK.

It's more important for them to realize how good a team McNeese State is.  But I know they'll be talking to students around town, and everyone will discount them, just like they belittled Austin Peay.  That's part of their environment, and so on Monday I also tell them, "Hey, McNeese has a very good ball club.  You're better than they are, but you're still going to have to do certain things to win the game."

Then we talk about their strong inside attack, about how we're going to need strong defensive help  if we're going to win. After that we just start getting ready.

Some schools prepare for the NCAA tournament.  We prepare for our Big Ten schedule, a schedule that's just filled with outstanding teams.  It is also a league that has coaches with different defensive philosophies, and that helps too.  There's Tom Davis at Iowa, who likes to press full force, to double- and triple-team the ball.  Jud Heathcote at Michigan State plays a little man, but he's a zone coach, always will be, because that's the way he thinks.  Then you have Gene Keady at Purdue,  Steve Yoder at Wisconsin, Bob Knight, and myself.  We all play very similar man-to-man styles, and Minnesota's Clem Haskins falls in there too. Northwestern's veteran  coach Bill Foster effectively uses more multiple defenses than anyone in the league.

We all do things a little bit differently, but the point is that we see a variety of offenses and defenses during the season, so nothing we might face in the tournament is going to surprise us. And this week, preparing for McNeese, we don't have to do anything special. They play a little triangle and two, but we've already seen that. We saw it against Norm Sloan's Florida team, and we already have an offense in place that's going to hurt that defense.

We even go the other way now, practice for only an hour or an hour and fifteen minutes, because it's so important to have good morale and to have your guys eager. You want them eager to play, not beaten down, which is something I learned about back at Las Cruces High School. One of our rivals always had unbelievable talent, better talent than most schools had. But they never won a state title and often got beat early in the playoffs. I always wondered why.

Finally, at New Mexico State, I recruited one of their players and I asked him about it. "You know, coach," he told me, "during the playoffs we worked out for as long as four hours. We worked on the two-three zone, on the three-two zone, on full-court presses, we worked on everything to make sure we were ready."

Well, it certainly is good to be ready, but look at what was happening: the long practices were taking too much out of them physically and mentally.

The media, they all want to know what the players think of the McNeese State Cowboys. That as much as anything makes this a difficult week for them. They haven't seen them, and we won't show them tapes until just before our game. So all their knowledge is based on what we tell them.

"Do you remind your players of the Villanova game and what happened there?" the media ask me.

They are associating that loss with failure, and so I say, "Now look, just a minute. Let's think about this. Do you realize we almost *upset* Villanova in the playoffs last year?" They scoff at that, but I'm serious and go on, "Villanova was a great team. They had done well in the Big East. They had beaten us earlier in the year, and after they beat us in the playoffs, they went on to defeat Kentucky and have a chance to go to the Final Four against Oklahoma. That was a 4-point ball game with four minutes to go, so they had a chance to win. And do you realize we almost beat them, which means we almost had a chance to go to the Final Four?"

I'm not sure whether I get through to them or not, but that's my way of getting out the message that our guys are not failures because we lost to Villanova. That's in the minds of more than a few people out there, and I know it's something that's going to be talked  and written about.

I want to dispel that notion. We have not been failures and I don't want my players thinking that way.


I know what the media usually want, most coaches do.  But I don't believe in being controversial or too emotional or overly analytical in hopes of calling attention to myself. Really, I don't even kid that much with the media any more, even though I do tell jokes and like to have a good time when I give talks.

I'm a little bit different from my true personality with the media, and that's why they perceive me differently than  do people who really know me. But I've got to be careful. I've said some things kiddingly in the past, and the writers who heard me thought I was serious.

Here's a good example: A few years back, Larry Smith skipped a practice, and we just assumed he had quit the team. But then he returned, and we were going to Wisconsin for a game. When we got there I asked Larry, "Do you want to discuss your situation with the media?"

"No, coach," he told me. "I don't want to talk to them because it's so embarrassing."

So I gave that news to our sports information office, but they failed to relay it to the writers. After our game, three or four press people went into our locker room to talk to Larry. When I saw them around him I went over and said, "Now, Larry, you remember what you told us? What do you want to do?"

"Really, coach. I don't want to talk to anybody," he said.

"OK, you can go," I told him, and after he left I turned to the writers. "Hey, you guys. You're just a buncha leeches," I said jokingly.

Now these media people were all regulars on our beat, they followed the team all the time, and I thought they'd understand that I was kidding. But I learned that a couple of them thought I was serious; so I called them. "Hey," I explained, "I wouldn't even say that about someone I didn't know or like. You guys should know I was just kidding."

So you've got to be careful that what you say isn't misconstrued. But at the same time I try to understand that they have a job to do. That's why I always try to return their phone calls, to give them as much time as I can. I think over the years my relationship with the media has been good. I might not always be as colorful as they would like me to be. But I think they understand that I'll always try to cooperate with them.

I believe it's important for coaches to think the way they want their players to think, so I try to keep my mind focused on the McNeese game. If I start thinking two or three games ahead, I'm afraid it will surface in some way.

But we, the staff, do feel we can beat McNeese; so during this week we also look at tapes of Ball State and Pittsburgh. One of them could be our second-round opponent. Because we could be facing them just two days after McNeese, it is important we do a little bit of preparation for them as well. We are aware of that, so often this week we drill on matters offensively and defensively, which will help us against both McNeese and our second-round opponent.

We score the game's first 8 points and with just under five minutes gone, we're already up on McNeese 14-7. But the next six times down the court, we get no points from a half dozen good shots. By the time we score again, we have gone nearly eight minutes without a basket, and we're trailing.

We are playing tentatively now, playing as if we're afraid to lose instead of playing to win. Only by scoring the last 6 points of the first half do we manage to go to the locker room with a 5-point lead. There we talk to the players about their attitudes, tell them to forget the past, and to play to win. They turn up their defense in the second half and outscore McNeese 8-2 at its start to open up an 11-point margin.

We build from there, and midway through this half we are up 15 and on our way. Our margin is 23 when I start substituting with a little more than three minutes left in this game. Although we win by only 6, it is that close because McNeese outscores us 24-6 in those closing minutes.

We think Ball State has a good chance against Pitt, and when they do beat that Big East upset specialist, we feel pretty good. We haven't used much emotion or energy in our win, and they have expended a lot. And I know enough about psychology to know what that means.

We get eight quick steals, totally knock Ball State out of any kind of offensive flow, and we're up by 14 midway through the first half. We know they can be tough in a slowdown game, but we won't have that here. We use our quickness and our defensive pressure to push it up to a tempo we enjoy more.

We are up 11 at halftime. When Ball State closes to within 6 with twelve minutes remaining in the game, we run off 6 points of our own and then coast to a 72-60 win. "We told each other we have to get past the Illini jinx, and we feel good about that," Nick says when it's over. "You couldn't help but think about losing last year to Villanova, a game we should have won. And Austin Peay. That's something you can't help but think about."

I have thought about it too, but I never believed this team would let down. I knew they would fight until they died, that their attitude wouldn't be a problem. Now that jinx isn't a problem either. We're on our way to Minneapolis.

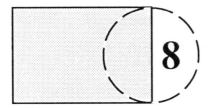

# The Yellow Brick Road

**W**e are flying home from Minneapolis as Midwest Regional champions, and Mary and I talk privately as we head happily back toward Champaign. For us it's a quiet moment of satisfaction.

Around us the plane is filled with our players and with personnel from the athletic department. They are loud and having a wonderful time among themselves. But we don't join them, we just sit together and share the moment. We talk of returning to the Final Four once more and of all that we have been through since we went there with New Mexico State back in 1970. We talk of the weekend just ended, of the injuries and the adversity and the emotion, of all the unusual circumstances surrounding our games.

We say how happy we are for our players and our coaching staff, who are now finally enjoying the fruit of all their hard labor, and how happy we are for all of our friends, those people who stuck by me even when I was being criticized for our tournament losses. We talk of that criticism and my feelings now; we know that subject is going to come up often in the days ahead.

But we also feel happy for our family and for ourselves, for we know now that even that type of criticism is behind us for at least a while. Look, I'm human, and so right now I can't help but think of those people on the national scene who said that Illinois always choked in the playoffs—and of those people who heard them and believed them.

I can't help but think of them and so right now, down deep, I can't help but also feel a certain sense of vindication.

When our plane lands at Willard Airport, I cannot believe the sea of people. There are something like 4,500 people there to greet us. They're all over the airport, and after we load onto our bus and head back toward Assembly Hall, we see even more in their cars, lining our path.

Some estimate the total crowd at 10,000, others at 8,000. I don't know how you can estimate the number of people out this evening. It feels great, I feel great for our players. As we ride past our fans, I get a tingle that will stay with me for a long time. I see the faces of many friends and can tell how happy they are for me, but I am just as happy for them.

"FINAL FOUR—WAY TO GO HENSONS" is the greeting printed on a huge handmade poster that covers a large portion of our garage door, and shortly we have gathered in our driveway a loyal band of neighborhood well-wishers. Among them are Glenn, Jo Anne, Jill, and Ellen Stanko, the artists in question; Tom and Judy Ruzicka, whose son Paul is an Illini yell leader; their daughter Mary, and her fiancee Adam Stell; next door neighbors Tom and June Tadler; assistant artists Donna and Gabrielle Giertz; Gene, Mary, Stephen, and Melissa Wurth, who live down the road; and Mel and Ann Parker, who live behind us. Neighbors such as Bill and Cheryl Thompson are themselves still enroute from Minneapolis. Those present are basking in the revelry of the success of our "Flyin Illini," a phrase used recently to describe the in-flight activities of this exciting group.  At times like this you appreciate the intimacy of your neighborhood and the warm friendliness and supportive fellowship.

Within a short time after our welcome-home group disbands, Mary and I and several members of the family, including my brother Ken, are sitting around chatting, and we decide to slip the tape of the Syracuse game into the VCR.  It isn't long before Ken and I realize that most of the others have gone off to bed, so we decide to do some serious film studying.  Ken is a former coach and understands the game as well as anyone I know.  Anyway, Ken and I get to looking at the Syracuse game,  and it's as good as I remember.  We often stop the tape and go back so we can discuss a play or a referee's call.  It is the latter that triggers the memory of a not too recent game at the Assembly Hall, so I tell Ken all about it.

It was on Christmas Eve afternoon of 1983 that the University of Kentucky basketball team coached by the highly successful Joe B. Hall was warming up on the Assembly Hall floor, preparing to meet my Illini team.  Outside the temperature was frigid, and the blizzard that had raged the previous night was quieter now; but still the snow blew and drifted.

A message was relayed to me in the dressing room that the three Big Ten officials assigned to work the game could not get through the impassable roads.  A hurriedly called conference resulted in a plea going out over the public address system for any experienced referee to please report to the scorer's table.  Several came forward, and at the tip-off three local officials were calling the game: Charlie Due, Bob Hiltibran, and Bill Mitze.  Although we lost a close one by a 56-54 score, we all felt that it had been one of the best refereed games we had seen.  It didn't take me long to get on the phone to our Big Ten Commissioner Wayne Duke and recommend that we select all game officials in that manner!

Ken enjoys being reminded about that Kentucky game, and we continue with our critique of the Syracuse game through the first half. We take a little break here and Ken remarks, "Boy, your guys sure played poor defense that first half!"

This observation tickles me and I retort, "You're a good one to be talking about defense!" That makes me recall another story for his benefit, the time he was the head basketball coach at Howard Payne College, located in Brownwood, Texas. He was scheduled to speak at a coaches' clinic being held at Baylor University in Waco, Texas, on a Sunday afternoon, and the subject of his talk was to be defensive strategies. Ironically on Saturday night prior to his speech, Ken took his Yellow Jackets to Stephen F. Austin College in Nacogdoches, Texas, where they scored 123 points and *lost* by 17! His comment to me on the telephone following the game was, "Aw, they just got hot on us!"

My reply was in the form of a request, "Ken, whatever you do, don't let those coaches know you're my brother!"

Lindsey and Lacey, two of our grandchildren, are at the house early on Monday morning waiting for me to drive them to school. "Hey, Lacey," I say when I see her. "We won yesterday."

"Yes, grandad, I know," she says. While she seems happy, she doesn't seem particularly thrilled.

I'm excited and so I ask, "Did you see the game?"

Now I just know she watched it and cheered and got into the game, but she says, "No, grandad."

"Well, why didn't you Lacey?" I ask.

"Grandad," she says, "I was just too busy playing."

Moments like that help you keep everything in perspective. She was just too busy playing to watch a basketball game.

There are going to be pressures this week, I know that, but I feel it's important to maintain a perspective and do my best to keep the tension off my players. As coaches we sometimes think we're the only ones who have them, and we often forget the tremendous strain that is placed on our players to perform athletically, academically, and other ways as well.

Most of them are teenagers, after all, and it's hard for us to understand just what can affect them. I remember a time when one of our girls had a pimple; for two days she was depressed and teary. Now does that make any sense to be so upset over a pimple? To me it didn't, but to her it was a real and true problem.

Another time, at Hardin-Simmons, we received a call at 11:00 one night from the house mother in the dorm that we supervised. This time the problem was much more serious. One of the students had shot himself in the shoulder in a failed suicide attempt. The wound had come very close to his heart, and three or four days later when I could speak to him in the hospital, I asked, "Joe, why would you do this?"

"Coach," he said. "I love Hardin-Simmons and I'm so depressed. I don't have enough money to stay in school next semester."

Now was that any reason for him to make an attempt on his own life? We can't imagine that. But to this young man, something he wanted more than anything else was slipping away from him, and the pressure was just too great. Another night a football player was up on top of the stadium, threatening to jump. He was going to commit suicide because he and his girlfriend had broken up.

Later on in life, he would have had a different perspective. But for him just then, that was a devastating occurrence.

Girlfriend problems, they can be tough on a teenager and ruin your team. Nevada-Las Vegas coach Jerry Tarkanian talked about that at a clinic one time, talked about his reaction upon learning that one of his players was having girlfriend problems during an important part of their season. "I didn't go to the kid," said Tark. "I went to the girlfriend. I sat down with her and told her how important the season was, and then I said, 'Now, Betty. Would you do just one thing for me? Would you hang in there until the season is over?'"

It's a humorous story, but it's also one that helps me keep perspective. It's one that helps me remember all the different pressures a player can be under.


As I drive Lindsey and Lacey to school this Monday morning, we sing the Illinois fight song and others as well. We do this most every time they're with me in the car; they think it helps us win games.

I'm not much of a singer but their other grandad, Dr. Ralph Nast, is pastor of our First Baptist church and our son, Lou, Jr., married Ralph and Lottie's daughter, Laurie. And Ralph is an excellent singer. So one time when I had the girls alone I figured I'd test them. "Lindsey, Lacey? Who's the better singer, Grandad Ralph or Grandad Lou?"

I saw them turn to each other and whisper, then you know what they said? They said, "Grandad, it's a tie."

I felt great I had registered a tie with the singing because I knew I'd have him beat with my next question. I asked, "And who's the better basketball coach, Grandad Ralph or Grandad Lou?"

Surprisingly, they whispered between themselves again, and again they said to my dismay, "Grandad, it's a tie."

Moments like that help you keep perspective too, although Mary says it only reveals my competitive nature.


I head toward my office after dropping them off, and when I arrive there I immediately begin watching film and preparing for Michigan, our opponent in Saturday's national semifinals. I am determined to make this week as normal as I can make it. I view this as just another game and will treat it that way, and I want my players to do the same thing. But at home, it's proving to be anything but a normal week for Mary: plants, flowers, all types of Illini paraphernalia, telegrams, letters, cards, notes, newspaper clippings, photographs, and other memorabilia begin arriving. She starts fielding congratulatory calls from an endless stream of well-wishers and from people who want tickets for Seattle. Some are regulars, old friends who have supported us over the years and want the chance to cheer us on in the Final Four. But many of them are long-lost acquaintances who suddenly want to be remembered, people who have never seen a game at Assembly Hall but want to be taken care of now that we're in the Big Show.

Mary will eventually get ten times the number of ticket requests she does for a normal game, and I'm sure it would have been worse if I hadn't heeded some of Bob Knight's advice a couple of years ago. Our phone number was listed for thirty-two years; anyone could call us and many did. Bob and I were talking one day at a time that we were getting all kinds of calls at all hours of the day and night. Mary was fielding most of them and trying to be nice, even if it was a stranger on the other end. But she was getting tired of not being able to get through a night or a meal without interruption. After Bob learned of this he said, "I can't believe that you have a listed number. Why would you do that? Look how hard it is on Mary."

Well, I told him, it wasn't too bad. We didn't get many negative calls, maybe just two or three a year. Other times fraternity students happy over a victory might call us from a bar and sing to us, but we didn't get those kinds of calls too often.

Bob listened and then asked another question. "And what do you do with your negative letters?"

"Well, I read them," I admitted.

"Do you answer them?"

"I may answer some."

"How do you feel when you get a negative letter?"

"I don't feel very good. Most of the time they're ridiculous, but I still don't feel very good."

"Why do you do it then?" he asked.

"Well," I answered, "I don't know. I just do."

"Let me give you some advice," he told me. "First of all, get an unlisted number, and you'll be surprised at how much better things will be. Secondly, tell your secretary that anything that comes through negative, you want her to dump it. You don't want to see it."

That was a year or two ago, and that's what I did. And hey, my life's been a lot less frustrating since then.

The round of interviews I will give during this week begins on Monday morning. Among the first people I talk to is James Brown of *CBS Sports*. One of the first subjects he brings up is my reputation for not being able to win in the NCAA tournament.

He's being negative and that bothers me a little bit. I'm very firm in my answer and tell him the way I really think it is. My feelings and my agitation at the question show through, though, and afterward he apologizes for bringing up the topic.

We played Michigan just right, defeating them twice during the regular season. And now, to a degree, I face the same situation I encountered before our game with Austin Peay. The players know they've twice beaten Michigan pretty badly, and they just feel they're going to beat them again.

We try to talk to them about Michigan. We tell them how great Glen Rice is shooting in the playoffs. We warn them that Michigan is playing harder now than they were during the season, that they're a different team now than they were the last time we faced them. It's the same approach I have used all during the year: I build Michigan up while being positive about our chances.

I review the reasons behind our success over Michigan, then I bring up a statistic I remember vividly. Over the course of the season, it's a fact that the team that won two games against an opponent went on to win the third one 83 percent of the time. I make them aware of that statistic to build their confidence.

This is the same process I follow every game week every year, and we never once mention the Final Four or winning the national title. Again I'm trying to treat this as just another game.

I'm positive this week, publicly very positive. But in private I see a number of factors stacked against us. Each of them combines to make me a little wary of Saturday.

I know we embarrassed Michigan the last time we played them, and while you never want to embarrass anyone, you certainly don't want to do that to someone you have to play again just three weeks later. That, I understand, can come back to haunt you. I worry about the toll of those two very emotional games in Minneapolis. And I realize again that whatever you get on emotion at one point you're going to have to give back somewhere down the line. We saw that only two months ago when our emotions carried us to number one with a win over Georgia Tech and then left us flat for our next game against Minnesota.

Michigan, I know further, has breezed into the Final Four with a 102-65 blowout of Virginia, and I fear they will be mentally fresher than we will be come Saturday. I am concerned about all of this, concerned enough to discuss it with both Mary and my assistants. Mary, always my sounding board, says little, as do my assistants.

Sometimes, when I am acting the pessimist (an optimist with experience), they tell me I'm overdoing it and overreacting to the situation. But they also know I'm more comfortable preparing this way. They understand and they usually let me express my concerns without comment. This is what happens this week as our trip to Seattle draws closer.

Two weeks earlier Bill Frieder had announced that he would be leaving Michigan to become the new head coach at Arizona State University. It was just a day before his Wolverines were scheduled to open play in the NCAA tournament, but the reaction of Michigan athletic director Bo Schembechler was swift and final. "I don't want someone from Arizona State coaching Michigan. I want a Michigan man coaching Michigan," he said. Then he declared that assistant coach Steve Fisher would guide the team in the playoffs.

Now Steve's a great guy. Many years ago I almost hired him for my staff at Illinois. But I personally think that Frieder should have been allowed to coach his team in the playoffs. It was Bill's team, he recruited them and molded them. I just think that it should have been Bill coaching his team.

It is my understanding that one of the reasons Bo was upset with him is that Bill allegedly failed to notify Bo of his intentions to interview at another school. But in my opinion, from what I could see, I think there was something of a personality clash between Bill and Schembechler. And after Bo succeeded Don Canham as athletic director, maybe Bill felt that Bo personally would have preferred that someone else coach the basketball team. Bo has denied this, has said that he didn't have any problems with Bill. But Bill certainly hinted at that fact when he said, "I was offered the Arizona State job three years ago. But three years ago, it was hard for me to leave Don Canham. Now Canham's gone."

So I think Bill was looking to move once he knew Canham was going to retire. I think someone said a year earlier that Bill was interested in the Texas job; yes, I think he was definitely interested. Then the Arizona State job opened up again, and Bill saw what Lute Olson had accomplished at Arizona, realized ASU was a good job, and wanted to be involved in that one as well.

Now I'm not sure Bill was the first choice this time around; I think Gene Keady over at Purdue was. But after Gene turned them down, Arizona State was under great pressure to hire. When they called Bill about the job, they told him he had only twenty minutes to make up his mind. Well, Bill had probably been thinking about this for weeks, so he knew what he wanted to do, and he told them. What he didn't know was that they were going to make the announcement in the papers.

But they had a board of trustees meeting shortly after Bill accepted, and you can't have a board meeting these days without it making the papers. His involvement with the job went public, and Bill was asked about it. He admitted he was going there, and then Bo made his move.

The timing was bad all the way around, but I think I understand it from all perspectives. I know Bill came out looking like the bad guy, and I couldn't believe the number of people who came up to me and said, "Can you believe Frieder running out on his team like that?" But Bill was in a Catch-22 situation, and much of what transpired wasn't necessarily his fault. So it was great for Steve, I was happy for him. But at the same time I was sorry Bill wasn't allowed to coach his team.


The University spirit groups ask if they can have a pep rally for us before we fly to Seattle on Thursday, and I say no. We haven't done that before, and I don't want to start now.

We know our fans support us, but I don't want to take the chance on anything affecting our play in the game. It's not that it would be a great distraction. It's simply the fact that it would be different. If we're not going to do it throughout the season, we don't want to do it the last week or two.

For example, at times during the season, Mike Haile, manager of local radio station K-104 with whom I have a weekly seasonal show, will fill every Assembly Hall seat with orange pom-poms. On other occasions, his sponsors place "Henson's Hankies" on the seats so they can be waved to indicate support of the team. These happenings have become something of a tradition.

But because of the number of games in a season, I don't wish to single out certain games when we try something new. As I said before, if we haven't been doing it regularly, I'd rather go along with the way we've been doing it. That's just being consistent.

We fly to Seattle on a charter, and with us on the plane are other athletic department personnel and some members of the media. We intentionally do not include alumni on this flight.

I have been around for thirty-three years, and I know what could happen if we had alums with us. They're so nice they would spend an hour and a half pumping up a player, telling him how good he is. And no guy can go out and play good ball after experiencing that. You can't control everything. But at this point in my career, I have a pretty good idea of what's going to work and what isn't. Some alumni don't quite understand, and unwittingly may say things they shouldn't—just like they did that Austin Peay year.

We tell the players not to give interviews during the flight. But once we land in Seattle, that's difficult to control. The media are everywhere, the media, a band, and a congregation of Illinois supporters. It's a problem just getting the kids through the airport without their being stopped several times.

But finally we get ourselves loaded onto the two buses that are waiting for us. And since the whole scene is so chaotic, we don't bother to get a good headcount. We usually do, but this time since we're riding in two buses it was difficult to get an accurate count.

One half-hour later, having been heralded along the route by a police motorcycle escort, we arrive at our hotel in Bellevue and begin unloading our luggage. That's when a white stretch limousine pulls up, and to the surprise of everyone, out hops Kendall. He had darted back to the plane to retrieve his wallet, which had slipped out of his pocket during the flight. He was embarrassed about missing the team bus, so he had commandeered the first vehicle available to him. I say nothing.

Nineteen years ago, when I went to my first Final Four with

New Mexico State, it was nothing like this. We had a nice send-off by our fans, but virtually no media coverage. We then just drove the forty-five miles from Las Cruces to El Paso and flew into one of the Washington D.C. airports. We landed unnoticed, and no one greeted us. We got on our bus, drove to our hotel, worked out the next day, and played a day later. I'm sure we were briefly interviewed by a few media, but it seems as if we never talked to anybody.

You never saw people at your workouts, but we will be jammed here in Seattle; back then you didn't have the endless requests for interviews either. So many people are around you now it makes it difficult to get things done. But the Final Four is a spectacle that is now equal to the Super Bowl or the World Series. I think the NCAA has been brilliant in its handling of the Final Four.

Every small conference in every part of the country is a possible participant in it, so in early March, colleges and their fans everywhere start thinking about it. Everyone has aspirations of getting into and maybe winning the NCAAs, and this spreads interest all over the United States. And television only heightens that interest.

That's another change. Back when my New Mexico State team played UCLA in a national semifinal, the game was televised in only a few areas of the country, not nationally. But our game with Michigan will be shown not only throughout the country, it will be shown in prime time as well.

CBS, the network now telecasting the NCAA tournament, is paying some $55 million a year for those rights, and that's why the payout to each Final Four team is $1.25 million. That probably influences the way some programs are run; and why we might be better off dividing the tournament money more equitably among all of the Division I basketball schools. That might take a lot of pressure off many of the people involved.

But while I may accept that idea as philosophically sound, in practical terms I can't support it; it would just be taking money out of our pockets. And in reality, in the Big Ten and most other conferences we're already doing that; we now split the money among the schools.

In the Big Ten, the competing school gets to keep 50 percent of what it earns, and then it receives a one-ninth share of what the other conference schools earn in the tournament. So we ended up with $820,000. Even those schools that didn't make the NCAAs wound up with between $250,000 and $300,000. They all benefited, and that's good.

So while I can't support spreading this money among all schools, I think it's good that conferences do divide it among their members. That way it helps everybody.


Our hotel in Bellevue, our last hotel of the year, also turns out to be the worst we encounter in our long season. A week earlier in Minneapolis we stayed at the Radisson, a magnificent place. Mary and I had a suite where I could watch film, and we could entertain our family and guests. This is a total contrast. Our room is dingy and small, and we are forced to rent an extra room just to look at film.

Everyone notices the contrast, and when I see the players talking about it among themselves I decide to bring up the subject. I don't mention it to the press; that would turn it into a policy problem. But I do tell the players, "I know your rooms are not as nice as usual, that there's a big difference this week. But don't let that bother you. You play better after suffering some adversity. You get a bad meal or hotel, you come out and play better. Adversity brings out the best in us."

That is often true, but we're still upset. Arlene Mackovic, the wife of our athletic director, wants to know how we ended up here. After she asks enough questions, she learns it was a mistake. She learns that Illinois was assigned two hotels, one for the alumni and one for our group. And someone who didn't realize the difference in the quality of the two assigned us to this one. The other one, the nicer one, was assigned to the alumni.

I am paging through some papers while resting and come across one of these Tales of the Tape comparing Michigan and Illinois. I quickly read over what they say about our guards and forwards and centers. But when I reach coaches, I'm dumbstruck. I am at the end of my twenty-seventh year in college coaching, and here's Steve Fisher having coached four games, and the writer has given the edge to Steve. Now Steve did a superb job of coaching in those four games, and my reaction in no way reflects on his ability. "Can you believe this?" I say to Mary as I show her the article.

"He's just one of those writers who didn't do his homework," she says, and then we spend some time discussing images and the stupidity of it all. I mean, you can't get mad. But how else should you react when you're fifth or sixth in the country in wins among active coaches and some writer intentionally insults you?

That same afternoon, this matter of image comes up again. A television sportscaster says that of all the teams in the Final Four, Illinois is the least disciplined and was not a "thinking team." Nothing can be further from the truth. This time I'm infuriated. I think of bringing up this announcer's name during a media conference and letting everyone know what he said. He's so wrong, I'm really mad about it, and I consider doing just that. But I don't operate that way. I don't want to jeopardize his job, nor do I want to expose my team to such poppycock before their Final Four appearance. I was sure they had not heard the despicable comment.

I really believe that the guy's job can be at stake, ala Jimmy the Greek. We're the only all-black starting five in the Final Four, and he says that our players aren't thinking out there. The misconceptions once again rear their ugly heads. The truth is that this team is one of the most knowledgeable and brightest groups I've ever had the pleasure to coach.

Thursday night, the night of our arrival, Mary and I along with John and Judy Nowak, Arlene Mackovic, Alvin and Mildred Griggs, Bruce and Marge Larson, and some of the members of our official party attend a lovely dinner honoring the Final Four coaches. And Friday is a whirlwind of obligations. Early on this day Dick Barnes, our highly competent assistant sports information director, shows me a list of things that I have to do and that I've been asked to do. I decide to try and handle them all. Tab Bennett, our popular veteran sports information director, was involved in a serious auto accident in Indianapolis during our regional games and was not able to accompany us to Seattle.

First there is a mass media conference at the Kingdome, the site of the Final Four. The questions center around the new Michigan under Steve Fisher and the recent remarks of Bob Knight. "If Illinois plays as well as it can play, no one can beat them," Bob said just hours earlier. Then he went on to effusively praise my coaching abilities and the talents of our players.

"Bob Knight said that?" I ask when his comments are read to me. And then I chuckle. "If Bob Knight said that, well, I put a lot of stock in what he says. I don't know if it's true or not. But he's one of the greatest coaches in the country, and that gives me confidence."

It is one of those rare times when I try to joke with the media, but I'm not sure if they understand that. Then we go into the Kingdome for an hour of shooting around. Then back to the hotel for a short break. And then I'm off to do interviews with a television station from the Quad Cities, then with a number of stations from Chicago, then with CNN and others. "This is a big moment for a lot of these guys," I think, looking at these reporters who have flown out with their own crews. I feel this is something I should do for them.

I do not think for one minute that my activities will have a bearing on the game. If I did, I wouldn't be doing them. But we have played Michigan twice, we have looked at their tapes, we know everything we can know about them. So while all these interviews are a hassle, no question about it, I do them and try to get through the hectic schedule and constant running from one media station to another. They're set up all around the exterior of the Kingdome.

Finally, late that Friday night I join Mary, my sister Rose Mary Yates, her son Steve, my niece Paula Long, her son Luke, and my nephew Barry Henson for dinner. I'm tired, and as we eat I keep drifting off into my own private world.

In public, when I'm with groups of people, I do a good job of staying involved with the conversations going on around me, and I try to keep up enough on current events to participate. But a big part of my living is talking. I talk in my office and to my coaches and while watching film. I talk at practices and at cocktail parties. So with friends I like to get others involved so I can just sit back and listen. With my family I sometimes drift so far away that Mary has to call to me to get my attention.

This Friday night, my attention is really drifting, drifting even further than normal. I usually don't get tired, but fatigue is a factor here. Mary told me later that I had looked so pale and exhausted that she was very concerned. "Go to bed," she finally orders me.

I don't argue and leave her and our children still sitting around the table. By the time she reaches our room, I am sound asleep.


I am up early on Saturday morning, and after my daily walk I watch more film of Michigan, prepare the crib sheet that will be in my pocket during the game, and jot down those subjects I want to discuss at our team's skull session. That's my routine, and I stick to it here.

At 12:45 p.m., exactly four hours and fifteen minutes before the scheduled tipoff, I join the players for our pregame meal. Again, as I always do, I sit apart from them, and I don't see the skirmish that breaks out between Marcus Liberty and P.J. Bowman. Marcus has been teasing P.J., but P.J. doesn't want any of that. He wants to be left alone so he can concentrate on the game.

Jimmy Collins, who was sitting with the players, sees this, however, and it bothers him. "We're going out to play the biggest game of our careers," he thinks, "and these guys are arguing and bickering over nothing."

Still, he says nothing to me about it. Instead he thinks, "It'll pass."

I return to my room after our skull session and it's empty, but not for long. Mary will be returning from her shopping spree at the local mall; the place will soon be running over. This is a time when I want to be alone. I want to be alone so I can just sit and meditate.

Early in my coaching career, I would have been nervous at a time like this, but you have to adapt or you won't last long. Years ago when I first started I talked with former Arkansas coach Glen Rose, who was around sixty at the time. "Lou," he told me, "I'm going to retire one of these days."

"Glen," I replied, "we'd all hate to see that. You've had such an outstanding career, we'd hate to see you go."

"I hate to go too, Lou," he admitted. "But I'm tired of going to bed before a ball game and jerking all night."

It was his way of telling me, a young coach, that it doesn't get any easier with age. But I think I have learned to control my feelings and not let myself worry. If I worry, I know I am going to be a little upset and on edge and won't be able to do my job.

But now, alone in my room, I do think of the game. And there's nothing wrong with thinking if it doesn't become an avenue to worry. So I think of situations that might arise, adjustments we might have to make. And then I give myself a silent talk. "Look," I think, "it's an important game. But ignore what's going to happen if you win or lose. Don't think about it being the Final Four. Keep your mind on those things you want to do."

"*Remember, it's just another game.*"

I am a stickler for detail and adamant that our players don't spend too much time in the locker room. I don't want them stuck in there for thirty minutes with nothing to do but think about the game. Already we know what the traffic will be like and how long our bus driver thinks it will take us to reach the Kingdome. At domes too it's important to know how long it takes to walk from your bus to the locker room, from the locker room to the floor. That has been figured out for us by one of our managers.

We are on a tight schedule as game time draws near, and an hour before our bus must depart the players start getting taped. On the bus during the ride, Jimmy Collins and Dick Nagy sit in the back and among the players. But I am up front in a seat next to Mary and across the aisle from Mark Coomes. After Mary is settled and we're on our way to the Kingdome I cross that aisle, sit down next to Mark, and begin discussing Michigan once more.

Hushed whispers are all you hear during this ride, and when we arrive at the dome the players walk silently toward our locker room. Before I join them on that walk I say good-bye to Mary. "Good luck. I love you," she says, and then she pecks me on the cheek.

I notice nothing unusual as our players warm up; they appear to be going about their business as they have all season long. To me they look ready to play.

But to Jimmy Collins the sight is unsettling. "They looked more relaxed than Michigan," he will later say. "Michigan looked very serious, and we looked too relaxed. But then, we've had other games like that, games where the guys looked too relaxed and then came out and played great."

In this game we feel we must control Michigan guard Rumeal Robinson. But less than thirty seconds into it, after a charging foul by Kendall, he penetrates and puts in a reverse layup. Lowell walks on our next possession, then Rice and Terry Mills miss for

Michigan, and Kenny bangs home an eight-foot turnaround to bring us even at 2.

Now Robinson misses twice and Rice misses a 3-pointer. But we're getting killed on the boards, and Rice gets it back again. This time he nails a jumper from the left baseline. That's seven shots for Michigan in the first minute and a half, and for us, one shot, one foul, and one turnover. "Fundamentally we're just not playing." That thought flashes through my mind here, but I'm already so into the game, I can't take time to reflect on it. That thought is like the crowd noise that you hear but don't hear, that you're subconsciously aware of but too busy to notice consciously.

But here Michigan keeps missing its shots. They hit just four of their first twelve, and we rush out to a 16-8 lead. "That score looks good, but we're not playing well," I think on our bench.

"Michigan's dying a little bit," Dick Nagy thinks. "But, well, there's a long way to go."

During a game, each of our assistants has a specific job. Jimmy, once a great guard, watches the guards. Dick, once a fine forward, watches the inside men. And Mark, formerly a very good guard, does all of our scouting and film work, watches the overall flow and any changes in our opponent's approach. I truly believe that I am blessed with one of the premier coaching staffs in the country.

I want to hear from each of them during a game. If our opponent is running different plays, using a different defense, I want to know then. I don't want to see that later on film. I want to know what's going on now, and they tell me.

What is going on now is not pretty, and we miss numerous opportunities to stretch our 8-point lead. Robinson commits a foul, but Lowell misses. Loy Vaught misses for Michigan, but Lowell misses again. Sean Higgins misses for Michigan, but Steve Bardo misses a 3-pointer. Higgins misses again, but Nick commits a foul. Finally, after going for over three minutes without a field goal, Michigan scores again on a Higgins 3, and after Nick walks, Rice hits to bring them back to within 3.

We get two of them back on Steve's free throws, but after Higgins misses once more, Larry Smith turns the ball over, and Mark Hughes knocks in a fourteen-foot jumper. Now Marcus misses and Rice hits, Kenny misses and Rumeal drives right by Larry for a layup. With 9:11 left in the first half, we are suddenly down 19-18.

We are but five of fourteen from the field, while Michigan is nine of twenty-two. We have five turnovers to their three, two assists to their six, eleven rebounds to their twelve. And we're this close only because we have seven free throws to their none.

We did a good job on Robinson in our two wins over Michigan, but here he's killing us. He's just killing us, and we're not getting it done. So I make substitutions early, just trying to get our guys pumped up.

On the bench the coaches are talking. Dick doesn't like what he sees in Nick—he isn't being as aggressive offensively as he is when he's at his best. We like to see him take the ball to the basket early, but here he's settling for shots from the perimeter. Kendall, who has played great for us since returning from his injury, is playing like you would expect him to play after coming back from an injury. It's not that he's playing poorly, he's just not playing great. So we put Larry on Robinson, who's in tremendous control here.

We know that two of our prime-time players are not really on their games; and we know too that we're not switching on picks, that we're not playing the drive, that we're letting them get behind us when we press. We see all this and none of us are happy, but we are careful when we discuss it among ourselves. You have a player's mentality and you have a coach's mentality, and you don't want some player on the bench to hear you saying, "Look at Kendall. He's really hurting out there." He may tell that to Kendall during the next timeout, and that could destroy his confidence.

We're having too many breakdowns in this game, and that tells me one thing. That tells me we aren't emotionally ready, that we're paying back for all the emotion we spent last weekend.

This is a 1-point game now and a 1-point game at halftime. Even though we're trailing then I am basically positive in the locker room. Our guys are not playing well, but they are playing hard, so I try to build on that and talk of all the adversity they've overcome to reach this point.

We have come back, we've made some great comebacks during this season, and I am confident we will win. I am confident we will win right up to the moment this game ends.

Michigan makes a small run at the beginning of the second half and is up by 7 five minutes into it. But then Lowell dunks and hits a ten-foot jumper to bring us back to within 3. At 11:27 Nick hits a baseline jumper to give us our first lead of this half. Then there's a layup by Robinson, a layup by Lowell, a 3-pointer by Rice, and two free throws by Robinson.

Now we are down 4, 60-56, and the message from the bench is pointed. "Hey, guys light a fire," Dick Nagy is screaming. "Guys, there's no fire, no spark."

"Guys, pick it up a notch," Jimmy Collins is screaming.

All season long we've had periods where bang, bang, bang— we run off 10 or 12 points in a row. But here we can't set off that explosion. Every time we get rolling, something happens to us, something happens and they come back on us. Now that moment seems to have arrived.

Kenny, as has often been the case, is the spark. He puts in an offensive rebound, and then after a steal by Kendall, a layup and a foul shot to give us the lead at 61-60. But immediately, just seven seconds later, Rice hits a sixteen-foot jumper, and this game is headed for a close finish.

We go up 1 on a layup by Larry, they go up 1 on a banker by Rice. We go up 1 on a jumper by Nick, they go up 1 on a Loy Vaught hook. We go up 1 on a hook by Lowell, they go up 2 on a layup and foul shot by Higgins. They are up 4 with 3:03 left after Rice dunks on a fast break. But then our defense tightens. Kenny hits for 3, Rice finally misses, and Lowell gives us a 79-78 lead with a jumper at 1:55.

This is a great game for the spectators, but from the coaches' point of view, we can't stand it. Our guys know what they should be doing, and they're not doing it. Our guys are not playing well, and they would be the first to admit that.

They are doing their best. They are playing hard. But fundamentally they are playing a poor game.

Rebounding, all season long we stressed rebounding. But here Terry Mills misses for Michigan, and there's Mark Hughes putting in an offensive rebound and getting fouled by Lowell. His ankle is bothering him, he didn't practice all week. But we can't think of that now, can't think of it after Hughes makes his foul shot to put us down by 2.

But we come back to tie when Kenny leans into Mills, and as their chests meet, he puts up a jumper that bounces once, twice off the rim and then in. Now Robinson has the ball with the clock under ten seconds, and we have him trapped in the left corner. Rice is covered and can do nothing but pass the ball across the court to Mills. Mills, a center, puts up a 3-pointer as this game heads toward overtime. Under the basket, Nick moves to block out Higgins and position himself for the rebound.

But that rebound bounces long, bounces over Nick and to Higgins. He calmly puts in a baby jumper that falls through the net with two seconds remaining. With one second remaining, we call time.

We can still do it, that is the feeling of our players as they gather on our bench. I quickly draw up the play that will give us our chance to do just that. It's a bit different from the one we ran against Indiana, but it is something we have worked on in practice, and it is simple in concept. Steve Bardo takes the ball out of bounds, and Larry Smith positions himself along the baseline to pick if Michigan decides to challenge Steve's pass. Up the court, Nick pops free behind two more picks, catches that pass, and shoots.

We coaches sense that our players are still confident when they return to the court, and out there the play works. Larry gets run over by Mills, but the call isn't made. "That's a foul. That's a foul," we're screaming from the bench. But the whistle doesn't blow, and our up-court picks break down. Rice intercepts Steve's pass, and our season is over.

Michigan has played hard, you can't take anything away from Michigan. But other than Kenny, we were a different team tonight. We didn't play as we had all season long.

It's not how you take a job, it's how you leave it. That's an old saying I strongly believe in. So I am not going to question that last noncall or talk about how poorly we have played. I'm going to be positive about our team, which has reached the Final Four, and about Michigan, which is going to win the national championship.

I first congratulate Steve Fisher, tell him what an excellent job he is doing, and wish him luck Monday night against Seton Hall. Then I begin the long walk to our locker room. It's going to be tough. One of the toughest moments for me is facing our team after a defeat like this. I know it's only a basketball game, that it's not comparable to a family losing a loved one. But at this particular time, a defeat like this feels very much like a death in the family. It's hard enough to lose any tough game, but to do it in the Final Four is an experience you don't want to go through very many times.

The players are sitting silently in front of their stalls when I finally do arrive in the locker room, and my assistants are making their way among them, patting a back here, offering a word there. Kendall is near tears, as is Lowell. Nick and Ervin, long-time friends, are consoling each other. Losses, the higher you get, the tougher they are to take. This one is even more disappointing, since we beat Michigan by 16 just three weeks earlier at their place.

Eventually I stand up among the players and start by telling them that the sun will come up tomorrow. That's an expression I use a lot, and I think everyone relates to that. Then I elaborate, tell them they lost a game, but it was just a game. It wasn't the game

of life, and no one was critically injured out there. Remember that,
I tell them, keep it in perspective, and remember the great job you
did all year. I tell them, hey, you're one of the most courageous
teams I have ever seen play. We appreciate that and we're proud
of you for all that you have given us this year. Michigan beat us
tonight, I tell them, but it wasn't because we didn't play hard. We
played hard and fought back and almost won. I pay special tribute
to the seniors, to Lowell and Kenny. Then I tell the others that they
have another chance, that I'm coming back and they're coming
back. And next year let's see if we can do something about tonight.

Look the season over, look at all the good things you've accomplished this year, I tell them. The Final Four, thirty-one wins,
all the records, all of that can be wiped out in ten seconds now if
you do something you're not supposed to. I worry about a group
of individuals after a season is over. Safety is a big thing to me, and
now that we have two days free in Seattle, I touch on that. We're
confident you won't get into any trouble, I tell them, but be aware
of what can happen and keep yourself away from trouble.

I am escorted to the mass media conference, and there I'm
asked what I think about the last play, what I think about Mills
running over Larry. I handle it the way I do any media conference.
I tell them I don't think anything in particular.

But most of this is a blur, something I just have to get through.
Finally I make my way back to our bus, where Mary and our family
are waiting for me. Mary is like me, she doesn't take losses like this
very well. As we ride back to our hotel, we try to talk each other
through the moment. Close game, wonderful season, a loss like this
shouldn't overshadow all the accomplishments—we look for positives, they are the tonic we use to get through.

Back at the hotel I have another meeting with the players, and there I tell them again what a great season they've had and how they won the admiration of people around the country. They go off together then. Some order pizzas and eat themselves sick. I go off to my room, and although my family fills in, little is said this night.

As a coach, I'm conditioned to think ahead immediately. As a coach, I know that if you spend too much time thinking about what might have been, you're going to live a short life. You can't survive that way, and I know it. But the truth is, this is a heartbreaking loss.

I know if one ball bounces a different way, we're possibly the national champions.

Most teams leave immediately after losing in the Final Four, but we decided long ago that we were going to stay through Monday's championship game. Many of the people on our charter had never been to a Final Four before, and we felt it would be wrong to deprive them of the opportunity to enjoy Seattle and the spectacle surrounding the event.

But while Sunday is tough, it turns out not to be as bad as feared. That control mechanism that helps me through troubled times is in place now. As a coach who teaches mental toughness, I know that I must exhibit it too. Both those factors help. Then my spirits are heightened as I meet people, as I talk to coaches, and they tell me how much they admired our team. Everyone seems to have followed our team, everyone seems to have liked our team, and at that afternoon's slam-dunk contest, it's evident when Kenny gets louder cheers than any other contestant.

That night Mary and I are scheduled to attend a banquet, and although neither of us particularly wants to go we are pretty consistent about fulfilling this type of obligation. At the banquet I bump into Mike Krzyzewski, the Duke coach who lost in the other semifinal game, and we spend some time sympathizing with each other. Each of us knows what the other is going through, and each of us tries to help the other by talking positively about his team. As coaches we understand.

"We were really pulling for you," other coaches tell me. Some mean it, and some say it even though they were pulling for Michigan. This is business, part of the job, just like a media conference; and although you would rather be somewhere else, you go through it. You go through it and don't get emotional about anything that's said. Don't get emotional about any questions that are asked. You simply answer and go on.

Players rarely attend another game after losing in any kind of tournament, but most of ours decide to go to the Monday meeting between Michigan and Seton Hall. "It was like this," Ervin Small will explain later. "We figured if we couldn't win the title, let's go root for the Big Ten."

Mary and I decide to go as well, and as we make our way to our seats, people stop me to talk. They ask me to discuss our game, they ask my opinion on the officiating, they ask my prediction on the game I'm about to watch. I think it will be close, I say in answer to that last question, but I feel Michigan will win.

I can go to football games and really relax and enjoy them. But at basketball games, I watch situations and always analyze the offensive and defensive patterns that develop. I am usually detached when I do that, but here it's difficult. The situation is pretty emotional, and I often find myself thinking about how we would be attacking a certain defense, about how we would be defending a certain offense. I think I'm pretty stable, but this is hard on me. I felt and all my coaches felt that we could beat Seton Hall. So now I catch myself thinking, "We could be there. We could be there, on our way to becoming the national champions."

With three seconds left in overtime, and after Robinson makes the free throws that win that championship for Michigan, I feel sorry for Seton Hall coach P.J. Carlesimo. He has come so far and was just three seconds away. When those three seconds are over and his championship is secure, I feel happy for Steve Fisher. I have known him a long time, and it's great to see him win.

It has been tough, but I enjoyed the game. I think I've enjoyed it as much as I could under the circumstances.

There was a time when not one person would be on hand to greet an Illinois basketball team on its return from a road trip. But now, when we land in Champaign, we know there's some sort of celebration planned for us at Assembly Hall.

As we enter, we see in front of us a yellow brick road. As we tread along toward the dais, the spotlights' shimmering rays stream down on us, and 14,000 screaming, cheering fans leap to their feet to salute their returning heroes. We have lost, so I cannot believe this is happening. We are humbled by it. The message that is clearly sent is that this Illinois program is all class.

President Stanley Ikenberry is there and he speaks. "It's true that 'Lou-can-do,' but it's also true that Lou has done," he says of me. Chancellor Morton Weir is there, and he too speaks. "Before the season even started we were told that you were too small to succeed," he says to the players. "Coach Henson even said so, and that your pants didn't fit either! But it didn't take us long to learn that your hearts were bigger than your pants."

John Mackovic is there, and he speaks in glowing terms of the team's accomplishments. And then it's my turn. I tell these people that I'm overwhelmed, that this is a special, special night. I mean that. I believe that everything is not measured by whether you win or lose a particular ball game. Now we lost and we are disappointed; we could just as easily have been national champs. But I bet no school or community shows more class or treats its players better than ours do when we return from Seattle.

I feel deep appreciation as I stand before these fans. I think we all are moved by the reception we receive. They are recognizing the players for all the right reasons. They are recognizing a group of young men who worked hard, who put so much into their year, who put it on the line every time they went onto the court. The coaches knew that, we knew that all the time. And by the end of the year, I think the nation realized it too.

The calls and the letters show that this was a team people enjoyed. Even now, in airports strangers come up to me and say, "Hey, coach, you know I've never enjoyed watching a team more."

Some of the players speak after I give my talk, and one of them is Nick Anderson. For months now, there have been rumors that he is going to leave school early and move on to the NBA. In my time at the microphone, I assure the crowd that Nick has promised to return to Illinois for his senior season.

Now, with a spotlight shining down on him, he looks out at them and echoes my comments. "I tell ya, I look forward to playing next year," Nick Anderson says. At this moment, I'm sure he means what he says.

**9**

# Back to the Future

I am happy to get back to work on Wednesday. I have been uncomfortable, uneasy, since our loss to Michigan. But now I'm back in my environment and more at ease.

So now in my office, I put my disappointment behind me and get down to our concerns of the moment. The biggest is recruiting, the recruitment of a pair of players who could help our program immensely. One of them is 6-foot-8 Andy Kpedi, an All-American up the road at Kankakee Junior College, where he played for that excellent coach Denny Lehnus. Kpedi, a Nigerian, has lived for two years with Lorrie and Mark Gibson, editor of the *Kankakee Daily Journal.* He has narrowed his choices down to Purdue and Illinois. The other is 6-foot-9 Deon Thomas, an All-State performer for the incredibly successful coach Bob Hambric at Simeon High School in Chicago. Deon's own choices are narrowed to Iowa and Illinois.

We were fortunate to sign four excellent prospects during the fall: 6-foot-4 Brooks Taylor and 6-foot-5 1/2 Tim Geers, both from DeLasalle High in Chicago, where they played for the outstanding coach Jim Tracy; 6-foot-8 Tommy Michael, who led his Carlyle team coached by Brad Weathers to the Class A state title; 6-foot-3 Ken Gibson, who played at Bloomington High School under the very successful Loren Wallace.

The two unsigned recruits are going to be the focus of my attention between now and next week's national signing date. But lurking in the back of my mind are those rumors concerning Nick and the NBA.

Agents are a problem for all college coaches, especially those agents who get their hooks into a player when he's still an underclassman. Sometimes they do it by contacting him directly and brainwashing him about the great deals they can cut; and sometimes they do it by having one of their clients who is already a pro befriend that player during the summer.

The pro gets to know the player, and then during the season he starts calling him. Now suddenly they're buddies. The college player looks up to the pro, and then the pro starts talking, talking, buttering up the player. "You're ready for the NBA now. Why go back to school?"

"If you go back to school, you might get hurt. Why take the chance?"

"My guy knows a lot of NBA general managers. He can help move you up in the draft and get you a good contract. Why not take the money?"

"I know you may hurt the feelings of your coaching staff, but you know, it's just in your best interest to come out now."

I know that Nick and New York Knick forward Charles Oakley have become good friends. I don't know how many conversations they've had or what has been said. But just the fact that they took place, combined with the whispers, makes me wary. I feel I have to talk to Nick again.

If I ever have a player who is certain to go in the top five in the NBA draft, I'd encourage him to go. But with Nick, everyone is telling me that he looks like a number ten to fifteen pick, so I think it will be a mistake if he leaves without playing his senior year.

I tell him that when we meet, and I tell him a lot of other things as well. I tell him that completing his college work is the best thing he can do for himself and his family. I admit to him that I'm biased, that I certainly would like to have him back on my team. But then I ask him to consider just what another year in our program could mean to him. "Look, Nick," I say. "This year you averaged 18 points a game and that very easily could have been 25. But that wasn't really in the plan. The plan was for you to become a better player and get some recognition. But you know that no player should get recognition above the team, that the team comes first. You know that if you push an individual before the team, it wrecks the team and doesn't do the individual any good either."

"In addition to that," I explain, "We had Kenny, a senior, a great individual, thinking of playing pro ball. We had to get him some points. We had Lowell, whom we also think could play pro ball. And Kendall was a good player, and it was nice for him to get a few points as well. Nick, even under those circumstances, you got a lot of recognition and weren't hurt at all."

"Now," I tell him, "Next year will be different. Next year's your senior year, and you know we always give seniors a break. That's just good business and fair to all. So where you played only twenty-five, twenty-seven minutes in some games this year, next year we're going to leave you in maybe five or eight minutes longer. Instead of scoring 18 a game, you're going to get maybe 25."

"So, Nick," I continue, "Don't even think in terms of Illinois. Just think about yourself and what that could mean to you. Say you go ten  to fifteen this year, which is where people are telling me you'll go.  You'll get a contract worth maybe $350,000, maybe $450,000.  But say you stay another year, get 25 points a game, continue to be a great rebounder, improve your defense.  The pros are going to be watching, and some of the guys I've talked to are saying you could go three or four.  Think how much more money that's going to mean for you."

Those are the things I say to Nick, and he tells me the same thing he told our fans on our return from Seattle.  He tells me he's staying.

We have been in on Andy Kpedi and Deon Thomas through-out the recruiting process, so this is not a rush job.  We just want to stay in touch with them regularly.  But we're thinking a lot about those two guys.  We need them to make this a really successful recruiting year for us.

We  felt good about Andy all along, but while we were busy playing in the tournament, we started hearing things about Deon that bothered us.  He didn't tell us that he was going to Iowa, but that's what we kept hearing.  It got to the the point where Jimmy Collins, who's recruiting him for us, became concerned. "Iowa for sure," that's what everyone was saying—everyone but Deon, his coach Bob Hambric, and his grandmother Mrs. Bernice McGarry.

Recruiting is sometimes much like an election, and the school that's in the lead is often cast as the front- runner.  Now we all know what generally happens to front-runners: they have trouble main-taining their standings in the polls. That can also be the case with the recruiting leader. So even though we heard all this and Jimmy felt  concerned, we still felt we were in there solid with him.

In late March, Deon and his Simeon team took a trip to play in Amsterdam, and there I think he started to think more about us. That happens often with players who are planning to go to school away from home—if you get them away from home for a while, they realize the advantages of staying close.

I think that helped us with Deon, as did our trip to the Final Four. But as we prepare to make our final push on him, we are by no means certain he is coming to Illinois.

In the recruitment of any player, there's always going to be a "significant other" who is going to have the biggest influence on his decision. In the recruitment of Deon, we felt that person was his grandmother Mrs. Bernice McGarry. Jimmy has telephoned and written her frequently as we pursued her grandson.

She was the key, that's what we believed. When Deon was in Amsterdam, Jimmy called her from the Minneapolis Metrodome after we made it to the Final Four. He stayed in constant contact with her because he knew she would be in touch with Deon. And he knew from her that she wanted Deon out of the city, but not too far out. She wanted him to choose Illinois; she felt Iowa was too far to travel to see him play. But for the longest time, she kept her preference to herself. She wanted Deon to make his own decision. Then some two weeks before the signing date, Deon sat down with her and asked, "Grandma, what school do you want me to go to?"

"Illinois," she told him.

We feel that's a huge advantage for us now, and we also believe Illinois is the best place for him. When Jimmy talks to him—and he's talking to him daily now—he pushes that point, pushes the advantages inherent in attending the state university. "If you're going to live in Illinois after you graduate," he tells him, "then obviously we're the best place for you."

There are other reasons for Jimmy to say that, and he points them out to Deon as well. We don't have much size. We're losing Lowell and Kenny, and that's forty minutes of playing time right there that must be filled. We can show you that on paper, and no matter what other schools are saying, they can't. Your friends from Simeon, Nick and Ervin, they're doing really well at Illinois, and they'll be there for you. They'll make sure you fit into the program. But if you go away from home where nobody knows you, who's going to look after you? Your grandmother has been to all of your high school games, and she wants to see you play in college. Are you going to deprive her of that chance?

Jimmy is telling him all of this, but Deon is a very hard person to read. He always talks to him, but if Jimmy starts pushing him into a corner he clams up. The weather, his school work. . . . Deon elaborates on subjects like that when he's talking to Jimmy. But if Jimmy asks him where he is going to college, Deon is adamantly noncommital.

He's considering Illinois, he tells Jimmy that. But he also tells him that he likes former Iowa player Kevin Gamble and is thinking about that school as well.

Jimmy is supposed to call me daily and tell me how he feels we stand with Deon. But days sometimes slip by without his contacting me. But even when he doesn't report we get information. It comes to us from a variety of sources. We want the feel of things, and Nick and Ervin sometimes give us an idea of how things are going. We want to know what Deon is telling his girlfriend, we want to know what he's telling the reporter who is covering him, we want to know what he's telling his closest buddies. His parents, his grandparents, his coach, his assistant coach, they are other sources of information, and we stay in touch with all these people. We want to know everything that's going on.

From these sources we get good vibes going into the home stretch. Nick and Ervin, they're sure he's going to come here. But we are still hearing differently from others.

The signing date is just days away now, and Jimmy is wrapping up another of his telephone conversations with Deon. "You know," Jimmy tells him jokingly, "the next time I come to Chicago, I'm going to be carrying a letter of intent."

"Bring it on," Deon says.

Jimmy pauses, just lets that remark hang in the air. Then both he and Deon laugh. "You know I'm going to bring it, don't you?" Jimmy finally says. Deon says nothing, he just laughs again.

"Coach, I feel really good about Deon," Jimmy tells me when he reports in that day.

"Tell me why," I say.

He tells me what's occurred and then says, "Coach, we really have to get on him. That means you have to call him more. We have to keep going into the school every week."

Jimmy believes you should talk to anyone at a recruit's school who will talk to you. He wants us to do that now. He wants us to be around Simeon during lunch period and while the other students are changing classes. He doesn't necessarily want Deon to see us on those occasions, but he wants his schoolmates to see us. He knows they're going to think, "They just got back from the Final Four and still have time to come here."

So we stay in constant touch with Deon now, and if I don't call, Jimmy does. If Jimmy doesn't, Dick does. If Dick doesn't, Nick or Ervin do. We just want to keep Illinois on Deon's mind.

On Tuesday, April 11, Andy Kpedi verbally commits to Illinois, and the next day he signs his official letter of intent. That Wednesday is the first day recruits can do that. But Deon, as expected, is not yet ready to choose his college.

On Thursday, I make my official visit to see Deon. Although I leave with a good feeling, I am still not certain we are going to get him. He has recruiting trips still scheduled to Iowa and Minnesota, I know that now. I know too that all we can do now is stay in contact with him and hope.

Less than a week later, our hope is fulfilled. Less than a week later, Deon Thomas signs with us, and there's a great sense of relief. It means a great deal to our program. It just means so much more to us to get a Deon Thomas out of Chicago or out of Peoria or out of Edwardsville than it does to get a 6-foot-9 player out of Los Angeles.

Hey, you don't think I'm feeling good? People are already picking us as one of the 1989-90 top four teams, and right now I have to agree with them. I think we're going to be an outstanding team. I think we're going to be the best team I've ever coached.

Now that's not to knock Ken Battle or Lowell, they've played great for us! But don't try to compare the strength and depth of the team that just finished playing with that of next year's team. In Lowell's spot, pick from Deon, Andy Kpedi, and Rodney Jones. Put Marcus into Battle's slot—he's going to do a good job there. Then Nick's back; and Kendall and Steve Bardo and Larry Smith, all veterans, all guys capable of playing more than one position. We're going to have so much flexibility. Right now we're very optimistic.

On Wednesday, May 10, I bump into Nick, and we exchange

some pleasantries while he autographs some balls. I'm very relaxed two days later as Mary and I drive to Chicago for a lunch date with *Sun Times* sportswriters Taylor Bell, Clyde Travis, and Brian Hanley. Sometime during the meal Taylor asks, "Coach, do you think there's a possibility that Nick will turn pro?" I confidently respond, "Taylor, if I thought there was a possibility of that happening, I wouldn't be sitting here talking to you fellas."

That Friday evening we are scheduled to attend a University of Illinois Foundation banquet at the plush Four Seasons Hotel as guests of executive director Bill Nugent and his lovely wife Clara. Then we are going to stay the weekend so we can help our daughter Lisa move into a new apartment and so I can speak at the Benji Wilson Foundation dinner. We are looking forward to a relaxing time and to enjoying all that Chicago has to offer. As we check into the Four Seasons, I chuckle to myself as I take in our surroundings. When I'm recruiting, when I'm on a strict budget, I always look for economical places to stay. But the University of Illinois Foundation is having this special annual event, so here we are in genuine splendor.

Those are my thoughts, that's how relaxed I'm feeling. But back in Champaign, Nick is talking with Jimmy Collins. Last January, Nick's mom was seriously injured in an automobile accident, and that's when his ordeal began. That's when he first started thinking that he might have to leave school early and turn pro. She couldn't work then, she still can't work. And now in Jimmy's office, Nick tells him that his family needs the money, that he must move on to the NBA to support his mom and his sister and his two brothers. There are some tears as they talk. Nick truly would like to stay. But Jimmy knows his situation as well as anybody and doesn't try to talk him out of it.

But I know nothing of this. I'm at the banquet, and afterward I'm surprised to find a stack of messages awaiting us when we return to our room around midnight. One of them is from Mark Coomes, and I call him first. "Nick's leaving," he tells me. I'm staggered.

I don't blame Nick. I know his mom's in bad shape, that this is a case of his desperately needing money. If a player feels in his own heart that he has to go on to the pros, he should go. It shouldn't make any difference how his coach feels.

Selfishly, though, it bothers me. I know we would have been a great team with him. But more than that, it bothers me because I think Nick is hurting himself. Now you have to understand this about a coach. A coach feels about his players much like he does about his own family. Even though you may get mad at them, even though you may chew them out, it doesn't mean you don't love them. You're together, and you spend as much time with them as you do with your own family. And just as you don't want to see your son or daughter hurt, you don't want to see one of your players hurt.

So I'm disappointed when I hear about Nick's decision. Not only is he not finishing his degree, I know he's giving up a lot of money. I know what I have planned for him next season. I know pro scouts are going to be coming out of the woodwork and drooling over him. I like Glen Rice, but Nick is better. I know Nick is better. But it looks like Rice will be a lottery pick and sign for a million dollars. And Nick's going to go between ten and fifteen and get considerably less.

I think the world of Nick, but this other guy's going to get twice the money that he will, and it gripes me. It gripes me to see one of our players hurt like that. This is the frustration that runs through my mind as I go to bed early that Saturday morning.

The weekend is rough. I want to be back in my office, where it's easier for me to forget adversity. But I'm committed to two days in Chicago, where I feel like doing very little after we help Lisa move, other than watch NBA games on television. So it's a relief to get back to work on Monday.

The phone rings in my office on Tuesday. It's Nick and the first thing he says is, "Coach, I want to apologize."

"Nick," I say. "You don't have to apologize for anything. We've had a great relationship, and you've done a magnificent job for us. We're so proud of you, proud of what you've done for Illinois and for yourself. But Nick, I've told you this before, and this is the only time I'm going to be negative with you. Nick, I think you made a mistake."

I then tell him what I told him before. I tell him that I don't *think* he's a better player than Rice—I *know* he's better. And it upsets me to know he's going to get less money than Rice. I just have to tell him that again. I have to tell him how I feel. Finally Nick says, "I know, coach, but it's something I had to do."

After that, I'm not negative again. After that, I just tell Nick how he'll always be close to our program and how much we appreciate all he has done for us.

It seems as if I talk to some pro at length about either Kenny or Lowell every single day. I tell them how Lowell has come along and improved tremendously, in spite of having to stay out six weeks during his junior year due to a severe sprained knee. I let them know that I thought he had developed into the best inside defensive man in the Big Ten. And of course, they're all aware of his great offensive ability, so I am extremely disappointed when he's not drafted.

Kenny is the subject of many pro inquiries, so I talk about his spirit and will to win and about the great effort he puts forth in practice and in games. I tell them about the annual Kenny Battle Hustle Award that we have begun presenting to the one player who comes the closest to demonstrating the type of hustle that Kenny exhibited every time out. I tell them that Kenny has greatly improved his outside shooting, ball handling, and penetration skills, and that he spearheaded our defense. Now that Detroit, the team that drafted him has traded him to Phoenix, I think he'll be an impact player for them. Even though Kenny was drafted in the first round, I was upset that he didn't go much higher.

I also get several calls from pro scouts concerning Nick during the six weeks that separate Nick's declaration and the day of the NBA draft. One of them is from Pat Williams, general manager of the Orlando Magic, and we talk for a solid hour. "You know," I tell each of them right at the start, "I feel sorry for you people. I feel sorry for you because you don't know Nick. You just don't know how good he is. If I were in your job, I would take him over Glen Rice."

"What?" That's the reaction I commonly get when I say that. But now I have their attention and can tell them what I feel. I always tend to be positive about my players, to try and help them move up in a draft. But I'm not going to tell a pro coach or a pro scout that a player is great if he isn't. But here I believe what I'm saying. I really feel Nick is going to be a better pro than Rice.

Sacramento has the first choice in the draft, and people say now that they may take Rice. If they do, they deserve to be in last place. That doesn't mean that I'm against Rice. No, Rice is the best 6-foot-7 shooter I've ever seen on the college level. But let's take Rice and Michael Jordan. Can Jordan shoot like Rice? I really doubt it. So what makes Jordan so great? He's a creator. Is Rice a creator? No. He's a shooter.

That's why I tell pro scouts and pro coaches that in the next ten, twelve years Nick is going to be a better pro than Rice. He's got the body, and he can create. He's hard to stop one-on-one. Shooters, you have quite a few guys who can do that. But creators, they don't come along very often.

On June 27, the NBA holds its draft at the Felt Forum in New York City. The Sacramento Kings, picking first, select Louisville center Pervis Ellison. The Miami Heat, picking fourth, select Glen Rice. The expansion Orlando Magic, picking eleventh, select Nick Anderson. Nick's position isn't unexpected, but it still hurts.

We talk of handling the pressures of the Final Four and of attending a media conference after a tough loss. We talk of demanding toughness from our players and of creating an environment where that trait can be developed. We talk of my own childhood environment on the farm and of rebounding from the unexpected adversity that often confronted us there.

We talk of all of that and more, and so there is only one way to handle this situation. There is only one thing to do. You do what you've always done.

*You go on.*